Social
Justice
and
Local
Development
Policy

*To the memory of
Mayor Harold Washington:
He used local development policy
to reach for social justice.*

Social Justice and Local Development Policy

Robert Mier

with
Robert P. Giloth, Kari J. Moe
and
Lauri Alpern, Bennett Harrison,
Howard M. McGary, Jr., Irene Sherr,
Thomas Vietorisz, Wim Wiewel

SAGE Publications
International Educational and Professional Publisher
Newbury Park   London   New Delhi

For information address:

SAGE Publications, Inc.
2455 Teller Road
Newbury Park, California 91320

SAGE Publications Ltd.
6 Bonhill Street
London EC2A 4PU
United Kingdom

SAGE Publications India Pvt. Ltd.
M-32 Market
Greater Kailash I
New Delhi 110 048 India

Printed in the United States of America

Library of Congress Cataloging-in-Publication Data

Social justice and local development policy / Robert Mier with Robert P. Giloth . . . [et al.].
   p. cm.
   Includes bibliographical references and index.
   ISBN 0-8039-4947-2. – ISBN 0-8039-4948-0 (pbk.)
   1. Economic development projects–Illinois–Chicago–Case studies.
   2. Community development–Illinois–Chicago–Case studies.
   3. Social justice–Case studies. I. Mier, Robert.
   HC110.E44S65   1993
   338.9773'11–dc20   93-15519
                                                           CIP

93 94 95 96   10 9 8 7 6 5 4 3 2 1

Sage Production Editor: Tara S. Mead

Contents

Acknowledgments

This book was written over almost two decades, and many people played important roles along the way. Pierre Clavel, Bill Goldsmith, Ben Harrison, Norm Krumholz, and Tom Vietorisz were early mentors who became close friends. Friends, allies, and counselors from Chicago City Hall include Steve Alexander, Hal Baron, Rodrigo del Canto, Art Cummings, Natalia Delgado, Helen Doria, Pat Dowell-Cerasoli, Milam Fitts, Deborah Frieson, Joe Gardner, Bob Giloth, Maury Grenly, Liz Hollander, Al Johnson, Kappy Laing, Judd Miner, Geri Mercola, Grayson Mitchell, Jim Montgomery, Kari Moe, David Naravsky, David Orr, Ros Paaswell, Buzz Palmer, Matt Piers, Jane Ramsey, Diana Robinson, Wayne Robinson, Irene Sherr, Howard Stanback, Bill Taylor-Garcia, Nena Torres, Art Vazquez, Judy Walker, Wanda White, Delores Woods, and Tim Wright. Colleagues encouraging the development of this book include Dick Bingham, Ed Blakely, Gene Grigsby, and David Perry. Relatives, friends, and fellow life travelers include Nina Beaty, Rich Blue, Fred Boehm, Bruce Carmen, Ingrid Christiansen, Donna Ducharme, Msgr. Jack Egan, Joan and Shelly Fitzgerald, Doug Gills, Edna Hamburger, Katy Hogan, Thelma Jackson, Kelly Johnson, Anne Kanengeiser, Jody Kretzmann, Cheryl Laperriere, Mike Leyden, Ruth Mahr, Bill Markel, Gordon Medlock, Brian, Brendan, Dylan, Lian, Jonathon, and Maggie Mier, Sharon Mier, Nell Newton, Alice Palmer, Linda Pascucci, Joanne Peterson, Virginia Ryan, Steve Saltzman, Christine Sammel, Lisa Sauber, Mike Sheahan, Nick Staller, Barbara Temaner, and Christine Williams. I particularly want to thank Bob Giloth for commenting on portions of the manuscript; Joan Fitzgerald for her constructive criticism of the entire manuscript; Harry Briggs from Sage for his quiet support; and Leigh Peterman for her research and production assistance.

Introduction

U.S. urban regeneration in the 1980s resonated with excitement over new forms of economic stimulus—festival gallerias, "world's" fairs, and exploding service sectors—engineered by an old urban development team, the "growth coalition," wearing a new cloak of "public/private partnerships" (Judd & Parkinson, 1990; Porter & Sweet, 1984). Yet beneath this glossy veneer of progress trickling out from the geographic heart of cities pulsated an antinomy between urban neighborhoods and their downtowns (Clavel & Wiewel, 1991).

This tension existed in many forms. It variously surfaced in fights over manufacturing preservation versus investment in the service economy; blue-collar jobs versus low-wage McJobs; job generation strategies versus real estate development; industrial expansion versus downtown growth; credit-starved neighborhoods versus the growth of the finance industry; targeted local hiring and purchasing versus advancement of a regional business climate; and opportunity for minority and female businesses versus sanctification of the market and economic efficiency. These new contrasts pulsated with the historical meanings of the downtown/neighborhood metaphor: City Hall versus the neighborhoods; the rich and powerful versus the poor and excluded; corporations versus small business; and business as usual versus good government (Barret, 1983).

In the end, this complex of ideas, most often emanating from African-American, Latino, and blue-collar communities and from emerging networks of community activists, yielded several new development strategies in Chicago during the tenure of Mayor

Harold Washington (Clavel & Wiewel, 1991; Rivlin, 1992). The first strategy opened government and its resources to previously excluded constituencies, such as neighborhood organizations, civic groups, and labor unions, while increasing accountability for those firms or institutions who received public incentives for development. The second was the exploration of ways to link downtown and the neighborhoods in a more redistributive relationship, including requirements for minority and female business purchasing and targeted hiring. Finally, an attempt was made to balance development across economic sectors, size of business, and areas of the city. As will be clearer as this book progresses, these strategies overlap in practice.

Balanced growth as a strategy to ameliorate urban inequities was rooted in the urban landscape in the late 1970s and early 1980s: downtown boom, industrial collapse, and neglect by the Reagan administration. At the same time that the U.S. Steel South Works and Wisconsin Steel plants on Chicago's southeast side were closing, laying off 13,000 workers and devastating nearby communities, a new futures exchange was being completed in Chicago's Loop, with the help of a $19-million federal Urban Development Action Grant (UDAG). This development spurred South Loop residential development with an upscale loft district and a new-town-in-town.

The pervasive experience of glitter and collapse brought together grass-roots constituencies with a new set of ideas. A long-gestating realignment of neighborhood activism toward economic development and redistributive/accountability strategies was unwittingly spurred by the reduced funding, privatization, and entrepreneurial ideology of Reaganomics. This led neighborhood and civic activists to reformulate notions about their role in development and governance, often relying upon the downtown/neighborhood metaphor as an analytical tool to design strategies and as an organizing theme (Mier & Gelzer, 1982).

Three ideas emerged: Chicago's neighborhoods, small businesses, and manufacturing were being neglected; downtown development and the service industry were overemphasized; and downtown development impacts, particularly the questions of who pays and who benefits, were not being addressed. These ideas joined a strong "reform as fairness" theme that came out of Chicago's black community, particularly during the 1983 campaign for mayor by then Congressman Harold Washington. That theme was not simply a reworking by a new ethnic group of "we want ours," but was based on principles of social justice and fairness (Grimshaw, 1984).

Thus Chicago's development during the Washington years (1983-1987) became an example of a social justice-based local development strategy. Norman Krumholz, the former Cleveland city planning commissioner recently said:

> The *Chicago Development Plan, 1984* seems to be the strongest indication thus far that American cities are willing to try to harness local economic development for the benefit of their disadvantaged residents. If economic development practitioners in other cities modeled their efforts along the lines suggested here, their cities might have a more viable local economy, their poor and working class neighborhoods might be less disinvested, and their resident populations might be better employed, more responsible, and more self-respecting. (Krumholz, 1991)

This book attempts to tell the Chicago story. For several reasons I have chosen the narrative form of story telling. First, stories are a particularly powerful means of attacking what Delgado (1989) calls an "ingroup reality." In local development, that reality is the constellation of real estate development, central area development, and trickle-down economics, all conceived in back rooms and boardrooms. Delgado says: "Stories, parables, chronicles, and narratives are powerful means for destroying mindset—the bundle of presuppositions, received wisdoms, and shared understandings against a background of which political discourse takes place" (p. 2413).

Second, stories are the bread and butter of development decision making. Seldom do developers and politicians relate their desires, successes, techniques, and the like, through studies and analyses (although techniques like impact analyses often play both legitimizing and obfuscatory roles). Rather, "war stories" provide daily staple (Beauregard, 1993). Thus, it is stories that connect development ideas to development practice (Mier & Fitzgerald, 1991; Mier & Bingham, 1993).

Finally, local economic development is a constitutive practice—it is concerned with building a different future.[1] It is an act of social construction concerned with attention shaping and persuasion, coalition building, and resource mobilizing behavior. These are communicative activities (Forester, 1989). The act of social visioning is replete with contradiction and paradox. Too often in local economic development, power is employed to resolve differences, and analysis is employed to justify the exercise of power.[2] Alternatively, story telling is a form that does not shy from paradox, and thus can be an effective means of realizing an alternative vision (Delgado, 1989; Throgmorton, 1992). Delgado (1989, p. 2438) reminds us that "stories are the oldest, most primordial meeting ground of human experience."

This book is a compilation of stories, most told with other people who have been my mentors, colleagues, and friends. They have been selected because I believe they build a broad and deep case for the place of a social justice agenda in local economic development practice. Most of the chapters have been published elsewhere, dating back to 1975, and, in most cases, have been only slightly edited for this volume. As the stories progress, they are less social scientific and more phenomenological. Also, the story line shifts from shaping policy to implementation and management. Both approaches represent an evolution in my own thinking and values about scholarship.

Chapter 1, "Full Employment at Living Wages," was written with Thomas Vietorisz and Bennett Harrison as part of a special 1975 issue of the *Annals of the American Academy of Political and Social Science* addressing the possibility of a national full employment policy. The article focuses attention on the connection between work and poverty, observing the large number of working poor and attacking the notion that poor people lack a work ethic. It introduces the concept of "subemployment" to attempt to capture the extent of inadequate work. It further wrestles with the concepts of adequate work and a living wage, arguing that official measures of family poverty grossly understate the numbers of Americans living in economic marginality. Finally, the chapter sketches the framework for national economic policies that attack the belief that people must be forced or coerced to work, building instead on policies that are more humane and just.

I believe "Full Employment at Living Wages" is worth examining again because so many of the issues it raises are relevant today. For example, working poverty still remains a major, yet often hidden, issue in today's social policy debates—a recent U.S. Census report shows 19% of the 1990 work force earned incomes inadequate to escape the shackles of poverty (U.S. Department of Commerce, 1992). The possibility of a middle-class life-style remains an economically elusive, possibly even more distant, target for nonwhite households (Harrison & Gorham, 1992).

But the chapter is even more important in that it forces any conception of social justice in a work ethic society to confront structural inadequacies of work. Ever since the research underlying this article, I have been skeptical of a service sector growth strategy with its concomitant bimodal distribution of skills and large volume of low-wage, low-skill, poor-future work. The research forced me to consider not only fundamental questions about the quality of work, but also ones about economic well-being.

Chapter 2, "Social Justice and Public Policy," written with Howard McGary, begins to address directly the question of how a conception of social justice could be incorporated in public policy debates, and whether it has meaning in the arena of local economic development. The chapter is an abridgement of a review essay of John Rawls's seminal *A Theory of Justice.* Rawls's conception of justice as fairness invites attention to the circumstances of the least-advantaged in society and demands addressing the question of whether their life circumstances would be enhanced by alternative collective actions.

After discussing the debate within philosophy over Rawls's theory, the chapter applies his construction of justice as fairness to particular national and local policies. The national policy is the Elementary and Secondary Education Act of 1965, which is again commanding attention in terms of policy as its renewal is being debated by Congress. The local policy concerns the overtly equity-oriented practices of the Cleveland planning commission under its then-director, Norman Krumholz. These Cleveland efforts through the 1970s continue to receive attention as a model of equity planning (Krumholz & Forester, 1990).

"Social Justice and Public Policy" finds the Rawlsian framework both seductive and problematical. Its strengths are focusing attention on the least advantaged and addressing their life circumstances. Its weakness is that neither concept is well defined. I have always found it a provocative framework because it complements the labor market analysis in "Full Employment at

Living Wages." My own point of departure in every public policy debate, ranging from subsidies to new development to targeted purchasing or hiring, has been to pose the question of who the least advantaged are in this issue, and what would genuinely enhance their life circumstances. Early in my career, the framework of subemployment helped answer these questions; later I have found race to be an essential supplement.

Rawls continues to refine his ideas about justice (1985, 1987, 1988), arguing that it is a framework capable of encouraging political consensus. My co-author of "Social Justice and Public Policy," Howard McGary (1992), an African-American philosopher, is now more sanguine about Rawls. He believes that Rawls's conception of fairness assumes the possibility of social harmony within a context of extreme social diversity. He questions this assumption, particularly with regard to racial diversity (McGary & Lawson, 1993). His sense of the limitations of the Rawlsian framework resonate with my own, an issue to which I will return in the last chapter.

Chapter 3, "Job Generation as a Road to Recovery," first appeared as a countervailing voice in a book celebrating public/private partnership and central city development strategies (Porter & Sweet, 1984). The chapter builds on the previous two by arguing that a strategy to rebuild America's cities could not assume away the interests of the work-needy. It challenges strategies that do not make the work-needy both central to the strategy and part of the process. It does this by briefly examining redevelopment efforts in Oakland, Washington, D.C., New Haven, and St. Louis, finding in each elements of a model that might achieve social justice goals.

The chapter was written at the time of Harold Washington's campaign for mayor, and was used as a counterpoint to the work under way in the campaign to formulate an alternative development agenda. Thus, it portends the Washington program with articulation of a variety of approaches to development that address social equity. Included are an emphasis on open, participatory processes ("meaningful partnerships"), targeted investment, linking training and development, and the necessity of an active public role. In emphasizing these aspects of a local agenda, the chapter rejected approaches so popular with the elite at that time, as well as development fads of the era, like high-tech development.

Chapter 4, "Political Experience in Chicago: From Campaign to Government," written with Kari J. Moe, is excerpted from a longer work, which appeared in the book, *Harold Washington and the Neighborhoods* (Clavel & Wiewel, 1991). It commences a series of chapters directly focusing on the experience during the tenure of Mayor Washington on attempting to articulate and implement a social justice-based development agenda. The chapter begins by tracing the Chicago roots of the development ideas, roots whose growth directly parallel the quickening debate nationally and in other cities chronicled in the first three chapters. The interconnected ideas include development focusing on the work-needy, development from the bottom up, and building a national agenda on local initiatives.

The development ideas embody the principle of social construction, or economic development as a constitutive practice. For this reason, the chapter goes to lengths, through extensive notes, to link people and organizations with the emerging development ideas. It particularly emphasizes the emergence of the Washington platform, "Jobs for Chicagoans," from *The CWED Platform*, the product of a broad-based community agenda-setting process that preceded the campaign.

Because the Washington "movement" (as it was known locally) was the first "rainbow coalition," the reality of race relations begins to take form and importance. Many of the coalitions out of which the Washington agenda emerged were themselves multiracial and struggling to broaden their base in the context of a campaign that epitomized racial divisiveness (Rivlin, 1992).

The chapter concludes by bringing the movement into City Hall and confronting the reality of implementation. The predicament facing us was threefold: delivering development with a team of people who were part of the patronage army of the mayor's staunch opposition; trying to modernize a bureaucracy that still functioned as if it were 1960 (my co-author, Moe, would say "1860"); and trying to open up the processes of government to the citizenry in the face of a rigid and self-protective bureaucracy.

Chapter 5, "Strategic Planning and the Pursuit of Reform, Economic Development, and Equity," written with Kari J. Moe and Irene Sherr, continues the story of implementation by focusing on the creation of a strategic plan, *Chicago Works Together*. Building from "Jobs for Chicagoans," discussed in Chapter 4, the process began with a search for new ways to approach existing programs and projects to achieve the mayor's goals. The story of building the plan relates the continued process of bringing diverse people together in an effort to forge consensus—in this case, the new team being assembled by the mayor.

The chapter focuses on two distinguishing features of the plan—its emphasis on a small number of goals and policies, and its redistributive thrust. Both features required making difficult choices. How these choices played out in practice is told in the context of an investment trade-off between a steel mill and a festival galleria. It also begins to talk about the Washington agenda as a local industrial policy, recognizing both the absence of a national one and the need to build it from the bottom up (Osborne, 1989).

Chapter 6, "Managing Planned Change," with Kari J. Moe, continues the discussion of implementation. It tells the story of the tension between large-scale projects and dispersed development, and the attempt to balance that tension. It observes the reluctant realization by the mayor that he could not ignore mega-projects, and the challenge to put them together in such a way that the benefits were more evenly dispersed. How this was accomplished is told through the stories of negotiations with three professional sports teams, and the development of a new central public library.

These stories recognize that there is broad-based support for mega-projects. For example, sports teams are a source of civic pride, and often play a large role in people's identification with their city (Mier, 1991a). What the chapter attempts to illustrate is that "deal making" for mega-projects does not have to be exclusionary (see also, Pelissero, Henschen, & Sidlow, 1992). Furthermore, the large deals illustrate the importance of building organizational capacity for achieving equity goals.

Chapter 7, "Decentralization of Policy Making," with Wim Wiewel and Lauri Alpern, is an adaptation of a chapter in the book *Politics of Policy Innovation in Chicago* (Wong, 1992). The chapter argues that the participatory genesis of the Washington agenda did not end with the formulation of *Chicago Works Together*. It relates how the goals and objectives of the plan were continually being reflected in the work of community organizations. This is revealed through examination of a broad-based effort to update *Chicago Works Together*, through the strategic plans of three advanced community groups working on local industrial retention, and in the plans of two city-wide networks of community-development groups. One of the networks, the Chicago Workshop on Economic Development, was the author of *The CWED Platform*, a progenitor of *Chicago Works Together*.

In all these strategic documents, there appears an emphasis on similar themes: targeting the work-needy, job development (over real estate development), neighborhood development (over downtown development), business retention and expansion (over business attraction), small business development, and targeting of such resources as purchasing. Similarly, there was an emphasis on like tactics: encouraging partnerships bringing diverse communities together with the traditional growth interests, and promoting a type of collective entrepreneurship.

The chapter posits that the Washington agenda became embedded in a type of civic culture of development. It attributes this to the pervasiveness of the grass-roots communications networks, the emergence within them of widely shared beliefs about development and a language embodying them. It considers some of the actions of current Mayor Richard M. Daley as reflecting constraints that culture has placed on his own interests (Mier, 1992). It concludes by noting a certain arbitrariness emerging that potentially limits the range of action, as when too rigid a focus on "jobs" may lead to missed real estate development opportunities.

Chapter 8, "Democratic Populism in the United States: The Case of Playskool and Chicago," written with Robert P. Giloth, tells a story that stands in stark contrast to negotiating with sports teams. It is one of a municipal lawsuit to prevent the closing of a toy manufacturing plant at Christmastime. Such action by a municipality is perceived as akin to suicide—a sure-fire way to undercut the local business climate.[3] Yet this lawsuit had business support.

The story has many elements—the cavalier use of public financing by municipalities to steal plants from each other, the emergence of an unusual alliance of grass-roots organizations and local manufacturers to pressure the mayor to intercede, the adroit use of organizing metaphors to build public support for bold action, and a solution that only "satisficed." In the end, the toy company moved, although the final move was delayed a year. Yet, a partnership emerged between a community-based industrial development organization and a private real estate broker to redevelop the site. It now is largely occupied, employing nearly the same number of people as when it closed. It is the story of a city government willing to take risks on a social justice agenda, a community/labor/business coalition, and serendipity.

Chapter 9, "Spatial Change and Social Justice," also written with Robert P. Giloth, continues the story of trying to build toward a national industrial and employment policy through local action. The chapter discusses Chicago's response to manufacturing displacement and shows how it utilized task forces to focus attention on basic industrial sectors.

The first case relates the emergence of an overlay on the municipal zoning map strictly limiting land use changes in specific industrial areas, called "Planned Manufacturing Districts." The districts emerged from a coalition of local industrialists, workers, and residents concerned about industrial gentrification—the dislocation of industry through upscale commercial and residential loft conversions. Like the story of the closing of the toy factory, this story emphasizes that bolder municipal action is possible when there is strong external pressure bringing attention to issues of social justice.

In contrast to the story of Planned Manufacturing Districts, industry task forces took a sectoral approach to industrial policy. Task forces on the steel and apparel industries were assembled from a wide range of stakeholders in order to address the question of the future of the industries in Chicago. Each task force addressed industries that had largely been written off by previous Chicago mayors, and for which there was a public climate of resignation. Yet, in each case, subsectors of strength were found, generative strategies were formulated, and broad-based public support was built to retain these industries.

The stories of both Planned Manufacturing Districts and industrial task forces stress the challenges of keeping diverse stakeholders at the table, of keeping pressure on municipal government to prevent it from getting risk adverse, and of framing the issues in ways that multiracial alliances are possible. Finally, the chapter concludes by attempting to link the Chicago experience with that in other cities, to construct a framework for a national industrial policy.

Chapter 10, a previously unpublished work written with Robert P. Giloth, begins to sum up the Washington experience by looking at the nature and role of progressive leadership. We began our work with Mayor Harold Washington with a bias against leadership, even while respecting the unique role he played. Much of the bias was resentment of top-down, nonparticipatory processes of public decision making that wore a cloak of "partnership." We concluded our Washington experience with new respect for a type of bottom-up, inclusive leadership often exhibited by community organization leaders.

This chapter reflects on leadership models, contrasting elite and more participatory models by looking at stories of leadership in action in four cases. Abstracting from those cases, it attempts to define more precisely a concept of "cooperative leadership." It looks in more detail at the characteristics of good cooperative leaders, observing 11 attributes of collaboration and communication. It briefly reviews traditional ways of training and nurturing leaders, and suggests a civic agenda for the development of cooperative leaders. It concludes by arguing that cooperative leadership and the pursuit of a social justice-oriented development agenda are intertwined.

The final chapter, "Community Development and Diversity," attempts to draw some personal conclusions from the experience of helping formulate and deliver an alternative development agenda. It begins by telling another story—one of implementing a neighborhood-oriented bond issue. It juxtaposes that experience, with its micro-impacts, against the higher profile efforts related in earlier stories, and begins to draw conclusions about the nature of progressive administration. Among the most important conclusions is the intractability of the issue of race in local development.

The chapter addresses the race issue by briefly sketching four more concrete situations that illustrate the issue. It concludes with an observation that race ought to be the central framework through which to see the essence of a local development challenge or opportunity. It argues that only such a framework makes a true social justice agenda possible.

As you read this book, you are invited to keep some of the words of Harold Washington in mind, words from his annual

State of the City address to the League of Women Voters shortly before his death. In his speech, he was reminding Chicagoans that meaningful social change is always contentious, and that progress comes in small steps:

> In years past, through some of the healthiest and happiest periods in our country's life, there was an active federal-urban partnership that flourished and nourished not only our cities, but the suburbs around them. But the spirit of those bright days has been eclipsed by a new ethic of sink-or-swim, a mean-spirited myopia that can focus only on the bottom line, blind to the crisis we are creating at our lowest income levels—or the growing sense of dread among those with fixed incomes—or the creeping anxieties of our middle classes.
>
> We must counter that specter of despair with the New Spirit of Chicago. We have proven to ourselves that change is possible in our own city. And we have taken the national leadership among cities, in working for change in Washington, D.C. The federal budget is our business. Our country's foreign trade policy is our business. Our country's economic policy is our business. Every policy that affects jobs, education, housing, is our business. We have a direct interest in federal policies toward the poor, the homeless, the aging, the disabled, mothers and children, and all those others who have been thrown at our doorstep by a federal administration in retreat from reality.
>
> And so I ask for your hand and for your voice. Lend a hand to help your city, in our efforts to "do for ourselves." And let your voice be heard as we make our case at the federal level, where the responsibility for our cities must ultimately lie. Working together, we can build on the progress of the past four years, to meet challenges of the years ahead. (Miller, 1989a, p. 186)

Notes

1. I would argue that even the strong preservationist tendencies in development, particularly in the suburbs of central cities, is concerned with building one alternative future by averting another one. In these cases, the fight to preserve the status quo lies in facing the negative impacts of growth and/or racial change, the ingredients of an alternative future that is being resisted.

2. My own realization of this truth occurred in 1967 in Vietnam.

3. We were so sensitive to this potential that the story was originally published in a British journal to minimize local attention.

1

Full Employment at Living Wages

with

·THOMAS VIETORISZ

BENNETT HARRISON

This chapter first appeared in a special issue of the **Annals of the American Academy of Political and Social Science** *devoted to "Planning for Full Employment." The issue focused on the potential of then proposed legislation titled "The Equal Opportunity and Full Employment Act," but popularly known as the "Humphrey-Hawkins Bill" after its chief sponsors, Senator Hubert Humphrey and Representative Augustus Hawkins. The bill eventually passed Congress as a tribute to Sen. Humphrey after his death, but any federal commitment to full employment had been diluted to the degree of ineffectiveness. However, the issues raised in this chapter about the intimate relation between poverty, work, and the quality of life remain relevant today.*

AUTHORS' NOTE: This chapter was originally published in the *Annals of the American Academy of Political and Social Science* written by Vietorisz, Mier, and Harrison (1975). It has been reproduced here with the permission of the publisher. Support for the research reported in the chapter was provided by a grant from the Center for the Study of Metropolitan Problems, National Institute of Mental Health, to the Research Center for Economic Planning. Opinions expressed are not necessarily those of the funding organization.

Introduction

Middle-class persons are subject to a curious double vision in considering what is a substandard job. At a public hearing on the housing component of flood relief in Elmira, New York, in 1973, the disadvantages of allowing trailer parks to proliferate in a community were discussed. The government people, business-people, and community leaders attending agreed that about $10,000 annual income was required for a family to afford nonsubsidized, permanent housing. As an annual income in 1973, this was felt to set a reasonable standard.

Yet, as an equivalent hourly wage of $5, the same income level horrified all those present, because they immediately recognized it as the effective minimum wage needed by family men if either trailer parks or public housing were to be avoided. The shock came with the realization that such a wage level was well above the prevailing local wage for many jobs in which family heads were habitually employed. Businessmen were aghast at the thought of having to meet outside competition while paying such wages, and civic leaders saw the specter of business flight, real estate value collapse, and a disastrous loss in tax revenues.

What is characteristic about this incident is that the group perceived the same labor market transaction so differently from the income side and from the cost side. From the income side, families and their needs were seen in relation to the social and physical structure of the community as a whole. From the cost side, labor productivity was seen as rigidly fixed and not responsive to wage level changes. Lacking the expectation that labor productivity would rise when wages increased, higher pay of necessity appeared as an unearned transfer that could be ruinous to individual businesses and to the economic health of the community.

Wages and Productivity

The prevailing work ethic locates the source of productivity in the effort and qualities of the individual. One of the strongest forces opposing the direct elimination of poverty by income transfers adequate to lift recipients into a modest lower-middle-class existence is the widely held notion that this would undermine the motivation to work. If people can live adequately while idle or unproductive, the argument goes, why should they bother to take a job or, having taken one, exert themselves to advance to more demanding tasks?

Ignoring the fact that many victims of poverty are unable to work at all—women with small children, the old and ill, the handicapped poor—this argument implies that the stick of widespread poverty is needed to beat workers into accepting productive jobs. The fact that a great many workers hold full-time jobs that leave them with poverty-level incomes has not yet fully penetrated public consciousness. At the level of professional discussion, the traditional economic view of the matter is that the worker is too lazy and ignorant or, using a more polite phrase, too deprived, through no fault of his own, to be worth more to his employer than the prevailing low wages.

The work ethic derives its political appeal from the moral standard that those who contribute more to the productive effort should get more in return. The standard establishes equity between individuals trapped to antagonistic social relations involving toil and possible privation, but it raises two fundamental questions. First, are individuals really in control of the productive contributions ascribed to them? Second, what makes for the prevalent antagonistic social relations? Are they inevitable?

With regard to the first question, there is widespread evidence that the productivity of workers is within a wide range of variation largely outside the workers' control. Productivity depends, rather, on the technical and organizational sophistication of the firm or industry. Levantine workers brought to German factories thus perform at German levels of productivity. When an industry or occupation pays low wages, it encourages wasteful use of labor and retards technical change; conversely, high wages stimulate labor-saving innovations. To be sure, the latter also involve on-the-job retraining and upgrading of the labor force, but higher wages provide a built-in motivation for worker cooperation. There are limits to mid-career retraining, but wartime experiences have shown, especially in England where at one point even the mentally retarded were brought into war production, that the obstacles to retraining have more to do with willingness to try than with ability to learn. In this regard, therefore, the work ethic is based on a false perception of reality.

So long as productivity is viewed as a fixed, personal characteristic of the worker and therefore unchanging in response to variations in wage levels, socially desirable wage increases will appear as unearned transfers. Yet unearned transfers are perceived by the public quite differently from earned income. A 1973 study by Lee Rainwater showed that the public perception of the minimum income needed for a family to "get along" is substantially higher than what the public regards as justified public assistance to the same family. Rainwater identified the "getting along" income as one producing a standard of living that puts a family just barely into the mainstream of society, whereas the publicly tolerable family assistance income is one enabling physical survival only under conditions of degradation and dehumanization.

Many people, in other words, regard it as fair not to meet minimum social needs of transfer income recipients. This attitude flows directly from the work ethic. Wage labor is plainly perceived as so alienating that it is regarded, in equity, on a par with very harsh privation.

Also, aside from ascribing social productivity to the merit of individuals, the work ethic is embedded in the perception of social relations as fundamentally antagonistic. Such antagonistic social relations are created and reinforced by the need for social control.

The control function arises from the need of business to reduce the bargaining power of workers by a policy of creating or reinforcing the formation of distinct qualities of labor. The subdivision of the production process into many educational and skill segments is only partly determined by technology; in part, it follows the logic of controlling the labor force by dividing it. The low-wage, low-productivity "secondary" labor force contrasts with the labor aristocracy of powerful unions and with persons working in the middle or upper echelons of public and private bureaucracies. Hierarchical organization demands low living standards for blacks and Puerto Ricans in order to enable the hiring of Irish and Italian (and now, progressively, some black and Puerto Rican) blue-collar workers, policemen, and clerical employees. The incentive is a lower-middle-class standard of living. The same segmentation permits the hiring of managers by cutting them in on the rewards of wealth, and the hiring of professionals whose duties in part serve the needs of production and in part help in maintaining the ideologies and control processes necessary for the continuation of the existing economic and social structure.

The resulting divisions, together with real or threatened upward and downward mobility of various groups, contribute both to the maintenance of social hierarchies and to the perpetuation of antagonisms between individuals and groups. Given a misconception of the sources of individual productivity, the foundation is therefore laid for the maintenance of a work ethic that opposes many measures that might reasonably be taken to eliminate poverty.

Concept of a Living Wage

The Elmira citizens were not unique in having a strong sense of a socially desirable family income. More than 30 years of Gallup opinion surveys revealed a public awareness of a minimally adequate income for a family of four, which in 1970 corresponded closely to the Bureau of Labor Statistics's (BLS) "lower" budget for an urban family of four of $6,960 per year (Rainwater, 1973; Kilpatrick, 1973). The BLS lower budget, representing the lowest of three standards of living, was based on the actual cost of a basket of goods that would enable a minimal socially acceptable level of subsistence. This budget was updated for autumn 1973 to an average of $8,181 per year for an urban family of four, over the 40 metropolitan areas surveyed.

The urgency for eliminating poverty is obvious; many social pathologies flow directly from poverty. We found in our research, for example, that much of the intercity statistical variation in substandard housing, crime, ill health, mental illness, drug involvement, and infant mortality can be explained by intercity differences in the incidence of poverty (Mier, Vietorisz, & Giblin, 1975). If there is consensus on a threshold income to break poverty and enable social participation, is full employment policy an appropriate vehicle for generating that income? Rainwater argued that public opinion has always supported a jobs strategy for confronting poverty.

Our research in the early to mid-1970s found in a 51-city sample of low-income areas, surveyed for the Bureau of Labor Statistics in the 1970 Census Employment Survey (CES), that more than 50% of the variation in poverty was explained by current employment difficulties—low wage or sporadic employment, or unemployment. A detailed micro-analysis of the Detroit, Michigan, CES survey area verified the above findings. It also yielded evidence that a substantial proportion of poverty unexplainable by current employment circumstances could be attributed to indirect and lagged effects, especially via family structures—illegitimacy, desertion, and problems of the aged—whose earlier work experiences precluded provision for their retirement years.

In considering employment policies to break the grip of poverty, there is a strong temptation to temper arguments for minimum wage legislation by relying on the employment of secondary family members. Evidence exists that many families whose members individually earn low wages can escape poverty if the structure of the family is favorable: multiple wage earners and no, or few, dependents (Lampman, 1971). Yet basing employment policy on the generation of family income from multiple sources ensures that families with unfavorable earner/dependent ratios will necessarily sink into poverty. In fact, poor families do have highly unfavorable dependency ratios. In the 1970 Census, families with incomes below $6,000 show up on the average with less than one (.89) full-time-equivalent wage earner.

In summary, there is strong public sentiment in support of eliminating poverty, yet the work ethic precludes the use of a direct income transfer program beyond providing for mere physical subsistence. The public favors, instead, a jobs strategy for attacking poverty. Evidence exists that a substantial amount of poverty is caused by employment difficulties; therefore, jobs policies are anti-poverty policies. There is a strong sense that eliminating poverty means bringing people into the mainstream of society by engendering some minimum sense of social participation. Because family heads can not begin to support their families at the prevailing minimum wage, the BLS lower budget better represents the wage necessary to bring a family into the mainstream.

The Target of Full Employment Policy

As an indicator of the magnitude of the full employment problem, the level of unemployment as currently measured is misleading. Although the Full Employment Act of 1946 addressed only unemployment per se, congressional debate preceding passage of the act made clear the rejection of employment on substandard jobs as satisfying national goals (U.S. Senate, 1945). This aspect of the full employment goal has, however, receded into the background over the intervening quarter century as the lack of a genuine national commitment to the high aspiration level of the 1946 act, set in a mood of postwar euphoria, has become amply obvious. The emphasis has accordingly shifted to plain unemployment, devoid of any wage standard, as a cause or indicator of not just labor market difficulties but, more generally, social distress.

The limitations of this approach are emphasized by a 1974 statement by the National Manpower Policy Task Force. This statement asserted that unemployment rates have become less useful for assessing the condition of the labor market as low-wage jobs, unstable work, welfare, and the hustle have grown increasingly important. As an indicator of social distress, the level of aggregate unemployment was deemed less significant than the prevalence of alternate spells of unemployment and substandard employment, with the resulting patterns of labor force exit and entry. The key factor identified was the adequacy or inadequacy of opportunities for gainful employment. In terms of assessing needs or realistically describing the labor force behavior of the disadvantaged, the task force statement concluded that the unemployment rate captured only the tip of the iceberg (National Manpower Policy Task Force, 1974, pp. 4-5).

The concept of subemployment was formulated primarily in response to the shortcomings of the unemployment measure as an index of social and economic hardship. The Equal Opportunity and Full Employment Act of 1976 recognized that opportunities for "useful paid employment at the highest feasible level of remuneration, productivity, and responsibility consistent with their abilities" were necessary to prevent workers from falling prey to family disruption, loss of social status and self-respect, physical and mental breakdown, and drug addiction and crime. The burden of our argument is that a full employment policy designed to eliminate unemployment alone will not attain that goal; only the elimination of subemployment will do so.

Subemployment

The concept of subemployment unites two major dimensions of labor market functioning that reproduce poverty and social distress: (a) the lack of opportunity for work, and (b) substandard wages. A number of economists and manpower specialists, following Willard Wirtz's 1966 initiative, began to develop subemployment indicators.[1] These various subemployment indices included the following detailed categories of workers:

– *The officially unemployed.*
– *The discouraged jobless.* This includes workers who say that they want a job now, but for a number of reasons are not looking. The reasons include such economic ones as lack of transportation or lack of a sense that jobs are available; also such personal ones as family responsibilities, which could be alleviated by day care; or ill health, which could be alleviated by adequate medical attention. The official unemployment statistics do not include such discouraged jobless in the labor force. They are regularly identified only in the Current Population Survey, although the Bureau of Labor Statistics defines only those who have given up searching for jobs as discouraged workers. This restriction reduces by 80% the count of those who say that they want a job now.
– *Involuntary part-time workers.* This estimate requires a separation of persons who work part-time because they are unable to find full-time work from persons working part-time by choice.
– *Workers earning substandard wages.* The Bureau of Labor Statistics's lower family budget, discussed above, is one possible wage standard; the "official poverty line" is another. The Social Security Administration set $4,200 as an average adequate annual income for a family of four in 1970, and this is the basis of

the official poverty line (Orshansky, 1965). Conventional economic theory, however, opposes the use of any wage criterion, stating that a worker is always paid the marginal product—all he or she is worth; hence, no worker can be considered subemployed on wage criteria.[2]

Despite an overall agreement about these general categories, conventional economics notwithstanding, several mutually inconsistent definitions of subemployment have emerged. The two most controversial issues confronting proponents of the various indicators were whether any member of a family whose income is adequate should be considered as subemployed, regardless of the quality of the person's job and the cutoff income level for inadequate jobs. The various indicators are compared by Vietorisz, Mier, and Giblin (1974).

The development of a standardized subemployment index has become the subject of continuing research, as a result of a formal mandate written into the 1973 Comprehensive Employment and Training Act (CETA). The creation of a single indicator may be misleading, however, because different conceptions of subemployment can be identified as follows:

– *Subemployment as a lack of individual opportunities for finding useful paid employment at a decent living wage.* The early subemployment calculations of Willard Wirtz (Spring, 1971) and of Spring, Harrison, and Vietorisz (1972) were first approximations to this type of subemployment index. Vietorisz, Mier, and Giblin (1974) have developed a new index, called the Exclusion Index, which makes the measurement of subemployment under this definition more precise and consistent.

– *Subemployment as a measure of family labor market difficulties, with the stress on family structure and the inability of family heads to support their families adequately.* The subemployment indices by Levitan and Taggart (1974) and by Miller (1973) were aiming at capturing this aspect of labor market functioning. Vietorisz, Mier, and Giblin (1974) developed a new index called the Inadequacy Index, which yields a more consistent test of the economic adequacy of earned family incomes.

– *Subemployment as the manpower waste inherent in labor market functioning.* This concept suggests a Manpower

Underutilization Index by quantifying the gap between the amount and skill level of labor supplied and that actually utilized. Berg (1970) has shown that a gap in skill levels can occur in two ways: when a worker is employed on a job below his or her qualifications, or when a job is made subject to higher credentials than are technically required.

Exclusion and Inadequacy Indices

We estimated only the Exclusion and Inadequacy Indices. These indicators are alike in that both aim to capture the lack of work opportunities, together with the extent of substandard wage employment. They differ in their coverage. The Exclusion Index covers every individual currently in the labor supply, including those who are omitted from the official labor force on the ground that they are not currently looking for a job. The Inadequacy Index covers only family heads or unrelated individuals and bases the criterion of wage adequacy on family size. Workers covered by each index are classified as subemployed if they are, at the time of evaluation:

unemployed;

employed part-time though desiring full-time work;

desiring to work, but for economic or social reasons not currently looking for a job; or

employed in a substandard job, as reflected in low hourly wages.

In other work, we have defined a substandard wage job by treating wage level as a parameter and estimating subemployment indices for alternative wage levels. The BLS lower budget, as discussed above, approximately corresponds to the popular perception of what a job should pay to enable a person or family to "get along" at a minimal level. Therefore, the hourly equivalent of that budget will be used hereafter as the criterion for wage adequacy. Because the Inadequacy Index focuses on family income, the wage adequacy standard is adjusted for family size in computing this index but not in computing the Exclusion Index.

The Inadequacy Index may be challenged because it focuses on family heads and because it considers as potentially subemployed even those family heads who have families with adequate incomes. These criticisms are actually two sides of the same coin, and they go hand in hand with employment policies whose success in confronting poverty depends on multiple family wage earners who are pooling income from several low-wage jobs.

The decision of secondary family members to participate in the labor force may be a matter of free choice for middle- and upper-income family members; however, it is more often a stark necessity for those in low-income families (Rainwater, 1970). In fact, across the entire family income distribution, labor force participation by secondary family members is frequently a response to job difficulties of the principal wage earner (Mincer, 1973). Lampman (1971) showed that the number of wage earners per family in each of the three upper quartiles of the family income distribution is greater than the number of wage earners per family in the lowest quartile. He argued that the mechanism of multiple wage earners has been successful in raising the income of many families. However, Thurow (1972) showed that this mechanism has nearly been pushed to its limit, and that this explains why black family income has failed to gain ground in relation to white family income.[3]

Policies designed to offset social distress by stimulating employment must recognize the force of these arguments. It is no longer desirable to rely on the mechanism of multiple wage earners, even in maintaining the position of families whose income adequacy is based upon the presence of such multiple wage earners. Therefore, the policy target must be the principal wage earner in a family. The Inadequacy Index focuses on that target. Our research has found the Inadequacy Index to be a much better correlate of a variety of social distress indicators than is any poverty index (Giblin, Vietorisz, & Mier, 1974).

Two estimating problems also warrant mentioning. First, estimates of an Inadequacy Index are distorted because surveys either conducted by the Census Bureau or patterned after Census procedures arbitrarily define any adult male in a household as the head. We are currently conducting research to measure the sensitivity of our subemployment computations to this remnant of sex discrimination. Second, procedures for determining if a person wants a job involve judgment. We adopt the principle that a person means what she or he says, and do not try to reduce

the set of people wanting a job by considering social or economic circumstances. For example, if a woman says she wants
a job but is not currently searching for one because of family
responsibilities, we assume that the availability of public child
care services or of jobs paying enough to make private child care
feasible would cause her to initiate a job search, and thus include
her in our base for the index.

We have computed Exclusion and Inadequacy Indices for a
number of urban poverty areas, using information from the 1970
Census Employment Survey (CES). This was a detailed sample
survey of employment characteristics of about 6,000 persons in
each of 60 urban and 8 rural clusters. (The 60 urban clusters
were located within 51 cities.) The sampling areas had been
selected owing to evidence that they were likely to contain high
proportions of persons with low incomes. The urban survey
clusters represented on the average 15% of the respective Standard Metropolitan Statistical Area population, and 33.5% of the
respective central city population. Much of the information from
the individual enumeration areas has been aggregated for each
survey area, and summary results were published in a special series
by the Commerce Department in 1971. For the purposes of our
ongoing research, the individual responses in the 24 survey areas
that were available within disclosure limitations were analyzed.
Table 1.1 is a comparison of the Exclusion and Inadequacy
Indices for an illustrative CES area in Detroit, Michigan.

A comparison of the two indices is important for full employment policy considerations. The Inadequacy Index suggests that
the creation of 75,000 jobs paying a minimum, which, at 1970
prices, averages $3.50 per hour, over all family sizes in the
Detroit poverty area is critical for raising entire families into the
mainstream of society. This should be the policy target. The
Exclusion Index, however, reveals that there is a labor supply of
180,000 who would compete for those critical jobs. Unless we
are prepared to introduce a far greater degree of control over the
movement of workers than seems compatible with prevailing
institutions, it becomes practically impossible to reserve all new
jobs for the family heads in critical need. Full employment policy
must therefore be addressed to all individuals excluded from full
participation in the Detroit economy. The policy must also
include a high minimum wage component—higher than the BLS

Table 1.1 Exclusion Index Compared to Inadequacy Index in Detroit, Michigan, Census Employment Survey Area, Fall 1972

Subemployment Category	Number of Subemployed Individuals	Percentage Subemployed	Number of Subemployed Family Heads or Unrelated Individuals	Percentage Subemployed
Unemployed workers	27,730	11.6	11,900	8.3
Discouraged workers	39,686	16.7	17,783	12.4
Involuntary part-time workers	9,231	3.9	5,365	3.7
Full-time employment at less than $3.50/hr[a]	103,017	43.3	40,300	28.2
Total	179,664	75.5	75,378	52.7
Labor supply[b] (used as a base in computing percentages)	238,086	–	143,049	–

a. Approximate hourly equivalent of the BLS lower-level budget for Detroit in 1970; adjusted for family size in computation of the Inadequacy Index; used without further adjustment in computation of the Exclusion Index.
b. Differs from the official labor force in that it includes discouraged workers.

lower budget applicable to the family circumstances of many individuals who would be competing for new jobs—if the target families are to be brought into the mainstream. A new approach to this problem will be discussed in the closing section.

How Many Jobs Nationwide?

It is possible to compute an Exclusion Index, but not an Inadequacy Index, for the nation by using published data of the Current Population Survey (CPS). The Inadequacy Index, if it could be computed, would reveal the number of family heads in critical need. Yet in order to reach these family heads under current policies, adequate jobs would have to be provided for the entire subemployed labor force. The Exclusion Index reveals the extent of the challenge to full employment policy.

Table 1.2 presents the national Exclusion Index based on the 1972 CPS annual averages. (The 1973 annual averages were not published at the time of writing.) The low-wage component of the Exclusion Index is broken into two segments: $2 per hour, the minimum wage prevailing at that time, and $3.85 per hour, the average BLS lower family budget for the United States.

We assert that 9 million jobs must be created for unemployed and discouraged workers, and 28 million more must be upgraded for the rest of the subemployed in order to meet the goal of full employment at living wages.

A Policy of Full Employment
at Living Wages

A 37-million-job full employment program, on first sight, appears an order of greater magnitude than even the most liberal policymakers are willing to consider. Some have argued that our estimates are unrealistic, that no wage standard beyond the minimum wage should be considered, and that even at so-called full employment there will be 4% frictional unemployment. Even those conservative standards would imply a policy target of more than 14 million jobs, compared to the 3.25 million public jobs provided at the peak of the New Deal's WPA, or the 300,000 jobs

Table 1.2 Exclusion Index for United States, 1972

Subemployment Category	Number of Subemployed Individuals	Percentage Subemployed	Cumulative Number of Subemployed Individuals	Cumulative Percentage Subemployed
Unemployed workers	4,840,000	5.3	4,840,000	5.3
Discouraged workers	4,462,000	4.9	9,302,000	10.2
Involuntary part-time workers	2,624,000	2.9	11,926,000	13.1
Full-time workers earning less than $2/hr.	6,100,000	6.7	18,026,000	19.5
Full-time workers earning $2 to $3.85/hr.	18,801,000	20.6	36,827,000	40.1
Labor supply	91,003,000	–	–	–

SOURCES: Employment and Earnings (January 1973); p. 60, no. 90: Money Income in 1972 of Families and Persons in the United States (December 1973).

provided by the recent Public Employment Program. Yet a 4-, 5-, or even 14-million-job employment program would be inadequate– it would not reach the critical families or individuals in poverty. It would still have to be supplemented by massive and unpopular welfare transfers. The public will not support welfare, however, no matter how efficiently managed, at a level of payments to families sufficient to bring poor people into society's mainstream.

This is why a full employment program at living wages cannot be constructed out of the materials of conventional wisdom. A three-pronged unconventional attack on the problem might include the following:

1. A large scale public service and public goods production program in which jobs would be targeted to the unemployed and underemployed.

At the time of this research, there seemed to be a special need for outputs in the areas of mass transportation, environmental protection, urban reconstruction, public energy, housing, light manufacturing (using local entrepreneurs), and public health. With a sufficiently large program (taking multiplier effects into account), it might be meaningful to discuss the government's "guaranteeing" every citizen-worker a job in either the public or the participating private sector.

2. The coupling of the job guarantee with a living wage level. The BLS lower budget is suggested as the standard.

Because the job guarantee is extended by the government, there is no obstacle to setting individual wage levels differenti- ated by the job seeker's family circumstances, as reflected in the BLS budgets for different family structures. Where equal work results in unequal pay under this system, the differential be- comes a family supplement. With public jobs, this raises no difficulties; with mediated private jobs, it may imply the public subsidization of family supplements.

Such a system of family supplements would be new for the United States, but it has been well accepted for years in a number of Western European countries. No increase in the birthrate has been observed as a result of such supplements. On the contrary, much evidence from cross-sectional sources has emerged at the recent World Population Conference indicating that the birthrate falls as people gain control over their lives with rising living standards. The burden of job and wage guarantees might be reduced if the job guarantee, instead of applying to all workers, were restricted to family heads and unrelated individuals.

A rough estimate of the direct reduction, based on the Detroit figures, is 40%. Of course, some of this reduction would be wiped out if secondary wage earners living in families decided to set themselves up as unrelated individuals in order to become eligible for the job guarantee. This would be more likely to involve grown children than working spouses.

3. A comprehensive framework of infrastructure, product, and man-power planning.

To keep the public job guarantee service from being crushed under a tidal wave of job seekers, the government must engage in far more expansionary macro-policies than were practiced before. This opens up jobs in the private sector for most workers; but to keep inflation under control, it implies the necessity for permanent price, profit, and wage controls. Owing to the restricted operation of market forces under controls, it also implies concern for production planning, at least in the core part of the economy represented by the few hundred largest firms. Moreover, to keep the subsidization of family supplements within tolerable limits, the government must reset minimum wages, perhaps after a period of trial and error, to a level reasonably close to the BLS budget level for the family structure most frequently encountered in the low-income range.

In raising the minimum wage, the government must strike a balance between the reduction of family supplement payments and elevation of the minimum wage above the BLS lower level for unattached individuals or small families. Raising the minimum wage, in any event, implies a series of required measures in the fields of direct public enterprise, technical upgrading of low-productivity firms, labor and management retraining, financing of the added working capital requirements of weak businesses, cushioning the foreign trade impacts, establishing guidelines for the revision of union wage differentials, and many other fields.

The basic elements of this three-pronged approach were present in early drafts of the Equal Opportunity and Full Employment Act of 1976. Yet the planning framework was never defined in enough detail, and the standard for living wages, above all, is badly in need of specification and strengthening. The number of issues raised by each of the three aspects of the overall approach is formidable and will require extended debate to explore in depth. Here we have been able to do no more than define the skeleton of the required approach.

Conclusion

In sum, a policy of full employment at living wages implies that the operation of market forces must be complemented by broad planning measures comparable to the ones that have already been established in Japan and most Western European countries. This represents a major institutional change for the United States but, for better or for worse, leaves the prevailing social relations of production largely untouched. In a private enterprise system, planning and the market are complements, not opposites, as they are popularly perceived. A change in the foundations of this system would require transcendence of both the market and of planning oriented to material incentives. This is not likely to happen soon.

Yet a full employment policy involving a public job guarantee without a standard for living wages could readily be turned into a device for exacting forced labor from the poor. As long as unemployment exists, refusal by many workers to take substandard jobs is masked by the job shortage. If guaranteed jobs, no matter how miserable, were known to be available to all comers, coercive institutional devices could be created that would force poor people to take and keep such jobs. Refusal to do so would then be seen as precipitating a crisis of social authority. Coercive measures against the poor, including criminal sanctions, might well appear legitimate to the large groups of people on the sunny side of the poverty watershed who live by the work ethic—and are alienated by it.

In short, such a policy could open the door to a truly dangerous authoritarian trend of development. Doors behind which monsters may lurk had better be locked and bolted. Full employment policy must mean full employment at living wages.

Notes

1. Wirtz was President Johnson's Secretary of Labor. William Spring (1971, p. 23) describes the political atmosphere that forced Wirtz to commence, then subsequently abandon, attempts to collect poverty area statistics. See also Spring, Harrison, and Vietorisz (1972), Levitan and Taggart (1974), Miller (1973), Vietorisz, Mier, and Giblin (1974).

2. A set of subemployment categories such as these is converted to subemployment rate or an index by examining some population of individuals and categorizing each as subemployed, not subemployed, or not in the labor supply. The subemployment rate is the number subemployed divided by the sum of those subemployed plus those not subemployed. The rate may be expressed as a fraction or as a percentage.

3. Thurow shows that there has actually been a loss of ground, because a deterioration in the black-white individual earnings distribution has overpowered the failing multiple-wage-earner mechanism.

2 | Social Justice and Public Policy

with

HOWARD M. McGARY, JR.

This chapter is a review of John Rawls's Theory of Justice. *It attempts to take the ideas of justice as fairness out of the esoteric realm of philosophical debate and examine their applicability to public policy issues. It particularly focuses on efforts at developing a just and progressive public planning agenda in Cleveland, Ohio, during the tenure of planning director Norman Krumholz. Krumholz began his work under Mayor Carl Stokes, the nation's first big-city African-American mayor. Thus the Cleveland experience served as an important precedent for Chicago during the tenure of Harold Washington.*

Introduction

The greatest single force changing and expanding the role of the federal government in the United States today is the push for equality. And although the orators of this movement still speak primarily in terms of rights, the goal increasingly is to level goods and powers in American society. Today's egalitarians want to use

---

AUTHORS' NOTE: This chapter originally appeared as Mier and McGary (1977). It is reprinted with permission of *Educational Studies*.

the federal government to redistribute wealth and incomes, to equalize differences in education and family backgrounds, and to override the classic principle that what a man consumes must be determined by what he produces or what he owns. The egalitarian movement is essentially authoritarian. It is highly critical of business and contemptuous of laissez-faire economics. (*Business Week*, December 1, 1975, p. 62)

This fear of social justice as representing equality opened a recent three-part series on "Egalitarianism: Threat to a Free Market" in *Business Week* (1975). The series particularly addressed education and employment opportunity as arenas within which government actions are "obviously egalitarian," and pointed to "the fight in the future" over government spending and taxation to support these and similar social programs. Title I of the Elementary and Secondary Education Act of 1965 (ESEA) is such an example of a redistributive program, because it (a) directly transfers federal funds to low-income areas to support the education of children in poverty; (b) attempts, over time, to ensure equality of opportunity by equalizing human resource endowments; and (c) guarantees employment for teachers in financially troubled school districts. The stated goals in Title I of ESEA are very much in consonance with the former two of these notions.

Business Week perceived the disparate forces striving for greater equality as constituting a "movement," and identified John Rawls (1971) as the movement's "guru." Since publishing *A Theory of Justice,* Rawls has indeed become broadly identified with critical social action. For example, *The Cleveland Policy Plan* focuses city planning activities on achieving social equity, and justifies that goal with references to Rawls's work (Cleveland City Planning Commission, 1975).[1]

The objective of *The Cleveland Policy Plan* is stated as follows: "Equity requires that government institutions give priority attention to the goal of promoting a wider range of choices for those Cleveland residents who have few, if any, choices." This goal directs the actions of the Cleveland planners in such issue areas as housing, transportation, and income.

Krumholz, Cogger, and Linner (1975) say that the egalitarian goal leads them to approach each issue with the questions of "who gets, who pays" and to endorse only those proposals that obviously benefit Cleveland residents in general and poor residents in particular.

This perspective has led the Cleveland planners to:

oppose public housing (they felt the supply was adequate);

endorse a housing allowance program;

oppose public fixed rail transit systems (which would not serve the transit-dependent population);

endorse demand-responsive systems;

and finally, oppose private acquisition of the public owned Cleveland Light and Power Company (the electric rates of the private system were higher than the public) in favor of public acquisition of the private system.

In each of these cases, and in numerous similar ones, a policy endorsement from the planning staff was predicated on a sense that the program activity would create more choices for poor residents of Cleveland (Krumholz et al., 1975, p. 301).

A Theory of Justice

The impact of *A Theory of Justice* has been profound and wide-ranging, and yet, as is suggested by the recent publication of Wolff's (1977) *Understanding Rawls,* it is a formidable book. The most provocative reviews have been directed to the interests of a specific discipline (Sartorius, 1975; Nozick, 1974; Arrow, 1973).

A number of Rawls's fundamental concepts have been called into question. For example, Sartorius and Nozick raise methodological issues, and Arrow epistemological ones (Scanlon, 1973; Arrow, 1973). We share some of these concerns, but propose to address certain of the philosophical issues from the more concrete perspective of public policy planning. In reviewing *A Theory of Justice,* we will briefly introduce some salient concepts from the book and then focus on policy questions raised by Title I of ESEA and by the policy actions of the Cleveland planners.

A Theory of Justice is a development of Rawls's (1958) earlier paper "Justice as Fairness." In the book he describes his account of social justice within his own novel form of social contract theory. In the history of liberal ethical theory, there are two contractarian traditions. The first is represented by the ideas of John Locke, and the second by Jean-Jacques Rousseau. Rawls, following in the tradition of these two great thinkers, substitutes his "original position" for the "state of nature" found in the older contractarian approaches. Rawls believes that the "state of nature" is an inappropriate initial choice situation, and that it will not ensure the fairness of whatever agreements are made.

"Justice" for Rawls refers to the process by which we ignore arbitrary distinctions and establish a correct balance between competing claims in relation to the distribution of benefits and burdens that form part of or result from social institutions. Rawls's account of social justice focuses on the macro-structure of society rather than individuals. Rawls believes that social institutions possess several virtues, (e.g., efficiency, stability, and coordination) and that justice is only one of them. Just social institutions will provide for a proper distribution of the benefits and burdens among individuals.

Rawls's contractarian account begins with what he considers to be an initial fair choice situation. He labels this the "original position." In Rawls's hypothetical original position, individuals meet to agree on principles of justice under conditions of uncertainty defined as the "veil of ignorance." The veil of ignorance prevents the hypothetical representatives in the original position from having knowledge of particulars. They lack knowledge of who they are or what their position will be in actual society. For example, they do not know whether they will be rich or poor, educated or uneducated. However, they do have general knowledge of the laws of psychology, sociology, physics, and the principles of human nature. Under these constraints, it is presumed they do not have a notion of justice, but they are capable of having a sense of justice.

The members of Rawls's hypothetical original position, acting behind the veil of ignorance, adopt the "maximin rule" for choosing a principle of justice under conditions of uncertainty.[2] They decide which principle(s) to choose from a finite number of alternatives. Rawls (1971, pp. 152-153) claims that the maximin rule tells us to rank alternatives by their worst possible outcome: "We are to adopt the alternative the worst outcome of which is superior to the worst outcomes of the others." In other words, the hypothetical parties in Rawls's original position play it safe by employing the maximin rule.

Rawls argues that under these conditions, representatives would choose his two principles as a matter of rational choice.[3] These two principles, in order of priority, are:

1. Each person is to have an equal right to the most extensive basic liberty compatible with a similar liberty for others;
2. Social and economic inequalities are to be arranged so that they are both
   a. reasonably expected to be to everyone's advantage, particularly to the advantage of the least well off, and
   b. attached to positions and offices open to all. (p. 60)

His first principle is usually referred to as his "equal liberty principle." The first part of his second principle is the "difference principle" and the second part is his "fair equality of opportunity principle."

The priority rules which hold among Rawls's principles are a crucial feature of his theory. The order in which his principles must be satisfied prevents liberty from being traded off for economic gain or greater opportunity. Preserving liberty and ensuring fair equality of opportunity, according to Rawls, allow us to maintain that whatever else social justice involves, it forbids the establishment of any social arrangement leading to the denial of self-respect for individuals or classes. For Rawls, self-respect is an essential part of his system and a crucial aspect of his argument.

Some commentators, like the authors of the *Business Week* article and the Cleveland planners, have labeled Rawls's conception of justice "egalitarian." This label is correct to the extent that it stresses Rawls's thinking that equality is an important factor to be considered in creating a just society, but it is inaccurate to the extent that it causes us to believe mistakenly that social equality is Rawls's basic principle for determining when a distribution is just.

Rawls is not a strict egalitarian, and believes that some inequality may be acceptable in a just society. It becomes crucial in his account to delimit what constitutes a just inequality. Rawls thus develops a concept of fairness which is one of the important factors involved in assessing whether an inequality is just. A just distribution must be a fair distribution, but inequality may be present in a fair distribution.

We might best understand what Rawls means by justice as fairness by considering the case raised by Rawls in Section 28 of his book. Here he tries to demonstrate that the principle of average utility is not a fair principle. The principle of average utility prescribes that over the entire community, we ought to maximize not the total but the average utility per capita.

Rawls imagines a slaveholder, confronted by his slaves, attempting to justify his position to them by claiming that, first of all, given the circumstances of their society, the institution of slavery is in fact necessary to produce the greatest average happiness; and second, in the initial contract situation he would choose the average utility principle while knowing the risk of justifiably being held a slave. Rawls points out that such an argument clashes with our intuitions concerning what is just. In fact, he finds the argument outrageous.

What is wrong with slavery, argues Rawls, is that it is unfair. Thus he concludes that a distribution must be fair if it is to be just. He contends that his two principles allow for fairness. Consequently, they should be favored over any principle that does not. Rawls provides three main reasons for contending that his principles of justice are fair:

1. the two principles preserve the basic rights of individuals and insure them against bad eventualities;
2. the principles motivate members of a given social order to support that order, because everyone's interests are considered; and
3. the principles regard persons as ends rather than means, a Kantian notion.

With these notions from *A Theory of Justice,* we return to our two policy examples. We shall ask, first, whether they correctly reflect Rawls's concept of justice as fairness, and, second, whether they represent tests of the universality of his conceptions. *The Cleveland Policy Plan* will be addressed first because it permits us to focus on Rawls's intent. Title I of ESEA, on the other hand, shifts the focus to means used to achieve just intentions.

Justice in Action

The goal of the Cleveland planners is the creation of more choices for those without options. They have seen their role as guarantor of choices for all Cleveland residents, especially for the poor. Within the Cleveland policy arena, employment issues have not received as much attention from the planners as housing, transportation, and income issues. Nevertheless, we wish to limit analysis to their employment activities, because as Lampman (1971, p. 53) and others argue, economic growth has had probably the most significant impact, directly or indirectly, on creating choices for the poor.

The Cleveland planners have been active opponents of Central Business District (CBD) development and proponents of neighborhood development. They oppose CBD development in large measure because it can offer little in the way of jobs to Cleveland residents. On the other hand, the planners have supported plant expansions and efforts to retain such local industry. Although this sort of activity reflects a concern for Rawls's liberty principle, it seems more strongly a manifestation of the difference and equality of opportunity principles.

Rawls (1971, p. 73) says that equality of opportunity ensues if "those who are at the same level of talent and ability, and have the same willingness to use them, should have the same prospects of success regardless of their initial place in the social system." However, standing alone, this principle would be rejected by an individual in the original position because it leaves the distribution of income and wealth to be determined by the distribution of natural abilities. The difference principle mitigates this effect by dictating that the higher expectations of those with more natural talent are permissible only if they exist as part of a scheme designed to improve the expectations of the least advantaged members of society.

Are the actions of the Cleveland planners, then, helping achieve social justice? The answer to that hinges on two questions: Are they serving the least advantaged population, and are they improving their life expectations? The former question raises the issue of defining and measuring poverty. In this regard, Rawls (1971, p. 98) provides little help, declaring that "it seems impossible to avoid a certain arbitrariness."

Rainwater (1974), however, has found that people's perceptions of the minimum income needed for a family to "get along," or socially participate in society, are substantially higher than what the public regards as justified public assistance to the same family. Incorporating that "get along" budget into a measure of work-related poverty called a "subemployment rate," Vietorisz, Mier, and Harrison (1975) have found that more than 40% of the U.S. labor force either desire full-time work or are employed in low-wage jobs. This subemployed population, earning less than a social participation income, is more than double the population of the "officially poor." By subemployment standards, the Cleveland planners are serving the least-advantaged population only when they broaden their focus beyond the poor.

The second question about enhancing life circumstances is probably more telling in the Cleveland case. Again, Rawls does not provide much help. He suggests construction of an index of "primary goods" with which to monitor life circumstances, and, in places, says that "self-respect" is the most important of those goods.

Low-wage, low-skill, unstable employment is part of the same social milieu as welfare and any number of other social support programs (Mier, Vietorisz, & Giblin, 1975; Braverman, 1974; Tussing, 1975). Unless one believes that all work brings with it self-respect, change is, then, in form only and means nothing in terms of life prospects. This is frequently the sort of "change," of course unintended, that emerges from the employment activities of the Cleveland planners. In their other arenas of action, the same question could be raised about the quality of choices they are creating.

In sum, the Cleveland experience suggests a confused notion of social justice, at least as Rawls defines it. Moreover, it suggests a confusion about social justice and self-respect in Rawls's formulations. We wish to address this latter problem from the perspective of Title I of ESEA. The redistributive goals of Title I are unambiguous:

> In recognition of the general education needs of children of low income families and the impact that concentration of low-income families have on the ability of local educational agencies to support adequate educational programs, the Congress hereby declares it to be the policy of the United States to provide financial assistance to local educational agencies serving areas with concentrations of children from low-income families to expand and improve their education programs by various means which contribute particularly to meeting the special educational needs of educationally deprived children.

After a series of amendments, more than $1.8 billion is now allocated annually, based on a formula counting the following special categories of school age children: (a) the number in families below the official poverty line as counted in 1970, (b) two-thirds of the number in families above the current poverty line (as escalated since 1970) who receive Aid to Families with Dependent Children (AFDC) payments, and (c) the number of migrants or delinquents, regardless of family income.

The allocation formula immediately raises the issue of whether resources are being directed to all of the disadvantaged population, and in this regard our observations on the Cleveland activities are still germane. Moreover, the Act, as a means for ensuring fair equality of opportunity, is fraught with both practical and conceptual difficulties. To an extent these difficulties are due to a confusion, transcending the Act itself, about what is equality of educational opportunity, whether it is necessary in a just society, and how far the state should go to ensure it.

Rawls gives fairly clear answers, as we noted above, to the first question. With regard to the second, Rawls and other egalitarians like Nagel (1973) believe emphatically that there is a general right to fair equality of opportunity, while other philosophers, such as Nozick (1974), deny that any such general right exists.

Rawls's fair equality of opportunity principle allows him to redistribute the holdings of some in order to ensure that everyone has an equal chance for desired offices and social positions. Nozick takes issue with redistribution to ensure fair equality of opportunity. He argues that any egalitarian, paternalistic, or utopian motivated redistribution is unjust. He believes that individuals deserve only what they are entitled to and that the just state should protect these entitlements.[4] Rawls, nonetheless, is unwavering in his adherence to the necessity of equality of opportunity. In terms of educational opportunity, he would reject the notion that some inequality is just.

How far, then, should the state go to ensure it? Rawls is, at best, vague about the answer to this question. In reading Rawls, one is not clear how he might answer some of the following sorts of questions: Should children from rich families be permitted to have private tutors? Would Rawls restrict the travel of students who are better-off if, for example, traveling abroad gave them a greater opportunity to obtain desired social positions?

With regard to Title I of ESEA, it is doubtful that increased resources would actually bring about equality of opportunity, although this and similar questions are the subject of ongoing Office of Education research. As long as there are "better" public schools in the middle and high family income residential areas, improving inferior schools without bringing them to par with others will not ensure equality of opportunity. In Rawlsian terms, offices and positions will not be open to all, because some will have less opportunity to achieve them. However, Rawls really provides little guidance on a better course of action other than to spend, "at least for a period of time," still more resources. In this regard, Rawls agrees with proponents of an unequal distribution of resources favoring "impacted" schools, a form of "affirmative discrimination" (Guthrie, Kleindorfer, Levin, & Stout, 1971).

Conclusion

We have tried to show that Rawls's precepts of social justice raise some provocative questions about the fairness of social policy. In focusing on the cases of *The Cleveland Policy Plan* and Title I of ESEA, we have found cause to question the justice of specific activities that on the surface seem acceptable. However, we have also found a certain vagueness in Rawls's work at critical junctures. We think, nonetheless, that further pursuit of Rawls's line of thought promises useful criteria for evaluating social policy.

Several concluding observations about *A Theory of Justice* might be offered. We have touched on only a few of its key conceptions—ones bearing most directly on the policy problems we have discussed. A number of topics are at once important and controversial, and we wish to address at least a few to convey the flavor of that controversy. For example, Rawls (1971, pp. 270-274) tries, unconvincingly we believe, to demonstrate that his precepts are equally applicable to differing social organizations of production. Harvey (1973, p. 15) suggests that this is a consequence of Rawls's insistence on analytically separating distribution from production. We agree with the Marxian notion that production and distribution are dialectically interwoven.

A second example concerns utilitarianism. Rawls spends a great deal of effort discounting utilitarianism, and yet, because he never clearly deals with the issue of *how much* redistribution and enhancement of life prospects are in order, he has been used by utilitarians to vindicate perverse pareto optimal actions. Phelps (1973), for example, analyzes the equity of wage taxes by maximizing the minimum utility and finds a regressive tax to be equitable—something Rawls would find unthinkable. This contradiction occurs precisely because Rawls (1971, pp. 277-280) equivocates on the issue of progressive taxation, fearing that it will cut too much into the efficiency of production.

A third area of ambiguity concerns the notion of self-respect in relation to other primary goods. This is never clearly spelled out by Rawls. Tussing (1975) observes that programs which redistribute social goods to the poor are designed to exclude a redistribution of self-respect. He draws attention to self-respect as the discriminating factor of a "dual welfare system" when he says,

> "Social insurance," the heart of the welfare system for the nonpoor, has been constructed in such a way as to be accepted as legitimate, to protect the integrity and dignity of the people involved. . . . "Public charity," or the welfare system for the poor, has been constructed in a way that reflects its "illegitimacy." (p. 101)

Rawls suggests a transfer branch of government to redistribute goods according to needs. However, he fails to recognize that categorical (as opposed to universal) programs whose delivery is delimited by need are the very mechanism used to distinguish "insurance" from "charity." Finally, some philosophers find Rawls's theory suspect in important places. For example, Sartorius (1975) (an actutilitarian) finds fault with Rawls's claim that utilitarianism can theoretically result in some people living a "miserable" existence in order to create the greatest average happiness per capita. In order for the utilitarian to meet this objection, from a Rawlsian viewpoint, he must assume that in a society acting in accordance with the principle of average utility, there will be a certain base level of primary goods. Rawls feels that such an assumption is unwarranted. Sartorius (1975, pp. 124-127), in turn, contends that Rawls also assumes a base level of primary goods in order to make his maximin strategy compelling. Sartorius claims that when a decision maker faces a choice, in which the minimum outcome is below the social base, he or she will become more of a risk taker and pursue a utility maximizing, or maximax, strategy.

There have been other interesting criticisms of Rawls's theory of justice. Nozick (1974), whom we mentioned earlier, challenges Rawls's whole strategy for arriving at principles of justice. He claims that Rawls's process for generating principles of justice is incapable of yielding principles that take into account relevant historical entitlements. Kenneth Arrow (1973) raises some epistemological worries about Rawls's hypothetical original position.

We do not think that any of these criticisms have rendered Rawls's theory unsound, but they have pointed out interesting issues that need to be resolved. In sum, we urge anyone concerned with issues of social justice and social equity to become familiar with Rawls's work.

Notes

1. This planning report is unique in the discipline and is considered to signal a radical departure from traditional planning practices. As a consequence, it has become the focus of a number of reviews, including the important "Journal Forum" of the *Journal of the American Institute of Planners.*

2. In facing decisions under uncertainty, a pessimist or skeptic would focus on the worst possible outcomes and choose among that set the one which would leave him or her best off. This is called a "maximin" decision. In other words, the decision maker would "maximize" his or her advantage among the set of "minimum" outcomes. See Baumol (1965).

3. Rawls (1971, p. 124) argues that the following alternatives would be considered and rejected by parties in the original position: the classical principle of utility, the principle of average utility, the principle of perfection, intuitionistic conceptions, egoistic conceptions, and mixed conceptions). Much of Chapter 3 of *A Theory of Justice* is devoted to the argument against these alternatives.

4. Generally stated, Nozick (1974) believes that a holding is just if it comes about through legitimate means. To be more specific, for Nozick, a holding is just if we (a) acquire it justly (according to Lockean property rights); or (b) obtain it from a just transfer (like legal sale, a bequest or a gift) or through some rectification of violations of (a) or (b). According to Nozick, in order to determine if a holding is just or not, we need to know how the holding came about.

3 | Job Generation as a Road to Recovery

*This chapter was written as part of a group of
essays documenting a national congress of
cities "on the road to recovery" held in
Cleveland, Ohio, in late 1982. The congress
extolled the Reagan-era goals of public-private
partnerships and breaking down dependency
on government. This essay was one of the few
dissenting voices, pointing to several
grass-roots-based initiatives that suggested
another path to recovery, if not a more
effective one than a more just one.*

Introduction

A city's recovery means: a regained ability to compete with its
suburbs as a place to live; a regained favorable climate for investment and a consequent growth for jobs; as a product of the above
two, a regained independence from external subsidies.

This definition of "recovery" included in the invitation to the
1983 Cities' Congress on Roads to Recovery in Cleveland immediately focused attention on the importance of job generation
(Porter & Sweet, 1984). It was somewhat disappointing, then,
to find among success stories presented at the congress by
delegations from 18 cities very little discussion about jobs. Most

AUTHOR'S NOTE: Originally published as Mier (1984b) in Porter and Sweet's
(1984) *Road to Recovery*. Reproduced with permission of Rutgers University
Center for Urban Policy Research.

of the shared success stories focused on capital investment, usually in real estate, and assumed that jobs naturally follow from such investment.

The absence of "jobs stories" comparable to the "investment stories" raises a series of questions that guide the following reexamination of the Cities' Congress. Is it too early on the "road to recovery" to observe the new jobs being created? Is the generation of jobs even necessary for successful revitalization? Were there any patterns of recovery shared among the success stories that suggest a greater possibility that new jobs will be created?

Although 60% of the cases presented claimed specific job creation objectives, only 40% reported success in this area, and only 27% that the jobs were being captured by the low-skilled and minorities. "Aldy" Edwards, executive director of the New Haven Downtown Council, reported that adoption of an employment strategy reaching those segments of the population with serious unemployment problems was the "next step" in New Haven. David Bergholz, Deputy Director of the Allegheny Conference on Community Development in Pittsburgh, put it more bluntly: "If you ask me candidly about where most communities have been least successful, it is around the issue of jobs. We aren't doing much beyond the usual things like summer youth employment."

Nevertheless, several approaches to job generation did emerge at the congress. However, I first want to argue that generating new jobs is an essential component of recovery. I will then examine four approaches to job generation: general service sector revitalization, high-tech manufacturing and research and development (R&D), public policy-induced job development, and self-help job development. In focusing on these approaches, I am attempting to be analytical rather than reportorial—excellent summaries of the success stories are presented in Porter and Sweet (1984). I also will be trying to draw some generalizations from the presentations that I observed.

The final section of this chapter will examine possible ingredients, hinted at during the congress, that might stimulate recovery. I will argue that the latter two approaches—public policy-induced and self-help job development, probably in combination—represent the best local strategy for true recovery, a recovery that genuinely attacks social dependency.

Jobs for the Unemployed as an
Essential Road to Recovery

The problem of "dependency" was a central theme of the Cities' Congress, beginning with Porter's assertion that recovery was synonymous with "independence from external subsidies." As Porter candidly points out in his preface to Porter and Sweet (1984, pp. xi-xv), the concept of dependency is complex and fraught with ambiguity.[1] Nevertheless, the clear linkage between local government fiscal stress and individual poverty emphasizes the need to focus recovery on those needing work. (After all, for every federal dollar spent in support of non-welfare-related state and local government programs, more than four are spent in support of welfare.)[2] James Rouse passionately argued this in his keynote address to the Cities' Congress.

Unemployment is a major social problem with both deep historical roots and ties to the national and international economies. Nevertheless, as long as we are a society that recognizes a responsibility for those either without work opportunities or unable to work, no city can afford to ignore employment problems. A city's self-sufficiency is integrally tied to that of its citizens.

If there is to be an effort to achieve greater self-sufficiency, is the stimulation of private investment sufficient? Many congress participants believed so. "Sandy" Taggart, president of the Near North Development Corporation in Indianapolis, most clearly articulated it when explaining the logic of the recovery strategy for the North Meridan Corridor area of Indianapolis. He said: "First, you've got to get the investment to create jobs. Then the jobs create a demand for better housing and retail services."

This reduction of the job problem to an investment problem was almost an article of faith at the congress. However, this supply side concept ignores the myriad problems that can get in the way of translating investment into job growth, including the technological reorganization of work, the need to retrain massive numbers of workers, and significant private investment in less productive enterprises that do not provide good-quality work opportunities (Harrison & Bluestone, 1983; Reich, 1983).

An example of the complicated interplay of these effects often looks like this. In order to compete in the international economy, a local manufacturer must invest in new computerized numerical-control technology. An adverse effect of this is technological displacement of many skilled workers. In order to reemploy them, both retraining and job creation efforts are needed. The short-run effect is probably fewer jobs and greater "dependency," with the long-run impact a matter of speculation (Choate, 1982; Eckstein & Tannenwald, 1981; Ginzberg, 1982; Magaziner & Reich, 1982, pp. 41-64).

An effective road to recovery must not ignore these interactions. Because they are highly idiosyncratic, every investment opportunity must be probed for its employment impact. The implication of this, to be developed in more detail, is that local governments can influence investment decisions to enhance job opportunities for the needy.

Approaches to Job Generation

This section begins to look at some of the approaches to recovery being undertaken by cities represented at the congress. To repeat, these include service sector, high-tech, public policy, and self-help approaches. The logic of distinguishing among them comes from the participants of the congress themselves, and represents differences in emphasis and understandings of local development conditions more than uniquely different strategies. Thus different approaches may overlap when viewed from the perspective of geography, sector of the economy, or key development factors. For example, high-tech development may affect the service sector and be public-sector induced.

Service Sector Emphasis

Virtually every city presenting cases at the congress reported significant developments in the service sector, usually in the central business district. Typically, the developments involve expansion of office and retail space, addition of hotels and convention facilities, and residential construction targeted to the professional class. Equally common was the presence of public money leveraging private investment. Examples include Oakland using an Urban Development Action Grant (UDAG) to finance a portion of a $48-million Hyatt Hotel, and Indianapolis using a $12.8-million UDAG for a variety of downtown development projects.

Nevertheless, little evidence of direct new job generation was presented in these success stories. This should not be surprising because such development often represents a job-holding action, yielding not net new jobs, but rather an expansion of office and retail space and an upgrading of its quality.[3] In other words, the space per employee expands, but not the total number of employees. Such activity is important to job retention, but does not open job opportunities to the dependent populations.

Creation of construction jobs is often pointed to as a positive indirect benefit of downtown revitalization. However, with the exception of Oakland, no city reported efforts to open the building trades to minorities, women, or low-income groups. Furthermore, few reported efforts to involve unions in the public-private partnership being formed to spawn recovery.[4] The Oakland exception, to be discussed in more detail below, consists of setting minority employment goals in any situation involving public financial support of private construction.

In sum, the revitalization of the downtown service sector probably received the most attention at the congress. Although it did show the ability of cities to mobilize significant capital investment—particularly when public funds are used to leverage private investment—it also presented, of all the approaches, the least evidence of creating jobs for the "permanently" unemployed.

High-Tech Emphasis

Although there was little direct discussion of high-tech development at the congress, it played an important role in the efforts of three cities: St. Louis, Indianapolis, and New Haven. The Washington University Medical Center Redevelopment Corporation in St. Louis was able to convince St. Louis-headquartered Monsanto Chemical Company to open a new research laboratory adjacent to the Medical Center. The key to Monsanto's decision appears to have been access, for research purposes, to Washington University Medical Center's fine science library.

A comparable strategy is unfolding on the near north side of Indianapolis, where the city and the Near North Development Corporation are using Methodist Hospital as the bait to attract medically related manufacturing to an industrial park being developed adjacent to it. No industry has, as yet, been attracted.

However, the site has been cleared, infrastructure installed, and the land cost "written down."

The third case of high-tech development is in New Haven, where Yale University has entered into a joint venture with Olin Corporation and the City of New Haven to begin development of an 80-acre research park on the site of a former Olin manufacturing facility adjacent to the University. Olin Corporation, a longtime resident of New Haven, will continue to operate R&D facilities on the site. Finally, the city promises considerable infrastructure improvements tailored to the needs of any prospective tenants.

Although none of the three cities promoted these high-tech developments as the central element of its recovery efforts, they are worth examining for two reasons. First, in each case they were presented as an approach offering great potential for new job creation. Second, throughout the nation, public attention is turning to high-tech development as a solution to the recession and heightened international competition.[5]

It must be noted that only in the Washington University/Monsanto case has any development moved to the implementation stage. Further, the jobs created there have largely been scientific and highly professional administrative jobs. In none of the three cases are sophisticated training programs being planned to attempt to open job opportunities to the local unemployed population, because the likelihood of these programs being successful is minimal. Even efforts to upgrade skilled and semi-skilled workers dislocated by foreign competition have not been successful (Corson & Nicholson, 1980). There is much less reason to be optimistic about the possibility of training the low-skilled for high-tech jobs.

Are the three cases of high-tech development useful approaches to providing meaningful employment opportunities, or are they examples of endeavors that have a high cost and a low probability of payoff? In a speech to the Cities' Congress Planning Committee in April 1982, Pat Choate cautioned that the technological transformation of production sweeping the world promises a significant net domestic job contraction in manufacturing, with employment as a percentage of the labor force decreasing by an order of two or three (also see Choate, 1982). In addition to high-tech production, the competition for new high-tech R&D

facilities is becoming intense, with virtually every major university or other research facility in the country developing adjoining research parks ("University Officials," 1982). Furthermore, business location decisions are complex, multifaceted ones (Schemmer, 1982). As James Rouse suggested in his keynote address to the congress, it is highly unlikely that high-tech industrial parks will be adequate magnets to high-tech industry, in isolation from a comprehensive effort to upgrade the quality of the urban environment including schools and social amenities. The sum of these negative effects doubtless would intimidate a even bold gambler.

An important recent study by Bennett Harrison (1982) charts other pitfalls of a high-tech road to recovery and suggests an alternative path to industry redevelopment. In discussions of high-tech development, Massachusetts, with its development along Route 128, is often cited as the prototype, along with California's Silicon Valley. Harrison shows that in a recent 2-year period, high-tech development in Massachusetts accounted for less than one out of four new jobs created, and high-tech R&D for less than 1%. This finding should be combined with David Birch's work, showing that most job growth comes from expansion of existing industry. The sobering conclusion is that the economic development payoff from focusing so much attention on attracting new high-tech facilities appears slight.

The same issue may be examined in another way. Despite almost two decades of significant high-tech development, Harrison finds that the shoe industry in New England, after being ravaged by international competition, still employs one-third more people than all of the combined industries defined as high-tech. A major problem for New England is the technological transformation of the shoe industry. The problem involves a range of activities, including adapting computer-assisted design to an industry with many small, individual manufacturers who lack the scale to adopt such new technology efficiently; developing vocational training that focuses on the new design and manufacturing technologies; and promoting development efforts that build on the skills of the workers who will be displaced by the new technology.

Although not discussed in high-tech terms, the best example at the congress of investment-facilitating technology transformation is the Washington University Medical Center itself. Interestingly, the medical-services sector is generally excluded from lists of high-tech sectors, even though it is a major consumer of new technology. As a consequence of WUMC's efforts, employment at the complex has expanded by several thousand. To me, this dramatically underscores the opportunities associated with high-technology catalyzed development once rigid and narrow approaches are abandoned (Mier, 1983).

Public Policy Emphasis

St. Louis and Oakland represent interesting contrasts, with respect to the role of local government in directly attacking the problem of unemployment. Former St. Louis Community Development Director John Roach attributed St. Louis's turnaround to a recognition that Community Development funds gave the city a competitive edge against the suburbs which "could not be wasted funding poverty." This theme was reiterated by Lynton Edwards, Executive Director for Development, Mayor's Office, City of St. Louis, who described St. Louis's development strategy as based on the dual premises that " 'poverty' is a national, not a local, problem" and that " 'profits' is not a dirty word in St. Louis."

St. Louis, then, chooses not to attack dependency directly, believing instead that reduced dependency will follow from improved nationwide economic performance and an improved local private investment climate. This view, of course, is quite in consonance with the urban policy of the Reagan administration presented at the congress by E. S. Savas, Assistant Secretary for Policy Development and Research of the Department of Housing and Urban Development. Following this thinking, St. Louis, for example, has invested its community development funds in public infrastructure improvements in places it believes likely to attract private investments, such as the one surrounding the Washington University Medical Center.

A critical question with regard to this public-private partnership is whether WUMC would have proceeded with its investment plans with less public investment in the area. In other words, in terms of a job-development payoff, could a lesser public role produce the same outcome, freeing public resources for investment elsewhere? Or, alternatively, could a more substantial social payoff have been derived from the public investment, such as firm commitments to targeting employment opportunities for needy St. Louis residents?

The Oakland approach departs dramatically from that of St. Louis. Mayor Lionel Wilson told the congress that employment, especially for minorities and youths, is the top priority in Oakland. Like other cities at the congress, Oakland tackles the problem by entering into partnerships with the private sector. For example, 30 local corporations, led by the Clorox Corporation, the *Oakland Tribune,* and the Kaiser Corporation, have joined to acquire a majority partnership in a new hotel development to be managed by the Hyatt Hotel chain. As was mentioned earlier, the city supported this development with an Urban Development Action Grant-based loan covering 12.5% of the development costs. However, at this point, Oakland began to depart from the norm.

More than most other cities, Oakland seemed to have recognized what James Rouse stated to the congress—that presently the urban real estate market is robust relative to that of the suburbs and that cities need not approach the bargaining table as weak partners.[6] They bargained for a return from their Hyatt investment, which is being used to capitalize a revolving loan fund available only to neighborhood-oriented small businesses.[7] Based on this early success at bargaining for profit sharing, the city has aggressively pursued its employment goals.

The city council has adopted a policy to promote minority and neighborhood organization equity participation in publicly assisted development projects. The policy states that any project receiving any form of public subsidy should strive for the following:

1. 26% of all construction expenditures should go to minority firms.
2. 50% of the construction work force should be minorities.
3. 40% of all professional work associated with the construction (architecture and engineering, legal, and so on) should be with minority firms.
4. In situations where the city acquires the land and writes down its cost for the developers, the land is transferred through a minority- or neighborhood-based local development corporation (LDC), such as the Oakland Local Development Corporation. The LDC uses the land to capitalize at least a 40% share in a joint venture with a private developer.

The city of Oakland has had considerable success in realizing these goals. Office of Economic Development and Employment Director George Williams reports that the goals have largely been realized in the construction of a new convention center adjoining the Hyatt Hotel and in new office buildings occupied by the Transamerica Corporation, Clorox Corporation, and the Wells Fargo Bank. Mr. Williams characterizes the goal of an equity stake in the development property the toughest to achieve and one that provokes the "hardest bargaining." Nevertheless, some modest successes have been realized here. Minority firms own 6% of the Hyatt Hotel and 8% of the new $21-million Third Office Building in the Civic Center complex.

The city's confidence in its ability to achieve its goals hinges on efforts of the Oakland Economic Development Corporation, a quasi-public, nonprofit group, to continue to attract investment to Oakland, and on the OEDC's threefold thrust of training the disadvantaged, providing direct small business assistance, and using downtown development to generate capital for stimulating the neighborhood's economies. They believe that this comprehensive approach is essential to increasing the attractiveness of doing business with the city of Oakland. Otherwise, it would merely increase the development costs and presumably the amount of necessary public subsidy.

Finally, Mayor Wilson said that the city places considerable emphasis on Oakland's neighborhood program for two reasons: to foster trust in the efficacy of public-private partnership, and to ensure that the benefits of the development process accrue to the needy. Although there is no formal policy of increasing resident employment, the city has aggressively pursued such a goal. It has recently signed employment agreements with the Hyatt Corporation and with developers of the Third Office Building.

Several lessons emerge from this public-policy approach. First is the possibility of an authentic bargaining process taking place in which the public sector recognizes that it has something to give and should not hesitate to get. Second is the possibility of directing the outcome of this bargaining process to upgrading local capacity, especially local ownership. Local control is viewed by Mayor Wilson as the best guarantor that the ultimate benefits of the development will reach Oakland's unemployed. Finally, as seen in both Oakland and St. Louis, public-sector professional staff are needed who understand business and development and are comfortable at the bargaining table.

Self-Help Emphasis

Several development efforts presented at the Cities' Congress included a neighborhood component. I have already described Oakland's neighborhood emphasis. An example of directly using the city's policy and program tools to promote neighborhood ownership is the development of a 13-acre industrial site. The city purchased the site for $1.2 million and is using a $1.5-million UDAG to finance site improvements. This $2.7-million public investment has been loaned to a neighborhood-owned local development corporation (LDC) to underwrite a 50% equity share in the development. The other 50% share is held by a private developer, who is granting the $2.7-million loan in exchange for entitlement, for tax purposes, to depreciate the assets. This project is too early in the development cycle to generate any jobs. It promises financial independence for the neighborhood LDC and may create the conditions for further self-help development.

A second case is the Near North Development Corporation in Indianapolis. A nonprofit entity initiated and subsidized by nearby Methodist Hospital, Near North is more directly concerned with neighborhood quality-of-life issues than with direct job generation. Accordingly, with assistance from the Planning Department at Ball State University, it has engaged in planning to promote housing and commercial revitalization.

The only case presented at the congress of direct job generation efforts by a neighborhood organization representing the needy, or dependent, population was Jubilee Housing, Inc., in Washington, D.C. (Lieske, 1984). The efforts of Jubilee Housing have been modest, but they represent part of a long community development tradition (Bowsher, 1980). The multifaceted neighborhood movement of the 1960s frequently turned to community control and autonomy as a solution to social distress and powerlessness (Goering, 1979; Levy, 1979; Hampden-Turner, 1975). Its major achievement lay in the creation of community development corporations sponsored by the Office of Economic Opportunity and the Ford Foundation.[8]

Although the self-sufficiency movement struck a low profile throughout much of the 1970s, by no means did it lose its intensity (Boyte, 1980). The economic development thrust of neighborhood efforts has been to intervene directly, either as partners or as activists, in as many local processes of job generation as possible to ensure that jobs reach the current, often unemployed, residents of a given neighborhood, thus minimizing involuntary relocation and yielding some modicum of economic and social justice (Berger & Neuhaus, 1977, pp. 8-18; Boyte, 1982). Their ultimate effectiveness is probably limited more by the sense of their local economic arena—a sense often sharpened in efforts at public-private partnership like those discussed at the congress—than by their own inherent capacity. In Oakland, for example, there seems to be a broad public consensus that most job generation efforts at least partially "belong" to the local constituency, and that the meaning of "partially" ought to be determined in public-private negotiation.

Several themes seen earlier, as well as some new ones, emerge in the self-help approach. First is a willingness to enter into partnerships and to engage in bargaining with other actors in the development process. Second is an emphasis on local control of the development process through ownership, training, and management. Finally, there seems to be the possibility, exemplified by Near North and Jubilee, of trying to view development comprehensively and engage in planning that goes beyond merely reacting to crises.

Conclusion

This review of the job-generating efforts and outcomes presented at the Cities Congress began with the observation that there was little to review and a question about whether the lack of success at creating jobs was important. I argued that a job-generation component of a recovery strategy, particularly one targeted to the unemployed, is important. Much of the congress focused on innovative ways to stimulate capital investment. I argued that capital investment, though necessary, is by no means sufficient to guarantee recovery because the development process is not a simple one. As Peter Drucker (1981) and many others assert, a variety of policies are needed simply to target investment to more productive enterprises and to retrain the technologically redundant workers.

The format of the congress precluded probing too deeply into why there does not seem to be much job creation in current local economic recovery activity. In any case, David Bergholz's frank self-assessment, "[We] have been least successful . . . around the issue of jobs," serves as an adequate standpoint from which to begin to look for threads of promises rather than proven successes in the congress stories. Several threads were present, and below I will sum them up. However, it is important to keep them in context, of which there are two dimensions that I believe are important. First, cities are intimately linked to the national and international economies, and will not be able to go it alone. Second, they will continue to need external support from state and national governments. Few of the success stories at the congress could have been told without the dependency of local governments on federal resources.

Although the Oakland case may come closest, no recovery model presented at the congress in and of itself represented a clear path to eliminating dependency by generating jobs for the needy. However, a mixture of elements from various cases begins to present a picture of what that path might look like. The picture can be partially shaped if one thinks of Jubilee Housing as being located in Oakland.[9] Seven items seem to emerge:

1. Meaningful partnerships in development must be constructed, involving not just the public sector, business, and civic leadership, as was so often seen at the congress, but also labor and neighborhood leadership. The test of the meaningful nature of the partnerships might be the degree to which different actors actually enter into contractual arrangements.

2. Conscious and planned efforts to use every development project as an opportunity to upgrade the human resources of a community through on- and off-the-job education and training. Oakland's employment goals policy and the training it offers might be examples of this.

3. Encouragement of local ownership, especially that which is more participatory in nature, such as cooperatives or community-owned development entities. Oakland promotes local owner-

ship, but seems to stop short of promoting Jubilee Housing-type models.

4. Development and utilization of professional capacity to implement development efforts. The prevailing model of the congress, as evidenced in St. Louis, was to turn the development over to the private sector. Jubilee Housing, supported by philanthropically sponsored technical assistance, shows the potential of neighborhood-based development entities that may be more responsive to the community.

5. A broad package of resources targeted to more comprehensively upgrading the local quality of life, including improving schools and rehabilitating public, physical infrastructure. James Rouse and Pat Choate stressed the importance of this dimension, and almost every city at the congress was struggling with the issues.

6. A capital pool to assist new business in capital formation, and existing business in technological transformation. Oakland's efforts to stimulate neighborhood-based, small business development is a partial example. (For an example involving insurance companies, see "Older Industrial Cities," 1982).

7. A key to bringing the preceding six elements together and, particularly, to activating partnerships, is a bargaining process between all parties affected by the development process.[10] To exclude the community or neighborhoods and labor from the bargaining process, during which significant development decisions are made, curtails both the spirit of participation and probably innovation (Mier, 1983). Few cities of the congress, Oakland appearing to be one exception, seemed to view bargaining as compatible with the spirit of partnership. Further, there was no evidence that the bargaining process, where it did occur, was an open one.

These seven approaches begin to illustrate just how complex the process is of moving from increasing urban investment to generating jobs for the needy. This outline is not intended to represent a comprehensive theory of recovery, but is rather a restatement of some things that seem to be working in a limited sense and should work better, taken together. Clearly, these elements cannot exist in a vacuum apart from national and state level recovery efforts. Furthermore, there seemed to be enough evidence presented at the congress that undertaking a few of them is not as effective as undertaking most of them.

Without asserting the sufficiency of the sevenfold attack on dependency, I think it is reasonable to say that until all seven are present through public or private efforts—especially the concept of a bargaining process providing authentic participation—there is reason to be pessimistic about the roads to recovery discussed at the congress. The challenge is to build a political consensus for an effective partnership in which all parties are treated as equals.

Notes

1. In fact, in a widely cited populist statement about public policy, Berger and Neuhaus (1977) argue that the concept of dependency is internally contradictory because of a continuing, strong public desire for public goods and services counterposed against an equally "strong animus against government."

2. "Welfare" includes providing direct aid to the needy, similar aid delivered through state and local governments, and state and local programs for the needy supported by federal grants. It does not include social insurance programs (Social Security, unemployment compensation, and so on) (Ellwood, 1982, pp. 35-37).

3. This is clearly the case in Chicago, as reported by Michael Young of Shlaes and Company and verified by the author. Other than in the high growth cities of the Sunbelt, I find no evidence to suggest that the Chicago situation is not a more general one.

4. A major difficulty with evaluating the success stories shared at the Cities' Congress is that each city had considerable latitude in choosing what to report. The meanings of a nonreport range from arbitrary or accidental omission to a lack of value attached to the event. Furthermore, the case of union involvement is thoroughly compounded by the often disinterested attitude of union leadership. It should be noted that only five union representatives were present among the more than 300 congress conferees.

5. "High-tech" is a colloquial expression covering all efforts to employ new technology to mechanize work processes. As such, it can and does permeate all sectors of the economy. Examples include the combine in agriculture, the continuous longwall miner, computer-assisted design in manufacturing, telecommunications in commerce, and information-age office technology. Whole firms or even sub-sectors of the economy often are organized around the new technology and have become the primary object of economic development efforts. For a comprehensive introduction to the mechanization of work, see Ginzberg (1982).

6. More and more cities are recognizing this ("Cities Seek," 1982, pp. 1, 7). Nevertheless, Oakland's robust real estate market is probably atypical in its strength because of two major events: the opening of the line to San Francisco,

and the flight of capital from Hong Kong, which Oakland has particularly skillfully exploited. As Paul Porter (1983) so aptly says, "luck and skill make any policy look better."

7. Because Oakland perceives downtown development so atypically—as intimately connected to neighborhood and job development—I have chosen not to review it under the earlier topic of "Service Sector Emphasis."

8. The ultimate success of these efforts to catalyze the local economy is an object of sore debate.

9. It has also been shaped by the author's efforts to evaluate the potential effectiveness of Enterprise Zone legislation (Mier & Gelzer, 1982).

10. Such bargaining is the essence of the negotiated and tripartite agreements, experiments of the past few years (Committee on Economic Development, 1980; Hinton, 1981).

4

Political Development in Chicago: From Campaign to Government

with

KARI J. MOE

This is an excerpt from a longer article first published in Harold Washington and the Neighborhoods: Progressive City Government in Chicago, 1983-1987, *edited by Pierre Clavel and Wim Wiewel. It begins the story of the Washington administration's social-justice-based urban agenda. This part of the story starts before the election, with the emergence of a grass-roots economic development platform developed by a network of community development organizations, the Community Workshop on Economic Development (CWED). The CWED platform incorporates and elaborates on the ideas developed in the last chapter. This chapter continues into the campaign with the development of Washington's plank,* The Washington Papers. *It ends with the dilemmas of delivering on the agenda after the election.*

AUTHORS' NOTE: Adapted from a chapter in *Harold Washington and the Neighborhoods* (Rutgers University Press) by Mier and Moe (1991) and reproduced here by permission of the publisher.

Paths of Development

April 12, 1983, marked a milestone in Chicago's history. Congressman Harold Washington was elected as the first African-American mayor of one of the most segregated cities in the nation. It was equally significant that his winning platform delineated commitments to jobs for Chicagoans, affirmative action, freedom of information, neighborhood development, fair processes for hiring and contracting, and an end to patronage—a reform program for a city that for decades had been dominated by an infamous Democratic political machine. Of particular importance here are the ways the commitments coalesced to constitute a neighborhood-based agenda for economic development and planning.

We played roles in Harold Washington's campaign for mayor, participating in the development of *The Washington Papers* (Committee to Elect Harold Washington, 1983). That document constituted Harold Washington's policy recommendations on local issues. Upon Washington's election we assumed key policymaking roles in the administration for development activities. Our perspective clearly reflects our extensive involvement in the planning and implementation of development policy in the City of Chicago.[1]

Chicago is a city that to this day has retained neighborhoods and wards as the locus of much organizing activity by politicians, local business actors, and community organizers. One legacy of 1960s Great Society programs had been the emergence of community-based organizations as local service providers. The range of services was broad, including counseling for elderly, drug and alcohol education, teaching of English as a second language, and youth activities. During the 1970s in Chicago, substantial cross-fertilization occurred among these community organizations. Organizations coalesced across class, across race, across issue areas, and across philosophy. The result was networks that formed the foundation of ideas and a constituency for Harold Washington's neighborhood agenda.

By the 1982-1983 campaign, several large and diverse neighborhood-based organizations and coalitions engaging in community economic development had emerged. The organizations included housing and commercial development groups, with a sprinkling of industrial development ones. Many of these neighborhood organizations and organizers had been influenced by experiences in the civil rights movement, antiwar movement, and Alinsky-style organizing philosophy, which focused on community empowerment.

These neighborhood development forces could rightly be called a movement in their own right. Several pathways of this movement are of particular importance to understanding the neighborhood form of the Washington platform and the agenda he attempted to implement once elected.

Community-Based Organizations Move Into Economic Development

By 1975 several forces in Chicago had converged to catalyze a sharpened discussion about economic development—in addition to housing—in community development. Community leaders were more clearly seeing the need move beyond simple protest and create jobs, promote skill training, and link people with jobs. As Gills (1991) has discussed elsewhere, formal and informal networks of community organizations were emerging to facilitate strategic discussions. A critical number of community development organizations existed by the latter half of the decade, and they frequently acted for a collective purpose through formal network organizations. Viable citywide organizations had been forming, which would provide support and assistance to the local community organizations and networks.

The Chicago Rehab Network, as Gills (1991) has pointed out, was a group of community organization leaders who coalesced around their commitment to rehabilitate housing in low-income neighborhoods. More important, they focused on the limitations of housing as a single issue and were beginning to explore broader community development approaches. Some of the Rehab Network groups were among the first to broaden their purpose, considering a direct job-generation approach to community development. The Eighteenth Street Development Corporation, the Bickerdike Redevelopment Corporation, the Kenwood Oakland Community Organization, and the Midwest Community Council in particular began to explore job training in rehabilitation construction trades as well as direct business development.[2]

The Chicago Association of Neighborhood Development Organizations (CANDO), started in 1978, was another important community institution. Some of the advocacy groups in white working-class neighborhoods had earlier taken up the issue of commercial revitalization. By 1978 there were about a dozen neighborhood commercial revitalization groups. Like the Rehab Network, they first came together as an informal network, then formally associated as CANDO.

In 1978 the graduate planning program at the University of Illinois at Chicago (UIC) formed the Center for Urban Economic Development (UICUED). UICUED became an important source of technical assistance to community development organizations.[3] By 1980 the School of Urban Planning and Policy (SUPP) at UIC had graduated a number of people specializing in community economic development. Many had joined the staffs of community organizations. Other support organizations included the Center for Neighborhood Technology (CNT), created in 1976. It worked within these networks of community organizations, trying to bring to them alternative production technologies. Their first venture was urban greenhouses for food production. Finally, the Associated Colleges of the Midwest Urban Studies Program, the Midwest Academy, and the National Training and Information Center proved to be important training grounds for many individuals who participated in the community organizing efforts.[4]

The downtown civic and philanthropic associations also increased their focus on housing and economic development issues in low-income communities. There was evidence of this shift in the Urban League; Community Renewal Society; the Latino Institute; T.R.U.S.T., Inc.; and the Jewish Council on Urban Affairs. In the late 1970s, led by the Wiebolt Foundation, the foundations shifted some of their funding to actual development activities. Once Wiebolt moved, the Joyce Foundation, the Chicago Community Trust and the Woods Charitable Trust, and eventually the MacArthur Foundation, followed.

Downtown Planning Initiatives

Interests primarily concerned with the development of Chicago's central business district began to advocate for or directly undertake development planning.[5] These downtown planning initiatives were important for what they revealed about corporate interests. They also stimulated a creative response from the neighborhoods. The "downtown versus neighborhoods" metaphor would emerge in the Washington campaign. The *Chicago 21 Plan* of the late 1970s was a catalyst that defined issues, interests, and relationships which endured into the Washington administration.[6]

The *Chicago 21 Plan* intended to shape development of a central area, which extended to Damen Avenue on the west, south to 35th Street, and north to North Avenue. These boundaries included several low-income communities that had experienced substantial housing and commercial disinvestment. The Plan envisioned those neighborhoods as extensions of the central area. To organizers and planners in those neighborhoods, it seemed as if the central area development advocates had a gentrification agenda. They began to raise questions and, through organizing efforts, formed a coalition against it.

The Chicago Central Area Committee (CCAC), the sponsors of the plan, responded by pledging matching planning grants to the affected neighborhoods. They sought input on the neighborhood components of their plan, with a pledge to incorporate them.[7] Two of the four communities were able to raise matching funds and undertake community plans.[8] One was done in Pilsen by the Pilsen Neighbors Community Organization, with Pat Wright, a SUPP graduate, as its planner. The other one was done in West Town, where the Northwest Community Organization (NCO) spun off a planning group led by another of former MUPP student, Maureen Hellwig.[9]

The planning grants may have played a cooptation role to the extent that these two groups began to focus on an agenda for their respective neighborhoods and diverted their focus from the overall approach of the *Chicago 21 Plan.* But the community planning processes also involved more people and organizations within each neighborhood in the debate about the future of their neighborhood.[10] Local residents could not visualize their neighborhood becoming an extension of the Loop without being gentrified. Gentrification became the organizing issue for the Coalition to Stop the *Chicago 21 Plan.*

Other events in these communities helped keep the issue of gentrification alive. For example, in Pilsen at that time, local developer John Podmajersky promoted a grandiose plan for renovating the historic Schoenhoffen Brewery as an upscale boutique development to be called Bathhouse Square. In addition, small artists' colonies emerged both in Pilsen and in West Town. Local groups perceived artists' colonies as beachheads for gentrification (Mier, 1988).

Issues similar to those provoked by the *Chicago 21 Plan* were emerging in other neighborhoods. For example, a major low-income housing displacement battle was being fought in Uptown in the late 1970s. On the west side, there was community conflict over the operations of a major hospital complex. People with specific experiences in their own neighborhood found common cause with people in other neighborhoods: Whites on the north side, Latinos in West Town and Pilsen, and African-Americans on the west side were experiencing the same organizing challenges and beginning to speak a common language of experience (Forester, 1989).

During this period a parallel set of community-based organizations and networks developed around health, human services, and education issues. These organizations were similar to the development organizations in philosophy, personnel, their networking, and in the way they visualized downtown's impact on the neighborhoods. The Alternative Schools Network, within which Moe worked from 1977 to 1980, was a parallel organization to the Rehab Network. In a lot of individual neighborhoods, the local alternative school worked directly with the local housing development group to train young people in carpentry. Where Moe worked in Uptown, her students trained at The Voice of the People, the local housing rehabilitation group. This represented one example of the multiple kinds of cross-fertilization going on within and among neighborhoods.

Business Alienation

A second countervailing force evolved through the 1970s. Businesses located out of the central area felt ignored by City Hall. This stimulated the formation of local chambers of commerce, business development groups, industrial councils, and eventually the CANDO network. In 1977 some of my students worked with the Economic Development Commission (EDC) doing a survey of manufacturing firms in the Pilsen/Little Village area (Nealon, 1977).[11] These firms were very much disenchanted with City Hall. This dissatisfaction lead to their creation of the Pilsen Industrial Council. The Council began to work with the Eighteenth Street Development Corporation. This networking between businessmen's groups and local constituency-based development groups was occurring in many neighborhoods.

Minority Political Empowerment

A third countervailing force also emerged beginning in the 1960s, that of increased independence and assertiveness within Chicago's African-American community. This history of rising minority dissatisfaction is well documented by Gills (1991). This movement was reinforced by the steady growth of Chicago's population of African-Americans and other minorities, and the verification of that growth in the 1980 census. This occurred in the national context of dramatic increases in the number of minority mayors throughout the country (Mier, Fitzgerald, & Randolph, 1993). Finally, contributing to all of this concern and protest was the cutback of social programs under the Reagan presidency, as well as the overt attack on civil rights policies.

The Paths Converge: 1982

Formation of the Community Workshop on Economic Development

The Community Workshop on Economic Development (CWED) emerged from a 1982 conference sponsored by the Community Renewal Society (CRS) to critique Enterprise Zones, the central Republican urban development initiative, and to focus the local urban development policy debate.[12] The participating community organizations were frustrated with President Reagan's cutbacks and the dismantling of urban programs. In addition, the specter of a World's Fair in Chicago loomed, an event threatening to absorb for the next decade all available discretionary public development resources. But they also understood that the times required strategies that moved beyond statements of opposition to Enterprise Zones and the World's Fair. The groups decided to coalesce in order to prepare a proactive policy and program statement that could undergird their fight for dollars and their critique of programs at the city and state levels. They also wanted a statement that would reflect the experience they had been gaining over several years of delivering community development projects.

The Chicago participants felt a sense, early on, that there was an opportunity, given a hotly contested governor's race under-way in Illinois, to produce a significant statewide policy state-ment.[13] The state also became the focus because Reagan was transferring the control of significant urban development pro-grams from the federal government to the states. State govern-ments would be designating Enterprise Zones. This launched the effort to put together CWED as a statewide organization.[14] CWED's formation was an acknowledgment that it was time for community-based organizations to get political at the state level, and it represented an awareness of common interests with sim-ilar groups in smaller cities.

The actual CWED policy statement (Table 4.1), a codification of the decisions of two statewide meetings, was written in August of 1982. The platform was subsequently modified, based on feedback from CWED members, and then ratified. Its seven goals emphasized the importance of neighborhoods as a social entity and their right to be authentic partners in any development process that affects them. They emphasized the importance of local actors—residents, businesses, and individuals—relative to external actors such as developers. They emphasized the importance of an aggressive, innovative public sector. Finally, they reflected a perception of social justice as targeting the work-needy.

At the time of its drafting, the significance of the policy defining effort was not fully appreciated. In fact, it failed in terms of being a political organizing device to influence the governor's race because it was completed too late. By November CWED was in transition. It had started as an ad hoc, short-term effort. There was an decision by the Chicago members to con-tinue the organization as the *Chicago Workshop on Economic Development* because of their belief that an advocacy organization focusing on development policy was essential.[15]

Harold Washington Decides to Run for Mayor

Chicago's African-American community was alive with politi-cal activity during the summer and fall of 1982. Operation PUSH

Table 4.1 CWED Goals

1. Full employment in every community.
2. An increasing ownership share by residents and workers in community development projects.
3. Meaningful community involvement in the planning and administration of economic development programs.
4. More public and private resources for community development projects.
5. Resource allocation through open negotiation.
6. Adequate management and technical assistance to enable communities to plan and manage development projects.
7. Allocation of resources and opportunities based on the philosophy of affirmative action, targeting resources to the most needy communities.

SOURCES: Community Workshop on Economic Development, 1982; Gills, 1991.

was leading a boycott of Chicagofest.[16] Chicago Black United Communities (CBUC) sponsored a straw poll to identify leading African-American candidates for mayor (Alkalimat & Gills, 1989). The census data revealed that the mayoralty was in reach. The traditional powers of the machine wanted to defeat Jane Byrne by supporting Richard M. Daley. Ed Gardner, owner of Soft Sheen Products, supported a voter registration drive called "Come Alive, October 5." Harold Washington, clearly the favored candidate of the African-American community, said he would run if the registration challenge he established was achieved. Finally, as Gills (1991) has discussed, with Washington's agreement to run, many community organizations like PUSH and CBUC coalesced, for the sake of the campaign, into the Task Force on Black Political Empowerment.

Campaign Issues Development

Moe received a call from Hal Baron in early November 1982. Congressman Washington had asked Baron to co-chair, with Vince Bakeman, his research and issues committee for the campaign. Baron asked Moe to be the staff director of research and issues, should Washington ultimately decide to run.[17] By November 15, Washington had made his decision and had approved Moe's hiring, and Moe left CWED for the campaign.

In the second half of November, Baron wrote a memo to Washington, suggesting alternative approaches to issues development. His favored suggestion was the formation of issues teams to bring together diverse viewpoints and constituencies and to produce a popularly generated platform. The second, more traditional alternative, was to assemble a few "experts" for a short, intensive effort to shape the campaign issues. Baron suggested to Washington that he would probably end up with the same policy papers, but the first approach would develop constituencies. Washington chose the broad-based issues teams approach. Baron, Bakeman, and Moe started to organize the teams in late November and early December. Each issue team was to represent the class, race, and neighborhood diversity of the city.

Washington's approach to issues development for the campaign was significant in that it later characterized his approach to issues development in government. The approach also reflected his tendency as a legislator to hear all views, and replicated the committee structure of his congressional district.

By early January about 15 issues teams had started working on topics, including energy, housing, jobs, senior citizens, women, fiscal policy, transportation, and neighborhoods, among others.[18] Washington appointed an oversight body, the Research and Issues Committee, to report to him regarding policy directions and to advise him routinely regarding work progress and schedule.[19] Each issues team produced policy papers; specific briefing papers for speeches, endorsement sessions, and debates; and campaign literature. The policy papers were published in the central policy document of the campaign, *The Washington Papers* (Committee to Elect Harold Washington, 1983).

The issues team assembled for economic development included several key participants in the CWED process. Not surprisingly, the economic development issues paper, "Jobs for Chicagoans" (Table 4.2), was an elaboration of the CWED platform. It articulated five main goals and eight complementary policies. Like the CWED statement, "Jobs for Chicagoans" emphasized neighborhoods, affirmative action, and targeting of work-needy people, and a need for an innovative and aggressive public sector. Going beyond CWED, it also emphasized job development instead of real estate development and business retention and expansion instead of attraction.

In essence, these goals and policies represented a substantial departure from traditional, growth-oriented approaches and evoked considerable controversy (Rivlin, 1992). There were

Table 4.2 Jobs for Chicagoans

Goals
1. Neighborhood development.
2. Preserving and expanding the existing job base.
3. A balanced approach to development emphasizing the strength of diversity.
4. An emphasis on maintenance and rehabilitation of housing and infrastructure.
5. Linking work-needy Chicagoans to local employment opportunities through coordinated training and education.

Policies
1. Retention and expansion of existing businesses.
2. Targeted local purchasing.
3. Expansion of the public and private capital base supporting development.
4. Elimination of business "nuisance" taxes.
5. Integration of employment training with development activities.
6. Affirmative hiring.
7. Early warning and preventative action for plant closings.
8. Emphasis on innovation.

SOURCE: Committee to Elect Harold Washington, 1983.

three elements to this controversy, all a reflection of the populist, participatory leanings of Washington's campaign. The strong emphasis on expanding employment (the rhetoric of "full employment" was used) evoked fears of government interference in business affairs. The emphasis on partnerships' including neighborhood and working people threatened a historical cozy relationship between City Hall and business and labor leadership. An emphasis on "jobs as the bottom line" threatened the real estate-based growth coalition. The economic development issues paper promised a departure from previous public economic development practice and set a context for strong business interest contention with the new mayoral administration of Harold Washington.

We are still impressed by the incredible energy and effort put forth by the more than 150 volunteers on these issues teams. On their own initiative, they gathered documents, conducted interviews, held substantive debates at their meetings, and worked under extremely tight deadlines to produce written documents for the campaign. In addition, the campaign research office coordinated another 10 to 15 volunteers per day who prepared the mayor's daily briefing packets for all his scheduled events. Along with every other aspect of the campaign operation, the core staff worked 14 hours per day, 7 days per week, from December to April. Resources were so spare that there frequently were not enough chairs for all the people who wanted to work.

Given all that had to be done for his campaign, Washington must be credited for allocating resources, talent, time, and status to the issues operation. He remained committed to a campaign of substance, even though often not covered by the media. He carried this concern for issues into City government.

The Campaign Trail

On the actual campaign trail, Harold Washington consistently transcended his written material. He embellished his briefing notes with history and a rich rhetorical flourish. The fact that Harold Washington was able to focus public attention on and elevate issues in the campaign provides an important insight into his history. This point is particularly significant because of the way in which the mainstream media and the political opposition characterized him as an exciting orator, but not a serious or substantive candidate. They ignored and misunderstood the content of his speeches.

Important dimensions of Harold Washington's personal history, such as his political weaning within the Daley machine, his break in the late sixties, and his successful resistance to machine attempts at his political annihilation, are well-known (Travis, 1989; Miller, 1989b). Less well-recognized by the general public at the time of his campaign was the quality of his record as an elected official.

He had always been, even as a regular Democrat, a strong issues politician. His state legislative record of accomplishments included currency exchange reform, education, promotion of minority and female business participation in government contracting (M/FBE), the Martin Luther King holiday, and funding for Provident Hospital.[20] His expertise on each issue was broad and deep in a way surpassed by few state elected officials. He maintained this pattern in the U.S. Congress, where he continued to score consistently high ratings from labor, women's organizations, and good government groups. He organized a variety of citizen-staffed issues committees in his congressional district. In a short time as a Congressman, he became one of the leading spokespersons for the Voting Rights Act renewal.[21]

This record had not escaped the African-American community. In their eyes, he had become a powerful symbol. He represented at once liberation, strength of convictions, achievement against the odds, and substance. He was seen as a giant intellect who possessed the humility and common sense to stay in close contact with his constituency. He was respected as a leader who could lead and listen. He was seen not only as a charismatic orator, but also as an elected official with a pragmatic, grounded agenda.

As a candidate, Harold Washington had a rare ability to integrate the emotional, political, and content aspects of all issues and to relate to any audience with whom he was talking. One of Moe's typical daily experiences, when traveling with him during the 1983 general election, was going from the west side El stops to the top floor of the First National Bank building to talk to bankers.[22] Then they went to the north side to discuss human rights with a predominantly gay audience, then to south side housing projects, then to the steel mills in southeast Chicago, and finally back to West Town to meet with Puerto Rican businessmen. There was not an audience that he did not move. He molded each issue into a message that connected with the disenchantment and desire for leadership of these diverse audiences.

The Transition Team

After the primary victory in February 1983, the base of support needed to be broadened (Alkalimat & Gills, 1989). Because it was too late for significant additions to the campaign steering or issues committees, Washington needed other vehicles to involve additional supporters. In addition, it was time to establish his ability to work with the broader networks that would be required for him to govern after the April general election and inauguration. In March 1983, he launched a transition committee, co-chaired by Bill Berry, longtime former director of the Chicago Urban League; and James O'Connor, chairman of Commonwealth Edison. There was an oversight committee, dominated by CEOs of Chicago corporations, but it also included substantial community representation, which was to become a Washington trademark. Sixteen individual issues teams were established, paralleling the structure of the campaign issues committees.

Although the structure of the transition team was similar to the campaign issues structure, and in some cases membership overlapped, many actors were included who changed the nature of the committee debate. As Gills (1991) has discussed, many of these debates foreshadowed subsequent discussions and controversies in the administration between varying interest groups.

Some of the teams, most notably economic development, were used by business leadership to advocate a particular policy position. In a pattern common to virtually every major city that had elected a minority mayor, the business leadership began a campaign to move the public development functions from under the control of the mayor into a quasi-public development corporation. They argued that this would provide development with "immunity from politics," but it was in fact a much deeper struggle over the control of development priorities and resources (Washington Transition Committee, 1983, pp. 129-152; Alkalimat & Gills, 1989, pp. 128-141).

In addition to generating policy recommendations, the staff of each Transition Issues Committee went to the City departments during April and May 1983, to conduct interviews and collect documents. The Washington team wanted to have as much information as possible. The final transition report was released to the public in September 1983. The recommendations of the *Washington Papers* and the transition report subsequently served as an explicit reference point for the administration's review of its progress up through the 1987 election.[23]

Taking Over and Starting Up

With the election victory, many of Harold Washington's supporters from the community and economic development networks and organizations—like us—began to think of taking roles in the new administration. To each of us, working for Harold Washington was an opportunity to implement the campaign agenda. It was clear Moe was moving from the car into the mayor's office. From the transition experience, the importance of getting someone who was committed to community-oriented development policies appointed Commissioner of Economic Development was clear. In the month after the election, I decided to make a push for it. Eventually, seven members of the economic development issues group would join the administration.[24]

Reflections on What Lay Before Us

Until the time we joined the City administration, we were both outsiders to local government, with our feet firmly rooted in community work.[25] We knew the transition from outside to inside was significant, but it was not possible at the time to anticipate all of the consequences. We vowed to not become bureaucrats. Contemplating the choice to join Mayor Harold Washington in government service, we attempted to be explicit about the major issues and our values and understandings toward them. We wish to share some of these understandings as a basis for ultimately judging what we accomplished.

Local Government. We saw local government as traditionally having several functions, or roles, which we understood would present both opportunities and constraints in the achievement of our objectives.[26] In terms of the local government as service provider, we recognized we had little ability to impact the macro-economy but were optimistic about our ability to improve the basic quality and distribution of service. We realized that the credibility of Harold Washington's ability to govern rested on his ability to deliver such things as garbage pickup and snow removal, and to deliver them fairly. Of course, basic development services were included in this calculus.

We believed that local government, by virtue of its proximity to local residents, provided the potential to be a laboratory of democracy, wherein city residents who had been alienated from government could experience a different relationship with government. We believed this could be done through freedom of information, community forums, citizen task forces, major speeches, and the like. We wanted to raise the local citizenry's expectations and have them set a standard to which they would hold the administrators accountable. With Chicago's history of having a dominant mayor who could command media, corporate, and business attention, we believed that Mayor Washington had a unique opportunity to influence the terms of the public policy debate at the local, state, and national levels.

We recognized the tendency of government to coopt challenging social movements as a way of maintaining consent for the basic structures of society. We recognized the danger before us that we might defuse the community actions that brought the mayor into office. We saw the opportunity, on the other hand, to use the cooptive power of government to broaden the base of support, both within and outside of government, for our goals.

We believed that local government often supported the corporate agenda, particularly when this agenda was expressed through "growth coalitions" (Mollenkopf, 1983; Mier & Sherr, 1984). We believed that local government was, more often that not, exploited by this relationship. We believed that we could alter this relationship through "public return on public investment" policies, like betting on basic industry (Markusen, 1989; Mier, Moe, & Sherr, 1986). We thought these policies would have a longer term impact on the macro-economy. We wanted to test the ability of local government to enlist the growth coalition's support for a broader public policy agenda.[27]

Finally, we also believed that local government, because of its closeness to peoples lives, played an important role in mediating social relations across race, class, and neighborhood lines. We believed that, by bringing people of diverse backgrounds and perspectives together, local government could promote at least understanding and perhaps decreased hostility among different interest groups. We were unsure about the ability of local government to develop consensus, except on a personal, issue-specific basis.

Social Issues. We believed that the two central social issues before us were poverty and race relations. We knew that local government, especially in Illinois where the welfare system is essentially state-managed, had only a limited capacity to address poverty. Nonetheless, we felt that we would have to keep the issue of poverty at the forefront of everything we would undertake. Similarly, we knew the racial divisiveness within Chicago would face us every day, even within the ranks of the Harold Washington coalition.

In addressing the issues of poverty and race, we knew that neighborhood-based organizations were a needed ally.[28] We hoped to bring our personal commitments to social justice into the government and to make it operational in our day-to-day decision making. In this regard, following the theories of philosopher John Rawls and the practice of Cleveland Planning Commissioner Norman Krumholz, we hoped to be able to focus attention on the least advantaged in any public decision-making situation, and to give their circumstances priority attention (Mier & McGary, 1977). We also thought that an economic development agenda that opened job opportunities to the most work-needy was a major means of achieving justice. This was tempered, as noted before, by our awareness of the limited ability of local government to effect such an agenda. We anticipated actively opening government decision processes to wide public participation. We believed that neighborhood organizations could be supportive of a broader social justice agenda, beyond their individual neighborhood concerns. To do this, we anticipated that much of the informal networking in which we had engaged as activists would still play an important role.

The Place of Planning. We each came from strong planning backgrounds and believed that public involvement in government decision making resulted in better plans, ones with a better chance of being implemented. We also believed that effective planning had to involve neighborhood-based organizations, because their perspective could not be represented by the government. During the campaign and our early years in the administration, we prepared discussion papers on local planning processes. Given the importance we placed on a strategy of neighborhood-based economic development as a means of achieving social justice, we believed that traditional local government planning should be driven by economic development priorities. Eventually, neighborhood planning grants, funded by both the Department of Planning and the Department of Economic Development, resulted in much planning activity being contracted out to local groups.

Personal Demands. We were clear on our beliefs about local government, social issues, and the place of planning. We probably were less clear about the personal commitment and sacrifice that would be required. Neither of us had ever shied away from hard work, and each had considerable confidence in our management ability. We went into government eager to face the tasks ahead of us. The Department of Economic Development (DED) would be a major testing ground for our ideas.

Economic Development:
From Activism to Administration

DED was an essential department to control. Although it had a relatively modest budget of $35 million, it had important legal authority and it carried out community development functions that could be significantly enhanced. It was a central department for reaching the mayor's neighborhood and small business constituencies. DED was a platform from which to set the terms of the economic development debate. For example, the Playskool plant closing case of 1984 dramatized a new direction for government/ business relations, which had national impact (Giloth & Mier, 1986). A paradox of DED's role was its limited spending authority versus its significant "setting the terms of the debate" authority.

There were a number of objectives we started with that were based upon our experience, *The Washington Papers,* the transition report, and the mayor's leadership.

1. *Direct Community Development Block Grant (CDBG) and infrastructure funds to support neighborhood development.* This objective was central to Washington's priority of neighborhood revitalization. The need for these program dollars was obvious, especially in minority areas that had been traditionally neglected. Byrne's concentration of CDBG funds and infrastructure programs on downtown projects and favored wards had been the subject of community protest.

2. *Enhance business retention programs focusing on small to medium-size businesses constituting the bulk of Chicago's employment base.* In this regard, we envisioned community development and businessmen's groups as a potential first point of contact with the more than 100,000 businesses scattered throughout Chicago.

3. *Develop and implement an overall program that was sensitive to the idiosyncrasies of particular economic sectors and could identify and seize strategic opportunities.* This challenge required understanding the enormous diversity of Chicago's local economy and recognizing that City government, with limited resources, had to invest carefully. We believed that we would find

low-cost, high-return projects by looking within specific sectors such as the steel industry.

4. *Increase the participation of small and minority-owned businesses in City loan and procurement programs.* These programs had been structured to favor large businesses or contractors, making it difficult for the vast majority of Chicago businesses to either get help or do business with the City. One consequence, for example, was that more than 60% of the City's $400-million annual purchase of goods and services was going to non-Chicago suppliers, thus resulting in the loss of a significant opportunity to stimulate local job generation.

5. *Advocate for an urban agenda at the state and national levels.* Given his rich experience in the state legislature and Congress, the historic political strength of the Chicago mayor's office, and a national leadership vacuum on urban issues, Mayor Washington felt that he could play a role in focusing public attention on such issues as housing for low-income and homeless people or jobs and training for the work-needy.

6. *Better coordinate economic development, employment and training, and education efforts.* Our goal was to change the public perception that training programs were little more than disguised welfare, and to make training and education central to business development. Beyond that, the goal was for the mayor to focus on the education bureaucracy, relating education to development. This objective, although certainly as pressing as all the others in the early debate, was overwhelmed by the day-to-day realities and did not surface as a strong agenda item until Mayor Washington's second term.[29]

7. *Improve government operations.* We knew that little attention had been paid to fundamental facets of management such as the development of personnel and information systems. We sought to modernize operations.

The overarching goal of these objectives was the need to provide jobs for Chicagoans needing work. As a result of the virtual hemorrhage of the city's manufacturing base during the 1960s and 1970s, combined with the severe recession of the early 1980s, Chicago's unemployment rate exceeded 12%, with a substantial concentration among minorities in general and minority youth in particular. We knew that there were substantial limits to the impact a local government could have on that, but were determined to gauge everything we did by the standard of providing jobs for the work-needy.

The Chicago Development Plan

As soon as I started in August 1983, then chief of staff Bill Ware asked me to form a subcabinet of commissioners from the development departments. Two were carryovers—Tom Kapsalis of aviation, and Jerry Butler of public works. The majority were Washington appointees: Brenda Gaines, housing; Liz Hollander, planning; Maria Cerda, MET; and Fred Fine, cultural affairs. Common to all them was minimal or no involvement in the campaign. They were professionals in their fields.

The development subcabinet was the first such grouping established in the government. The mayor wanted a forum for information transfer both up and down through the hierarchy, as well as a forum for policy debate and coordination of programs and projects. He did not want department heads running their operations as fiefdoms, which had too often occurred in the past.

I had a large task on my hands, and recruited Moe from the mayor's office to staff the development subcabinet. The early meetings consisted of gathering information, defining an agenda, and attempting to get all the commissioners on board with *The Washington Papers.* The subcabinet became focused when we undertook production of *Chicago Works Together: The 1984 Development Plan (CWT).*

The effort began when I woke up one morning in January to hear on the news that the mayor had announced the release of his development plan in about 60 days. So I walked into Washington's office that morning and asked, "What's this development plan you were talking about?" The mayor quietly beamed with the smile he wore when he was about to ask for something impossible, with the complete confidence it would somehow get done. He said, "I figured you'd fill in the blanks." We had 60 days to produce a development plan.

We met his goal with *Chicago Works Together. CWT* was a policy plan that laid out five broad goals (job development, neighborhood development, balanced growth, efficiency, and a state legislative commitment), which set the framework for more than 45 specific policies. Finally, the policies were to be implemented with more than 200 specific projects.

The R&D Division of DED was by then directed by Moe, and in the course of preparing the development plan, she emerged as the chief of staff for the development subcabinet. All the departments contributed staff to support the effort, and it turned out to be a great device to motivate the rest of the departments in the development cluster. Because the matters of the development subcabinet closely involved DED, they served to reinforce the goals and directions of the department.

With the completion of the development plan, it was reasonable to expect a clearer sense of purpose and more pointed output from DED and the other development subcabinet departments. All the pieces were in place for delivering the Washington agenda.

Notes

1. I served as Commissioner of Economic Development from 1983 to 1987, then from 1987 to 1989, as Assistant to the Mayor for Development, overseeing the Departments of Economic Development, Planning, Housing, Employment and Training, and Cultural Affairs. I also chaired the development subcabinet, a policy advisory group, from 1983 to 1987. Finally, I served on the Mayor's Policy Advisory Council, the highest policy group in the City government, from 1984 to 1989.

Moe joined the mayor's staff the week he was inaugurated in 1983, then in early 1984 moved to the Department of Economic Development, where she was first Assistant Commissioner then Deputy Commissioner in charge of Research and Development. In late 1985 she returned to the Mayor's Office as Assistant to the Mayor for Community Services, overseeing the Departments of Health, Human Services, Aging and Disability, and Information and Inquiry, as well as the Chicago Public Library, the Municipal Reference Library, and the Commissions on Human Relations, Women, and Asians. During that period, she also sat on the Mayor's Policy Advisory Council. Under Acting Mayor Eugene Sawyer in 1988 and 1989, she served as Commissioner of General Services.

2. Several authors of chapters in *Harold Washington and the Neighborhoods* have played prominent roles with several of these organizations. Bob Giloth directed Eighteenth Street, Bob Brehm directed Bickerdike, and Doug Gills has worked for KOCO.

3. A founding staff member and the director since Mier went to the City is Wim Wiewel, co-editor of *Harold Washington and the Neighborhoods*.

4. Moe and Donna Ducharme were students, and Jody Kretzmann, Hal Baron, and Lou Palmer were professors at the Urban Studies Program. Ducharme and

Kretzmann are authors of other chapters in *Harold Washington and the Neighborhoods*. Baron was Washington's Chief Policy Advisor. Palmer headed an organization, Chicago United Black Communities (CBUC), which played an important role in Washington's candidacy.

5. These interests included the Chicago Central Area Committee, the Metropolitan Planning Council, and T.R.U.S.T., Inc. The *Chicago Tribune,* a long-standing growth advocate, did a critical series that examined the City's Economic Development Commission and its lack of a comprehensive game plan (Longworth, 1981). Such corporate-led planning initiatives have occurred in many cities (Porter & Sweet, 1984).

6. For example, the coalition to stop the *Chicago 21 Plan* proved to be a training ground for some of the key leaders of the coalition that fought the World's Fair (Shlay & Giloth, 1986). The plan was prepared for the Chicago Central Area Committee (CCAC) by the architectural firm of Skidmore, Owings and Merrill (Chicago Central Area Committee, 1973). The CCAC historically has been composed of the major central area property interests—real estate developers, banks, utility companies, the newspapers, and so on.

7. Organizers in the four communities were sensitive to the possibility that this was a cooptation agenda, but nevertheless set out to use the money offered by the Central Area Committee.

8. The two that failed to failed to receive grants were Chinatown and the near north side, both neighborhoods with high concentrations of public housing.

9. NCO contracted with the National Council on Urban and Ethnic Affairs (NCUEA) to provide professional planning services. NCUEA assigned a young woman planner, Marci Kaptur, to direct the effort and to work with Hellwig. Several years later, Kaptur would be elected to the U.S. Congress from her home town of Toledo, running on a neighborhoods and planning platform.

10. New organizations emerged as a consequence of that broadened debate. In Pilsen, the Pilsen Housing and Business Alliance, lead by Arturo Vazquez, was created to focus on the gentrification issues of east Pilsen, the area closest to the central area.

11. The team included Giloth; Greg Longhini, currently the Assistant to the Commissioner of Planning at the City; Joel Werth, former Deputy Press Secretary to Acting Mayor Eugene Sawyer; and John-Jairo Betancur, currently a Research Assistant Professor in UICUED.

12. CRS is a civic organization sponsored by the United Church of Christ. Its mission throughout its 100-year history in Chicago had been the care for and development of low-income communities.

13. The race, between incumbent Governor James Thompson and U.S. Senator Adlai Stevenson III, was decided in Thompson's favor by approximately 6,000 votes, the closest in Illinois history. Close to Election Day, polls predicted a quarter-million-vote victory for Thompson, but did not take into account the substantial voter registration occurring in Chicago's African-American community.

14. CWED was chaired by Arturo Vazquez of PHBA and Squire Lance of the Englewood Businessmen's Association. Vazquez, then the Director of the Mayor's Office of Employment and Training under Acting Mayor Sawyer, would subsequently become a Deputy Commissioner of Economic Development. Lance was a former Executive Director of The Woodlawn Organization.

15. Its incorporation papers were signed by Mier, Vazquez, and Douglas Gills (whose work is frequently cited in this chapter). Moe stopped working for CWED in November and was replaced by Tom Carlson. Carlson, an ordained United Church of Christ minister, had previously worked at CRS, CWED's original sponsor, where he had undertaken a variety of community-development projects.

16. In an effort to broaden the base of support for the boycott beyond the African-American community, the "Committee of 500" was formed of white, Latino community, and labor leaders. It was co-chaired by Vazquez and Uptown activist, Slim Coleman.

17. Baron was a former research director for the Chicago Urban League and was a faculty member of the Urban Studies Program of the Associated Colleges of the Midwest when Moe was a student there. He coordinated program development for Washington during his unsuccessful 1977 run for mayor. He later joined the administration as the chief policy adviser. Bakeman was the president of a social service consulting agency, a faculty member of Kennedy-King College, and chair of the coordinating body of Washington's issues teams in the 1st Congressional District. He also served as an ad hoc adviser to the Mayor's Policy Advisory Council (MPAC).

18. I chaired the economic development issues team.

19. This committee, of which I was a member, was co-chaired by Bakeman and Baron.

20. Provident Hospital was a private, minority-owned and -operated, full-service hospital located on the south side of the city.

21. Washington had clearly impressed the members of the Congressional Black Caucus. To his credit, several of them campaigned and raised funds for him during the primary and general elections. Beyond the Black Caucus, leaders such as Congressmen Claude Pepper campaigned for Washington because of his commitment to the issues.

22. In mid-March, Moe began riding in Washington's car in order to personally brief him on issues relevant to his ensuing stop.

23. Moe served as the keeper of the "Washington record" from the beginning through the 1987 election. Much to his credit, Washington supported the generation of both internal and external reports on the Washington record in comparison to his campaign commitments in years two, three, and four. We know of no other elected officials who were so willing to be held accountable. Moreover, the public release of this information helped him create a constituency to hold his own cabinet members accountable.

24. Mier, Ros Paaswell as First Deputy Commissioner of Economic Development, Milam Fitts, Rodrigo Del Canto, and Steve Alexander as Deputy Commissioner of Economic Development, Wayne Robinson as First Deputy Corporation Counsel then Chairman of the Plan Commission, and the late Winston Mecurius as Director of Research in the Mayor's Office of Employment and Training.

25. We came to the Washington administration experience on community paths, ones that had frequently intersected. Moe arrived in Chicago in 1972 as a Carleton College student in the Associated Colleges of the Midwest Urban Studies Program. She returned in 1974, and until 1980 was employed as a social worker and teacher, while also working with several community-based organizations in the politically active Uptown community (Gitlin & Hollander, 1970). We met in

1976 when she enrolled part-time in the School of Urban Planning and Policy (SUPP) at the University of Illinois at Chicago (UIC). She later completed a Master's of City Planning degree at M.I.T. and returned to Chicago in 1982 to become Executive Director of the Community Workshop on Economic Development (CWED). She had broadened her focus on social welfare and youth policy issues to include community development, employment, and economic development.

I came to Chicago in 1975 to teach community development and planning at the University of Illinois at Chicago. In the preceding decade, I had served a tour of duty in Vietnam as an adviser to the Vietnamese Navy, and had been actively involved in both the antiwar and the community-development movements in the Oakland, California, area and in St. Louis. I was the founding director in 1978 of the Center for Urban Economic Development (UICUED) at UIC. My teaching emphasis on community economic development, pedagogical emphasis on social action as a means of learning, and technical assistance activities at UICUED brought me into close working contact with a number of community-development organizations. I was a founding member of CWED with whom I helped articulate a community-development policy statement. We both joined the Washington administration in 1983 (Mier, 1986).

26. In fact, like O'Connor (1973), we believe that some of those functions are inherently contradictory.

27. See Hollander's (1991) discussion on the players who eventually coalesced to push school reform in Chicago.

28. We say this fully aware that the history of neighborhood organizations in Chicago contains a strand that is built on institutionalizing racism. Philpot (1978) reports that Chicago's first neighborhood organization was a "conservation association" organized to fight for restrictive property title covenants.

29. Beginning to get control of the core City departments was extremely difficult; by comparison, getting even the most basic of information out of the "other" local governments (the Board of Education, C.T.A., C.H.A., City Colleges, and the Park District) was next to impossible. The City Council effectively blocked the mayor's appointees to these boards until 2½ years into the first term.

5

Strategic Planning and the Pursuit of Reform, Economic Development, and Equity

with

KARI J. MOE

IRENE SHERR

This chapter, which appeared in the Journal of the American Planning Association, *details one of the first priorities after the election—transforming the mayor's economic platform,* Jobs for Chicagoans, *into a working strategic plan,* Chicago Works Together. *It thus picks up where the last chapter left off. In addition to incorporating a participatory planning process, a challenge of the process was balancing sectoral and area development strategies. The inefficiency of government bureaucracies in supporting a strategic planning process emerge in this chapter, and are developed more fully in ensuing chapters.*

AUTHORS' NOTE: This chapter is adapted from Mier, Moe, and Sherr (1986). It has been reproduced here by permission of the *Journal of the American Planning Association* (JAPA). We would like to thank the people who reviewed earlier drafts of this chapter, especially Robert Giloth (whose comments were particularly insightful), Ed Bergman, Harvey Goldstein, and Diana Robinson, as well as A. J. Buckingham for her editorial assistance. We also appreciate the comments we received from the then JAPA editorial staff, Edward Kaiser, Scott Verner, and three unidentified reviewers.

The Challenge of Reform

From the beginning, the Washington administration was confronted with a volatile, adversarial political situation; extremely high expectations from constituents; limited funds to deliver programs; and an urban economy undergoing major structural change. Forced to grapple with difficult decisions necessary to achieve its reform commitments within the relatively brief period of a 4-year term, the new administration found that traditional planning and public administration approaches were inadequate.

In the early to mid-1980s, Chicago's socioeconomic environment resembled that of many northeastern and midwestern industrial cities. Throughout 1985 unemployment remained high, at 9.6% in the city and 8.9% statewide, despite the nation's so-called economic recovery. Consistent with national patterns, joblessness and underemployment most affected minorities, the young (under 21), and the mature (over 45). Chicago was still losing manufacturing jobs, and the addition of service-related jobs only partially offset these losses. One consequence of the partial substitution of service for manufacturing jobs was a general decline in wages, benefits, job security, and skill levels, to which we refer collectively as "quality of work" (Mier & Giloth, 1985).

Many of Chicago's neighborhoods are poor and deteriorating, following decades of disinvestment (Giloth, 1981). The departure of businesses from the city, losses in the number and quality of housing units, and rising unemployment have contributed to the city's fiscal stress. That stress is compounded by national economic policies and the excesses of previous mayoral administrations (City of Chicago Office of Intergovernmental Affairs, 1985a, 1985b).

Because Washington's victory was directly related to his promises of jobs and political reform, the voters demanded, first, job opportunities and, second, openness, fairness, and accountability in local government. These policy demands represented the central challenge for the new administration. Because the mayor was committed to responding to these challenges through the local government bureaucracy, a strategic approach to economic development was required. We argue that municipal reform, local industrial policy, and progressive planning are interdependent and, in an urban environment as turbulent as Chicago's, may be accomplished only through strategic planning.

We define *strategic planning* as a process wherein key actors agree on a limited number of goals, based on a careful analysis of the wide range of strengths and weaknesses in the organization's internal and external environment.[1] Then they develop strategies to achieve the goals and deploy resources to support the strategies. We trace the development of Chicago's first municipal strategic plan for economic development, *Chicago Works Together: 1984 Development Plan* (City of Chicago Department of Economic Development, 1984). We then illustrate the city's first steps toward ongoing strategic planning and what we believed was a substantially improved economic development practice in Chicago. Viewed out of the context of Chicago politics, the city's efforts might seem like a hybrid of various pragmatic planning approaches (Hoch, 1984; Malizia, 1982). Although the Washington administration was pragmatic about the need to distribute basic city services, its approach to economic development programs was strategic because it delineated limited goals and set new terms for the debate about development priorities.

Reform, Industrial Policy, and Progressive Planning

Under Harold Washington *municipal reform* had both traditional and new meanings. On the traditional side, Washington was committed to eliminating waste and patronage, promoting municipal efficiency, and making government accessible and responsive to all citizens. But for this African-American mayor elected by a populist electorate, reform had a distinct new meaning. It meant working toward equity—a better deal for those who had been shut off from society, suffered economic harm, and experienced powerlessness. Further elements of Washington's reform agenda were for the mayor to be a policy leader and to implement state-of-the-art policies and programs for local government.

Industrial policy also is a popular but ambiguous term, usually applied at the national level. But municipal government, despite its lack of constitutional powers related to economic development, also can make choices aimed at spurring growth in areas and economic sectors; nurturing cooperative problem-solving by business, labor, and community; supporting nontraditional enterprises such as waste recycling centers; and targeting job opportunities generated by development to people who need work. Municipalities ultimately may provide the arena in which new contracts for equitable economic development will be hammered out (Mier, 1984a).

A variant of planning practice and theory that focuses more on economic development gained legitimacy in the 1980s because of experiments in Cleveland, Hartford, Santa Monica, and a host of other smaller cities. Because administrations in those cities began to address the claims of constituencies heretofore ignored in the planning process—among them tenants, poor people, and neighborhood residents—this planning variant was considered "progressive" (Clavel, 1985). This new approach to planning tried to bring more people into the planning debate and argued for a new public balance sheet to evaluate public-private projects, in contrast to a tendency in the late 1970s to more private, closed planning processes (Einsweiler, 1980; Krumholz, 1980).

Formulating the Strategic Plan

Within 6 months after Washington's election as mayor in April 1983, he initiated the organization of representatives from the mayor's office and relevant development and planning departments.[2] As recently as the late 1970s those units had been parts of a single planning department. The mayor asked the subcabinet to prepare a policy plan (consistent with the policies articulated by *The Washington Papers*) to guide the administration in the design, implementation, and evaluation of development programs and projects.

The Formulation of Goals and Policies

When the subcabinet began to meet, its commissioners quickly identified several interdepartmental development projects and policy issues that required attention. The commissioners agreed to participate in a series of weekend retreats to address those issues and lay the groundwork for the statement and plan requested by the mayor. The plan eventually was published in May 1984 as *Chicago Works Together: 1984 Development Plan*.

The planning process merits brief recounting. An initial briefing document was prepared by staff of the subcabinet; that document identified all of the development objectives stated in *The Washington Papers* and in a transition team report developed by business and civic leaders immediately after the election (Washington Transition Committee, 1983).[3] The commissioners reviewed the briefing document and, during a lengthy consensus-building process, distilled its long list of objectives into 13 priority goal statements.

The subcabinet used the list of 13 goals as a yardstick to evaluate existing city programs and projects. For example, the subcabinet examined a proposed expansion of O'Hare Airport, a $1-billion investment anticipated to generate (directly and indirectly) 50,000 jobs in the ensuing decade. In light of the goal of more jobs for Chicagoans, the subcabinet asked whether most of the new jobs provided by the O'Hare project, as designed, would go to Chicagoans. The fact that suburban residents then held more than 90% of the jobs at O'Hare dramatized the importance of that question. The subcabinet discovered that the Mayor's Office of Employment and Training—the agency best able to refer Chicagoans to jobs—had no involvement in the O'Hare project. Hence City resources such as revenue bonds were subsidizing the construction of private aviation facilities, but no one was giving attention to linking new employment opportunities in those facilities to any specialized training and placement effort.

The subcabinet began to identify new approaches to current programs and projects to advance administration goals. Then they identified the goals—such as affirmative action, citizen participation, and neighborhood development—that required the design of new programs. For example, a new transit line was planned from downtown Chicago to Midway Airport, but the preceding administration had given no thought to housing or commercial development opportunities around the transit stations. The subcabinet added an investigation of such opportunities to the plan.

The result of these retreats and subsequent discussion was an outline for *Chicago Works Together* (*CWT*). The subcabinet reduced the 13 original goal statements to 5 and identified a total of 14 policies associated with the various goals (see Table 5.1).

A distinctive quality of *CWT* was that it committed the mayor to delivering on annual numerical targets, such as 6,000 units of rehabilitated housing, 10,000 jobs retained or created, and 12,000 persons trained in job skills. The key programs and projects

Table 5.1 Goals and Policies of *Chicago Works Together*

Goals
1. Target job opportunities.
2. Promote balanced growth.
3. Neighborhood development.
4. Public participation.
5. Legislative agenda.

Policies
1. Targeted business investment in support of job development.
2. Local preference in hiring and buying.
3. Skilled labor force development.
4. Infrastructure investment for job development.
5. Affirmative action.
6. Balanced growth, downtown/neighborhoods.
7. Public/private partnerships.
8. Equitable distribution of tax burden.
9. Strengthened tax base.
10. Neighborhood planning.
11. Expanded housing opportunities.
12. Linked development.
13. Increased citizen access to information.
14. Increased opportunities for citizen involvement.

SOURCE: Chicago Works Together Planning Task Force, 1987.

designed to deliver these goals were described in a lengthy appendix, including information on estimated program effects, program cost, source of funds, and estimated timing for more than 85 programs and projects.

Chicago Works Together as a Strategic Plan

The strategic planning process of the Washington administration did not originate with *Chicago Works Together*. Rather, that document represented an important stage in a longer effort to articulate a development policy driven by a philosophy of reform. As was related in the previous chapter, the development of the CWED Platform (Table 4.1) and *The Washington Papers* (Table 4.2) were important precedents. Yet, *CWT* was a self-contained strategic plan in terms of its process and content.

The creation of the Mayor's development subcabinet was another important step in the organizing phase of the strategic planning process. Compelling bureaucratic competitors to meet weekly and agree on program boundaries and resource distribution was a major accomplishment. This coalition of departments has proven to be an essential forum for the planning, refinement, and implementation of strategic goals.

In writing *Chicago Works Together* the subcabinet conformed to the steps of a standard strategic planning process. After many hours of discussion, it identified key issues; agreed on a mission statement; and established goals, policies, and strategies. The subcabinet also used its members' broad knowledge of the city, as well as the information in *The Washington Papers* and the mayor's transition team report, to evaluate the local environment and identify strengths and weaknesses of existing government activities. Time and resource constraints prohibited extensive research regarding specific short- and long-term economic trends or trends in different neighborhoods in the city. Finally, the last steps of a typical strategic planning process—developing the action plan, implementation, and monitoring—are occurring continuously and have become the central element of a management-by-objectives system.

Like *The Washington Papers, CWT* emphasized jobs, neighborhood development, and citizen participation. Several policies and programs highlighted in *The Washington Papers* remained in the development plan, including affirmative action, preference for Chicago businesses in purchasing and Chicago residents in hiring, neighborhood planning, and industry task forces. *Chicago Works Together,* however, improved on *The Washington Papers* in two important ways. First, it set a small manageable number of goals and policies—a characteristic that often differentiates strategic plans from comprehensive plans. Second, *CWT* recognized the difficult choices the city must make to distribute the benefits of development to citizens, businesses, and neighborhoods with demonstrated need. Unlike comprehensive plans, which attempt to provide something for everyone, the development plan specified priority beneficiaries and focused on a few programs designed to benefit them. The result was a somewhat unusual plan. In a contemporaneous review of the plan, Norman Krumholz, Patrick Costigan, and Dennis Keating (1985) said:

> The Chicago Development Plan 1984 is the strongest indication thus far that American cities are willing to try to harness economic

development for their disadvantaged residents. It is virtually certain to
be the forerunner of similar plans, especially in cities where the political
power of African Americans and Hispanics is on the rise. (p. 396)

The existence of the subcabinet and *Chicago Works Together*
represented substantial organizing and planning accomplishments, especially compared to their starting point. We attempt
below to illustrate their significance to municipal reform, strategic
planning, and industrial policy through a complex of public investment decisions that evolved as the local planning process matured.

Navy Pier or South Works?

The Developments: Phase 1

During the fall of 1984 the Chicago Department of Economic
Development found itself negotiating simultaneously with The
Rouse Company[4] for development of a major retail and entertainment complex and with U.S. Steel Corporation over a major
investment. Both projects were inherited from the previous
administration.

The Rouse plan would have resulted in the rehabilitation of
Navy Pier, which projects two-thirds of a mile into Lake Michigan, north of the Chicago Loop. Built just before World War I,
Navy Pier is the most visible artifact of the original Burnham Plan
for the city. The development projected leasing and rehabilitating the pier to accommodate 400,000 square feet of retail and
entertainment space and a 250-bed hotel. The total investment
required would have been $280 million, and it was estimated
that it would produce, upon completion, 5,000 jobs and more
than 100 business opportunities. Besides leasing public property to The Rouse Company, the City was considering a package
of public improvements that would have cost $60 million. We
contemplated financing $30 million to $40 million of it through
an Urban Development Action Grant (UDAG).

At the same time, on the city's south side, U.S. Steel had been
planning for several months to build a new rail mill at the historic
South Works. The South Works is the region's oldest fully integrated steel-producing facility, dating back to the 1870s. Today it

is merely a shadow facility, with more than 7,000 workers laid off in the past 6 years. This formerly awesome plant had one remaining operation—an electric furnace that would melt scrap steel to feed a beam rolling mill. U.S. Steel planned to upgrade the electric furnace to increase its productivity and add a rail mill. The melted scrap then would produce two products, beams and rails. The proposed investment was $250 million; a public contribution of about $45 million was proposed, $40 million of which might come from a federal UDAG. The rail mill would have expanded employment at the South Works to slightly more than 2,000 people.

Each project attracted its own advocates and political constituencies. Behind the Navy Pier plan was a nationally renowned developer with an impeccable reputation and the support of some Chicagoans eager to see an underused local landmark put to productive use. The prospect of keeping the South Works operational mobilized a unique coalition of union representatives, community groups, and local, state, and national politicians.

Each project required a large UDAG to proceed. Although there had never been a UDAG award of $30 million to $40 million in the country, the City had confidence that it could get one such grant, but definitely not two. Alternative approaches such as tax increment financing were uncertain because of the City's fiscal situation. Thus the City had to choose which project to support with public financing.

Mayor Washington decided to proceed with the UDAG application for the South Works project because of his commitment to the preservation of the local steel industry, to manufacturing jobs over retail jobs, and to projects that would benefit neighborhoods. In choosing South Works, however, the mayor did not abandon the Navy Pier project. Instead, he directed the commissioners of the development departments to pursue other approaches to financing the development.

The Capacity for Complex Decisions

Because the South Works and Navy Pier projects were legacies of the previous administration, the choice confronting Mayor

Washington was not of his making. The planning process of the campaign partially prepared him to make the choice, but he was clearly in a reactive mode. One of the problems the Washington administration encountered was having to rely on incomplete information about the comparative costs and benefits of projects that were molded by the goals and values of the previous administration. For example, the previous analysis did not give any priority to quality of work, so occupational information was not available to test the hypothesis that South Works offered better jobs.

Because this decision confronted the mayor while he was still assembling his administrative team, he did not have in place a level of teamwork to orchestrate political events around the projects. Consequently, key constituencies could not be mobilized.

These factors—being in a reactive mode, having incomplete information, having a new team, and not being able to mobilize constituents—raise the question of whether Washington should have made any choice. After all, he could have allowed the federal government to make the decision. We hypothesize, on the basis of UDAG administrative criteria, that the federal decision would have supported the Navy Pier project. (These criteria consider the total number of jobs, the ratio of private to public investment, and the likelihood of project success.)

Shortly after the mayor made his decisions, U.S. Steel canceled its plans for the rail mill. While bargaining with the Washington administration for financial incentives, U.S. Steel simultaneously was bargaining with the United Steel Workers of America for substantial work rule concessions. USWA had made substantial concessions to U.S. Steel the year before to support the prospective rail mill development and refused to concede more. U.S. Steel canceled its expansion plans.

As the Washington administration regrouped and reconsidered the Navy Pier opportunity, local politics struck. In what is widely interpreted as an action solely designed to damage and embarrass Mayor Washington, his opposition on the City Council directed that negotiations with the Rouse Company be terminated. That experience, in combination with several similar economic development decisions, underscored the need for a strategic plan with more depth and detail than *The Washington Papers.*

The Developments: Phase 2

By early 1984 the process of preparing *Chicago Works Together* was well under way. The mayor had developed the administrative apparatus to reexamine the two projects through a fresh lens. In keeping with his desire to open complex decision processes, he created two task forces focusing, respectively, on Navy Pier and on steel and southeast Chicago. Each constituted a representative cross-section of interests: the Task Force on Steel and Southeast Chicago included industry, labor, community, real estate, and civic groups; the Task Force on Navy Pier included retail development, civic, community, and architecture and planning groups. The charge given to each task force reflected the goals and policies that were emerging from *Chicago Works Together.*

The efforts of the Task Force on Steel and Southeast Chicago ranged widely across the industry and the area (Markusen, Lerner, Patton, Ross, & Schneider, 1985; Task Force on Steel and Southeast Chicago, 1986). With regard to the South Works site, the task force, working closely with the company and the union, analyzed and rejected the feasibility of an employee buy out of the facility. It also rejected several nonmanufacturing land use proposals, ranging from a World's Fair to an airport. Working with the City and the state, U.S. Steel now is redeveloping approximately half of the site as an industrial park and has begun making a multimillion-dollar investment. In addition, a training program sponsored jointly by the City, the state, and U.S. Steel is being developed to try to link dislocated steelworkers to the new employment opportunities. Meanwhile, the remainder of the site continues to house a steel-producing complex that employs more than 1,000 people.

The Task Force on Navy Pier rejected the idea of a Rouse Company-type development for Navy Pier on several grounds. First, it would require an up-front public investment that they thought should be targeted for retail revitalization in more needy areas, a policy of *Chicago Works Together.* Second, they did not think the resulting facility would have the broad public appeal formerly enjoyed by the pier. After considering options ranging from a gambling casino to housing, the task force recommended redevelopment of the pier as an urban park with a strong cultural and recreational orientation (Task Force on Navy Pier, 1986). By pursuing their work through a consensus-building process, the task force built such a degree of public support for their recommendations that the City Council unanimously approved $15 million to begin renovation.

Lessons of *Chicago Works Together*

1. Reform goals can be implemented successfully through strategic planning. As of February 1986, the programs of the development subcabinet had been guided by *Chicago Works Together* for about 18 months. As mentioned above, the subcabinet was successful in achieving key performance objectives. The subcabinet periodically assessed its performance on the 85 programs and policies discussed in *Chicago Works Together.* Within 18 months after the release of the plan, for example, the City had exceeded its performance targets in 12.8% of its programs and projects, had at least realized its targets on 20.9% of them, and had made at least partial progress on more than 90% of the programs and projects. In only 5.7% of the City's development efforts was no progress made.

The accomplishments touched all aspects of government, including increased public participation, increased job creation and retention activities, increased technical assistance to nonprofit economic development organizations, and increased placement of poor people into jobs. The administration's successful delivery of programs directed to benefit minorities and low- to moderate-income people is particularly important. For example, 53 minority- or women-owned businesses received financial assistance from the City during Washington's first 2 years as mayor, compared to 9 such businesses in the preceding 10 years.

2. There was great value in limiting the number of clearly stated goals and policies. One of the key flaws in traditional comprehensive plans (and even some recent strategic plans) has been the large number of goals identified.[5] Studies or plans with 10 or 15 goals and 50 to 100 policies and other recommendations have been common. Those types of plans often encounter difficulties at the implementation stage for several reasons. Adopting a multiplicity of goals may please everyone, but it avoids the tough process of building a necessary consensus around priorities among key actors. Chicago's development subcabinet, mirroring public debate, struggled internally with the question of

job generation versus wealth generation as the main priority of development ("New Development Chief," 1983). The debate over downtown development versus neighborhood development resulted in a consensus about the goals of balanced growth.

By limiting *Chicago Works Together* to five goals, the Washington administration made it easier for the public to understand and accept the plan. Within 6 months of the publication of the plan in May 1984, the development subcabinet commissioners had completed more than 200 presentations on the plan to the public. The commissioners, backed up by a slide show, lapel pins, and brochures, were able to deliver a concise and consistent message about the mayor's five-point development plan.

Direct public communication of the goals began to influence priorities and plans in other government departments and in nongovernment groups. For example, the business group that sponsored the original Burnham Plan also sponsored a metropolitan area strategic development plan, which concluded by focusing on job generation as the predominant goal (Longworth, 1984, 1985). In other words, *Chicago Works Together* set the parameters of the local policy debate. Similarly, as will be shown in more detail in the next chapter, community organizations designed their own strategic plans or priority projects to conform with the City's goals (United Neighborhood Organization of Chicago, 1985).

3. A strategic approach to economic development must contain sectoral and area development strategies. The achievement of goals such as job creation and neighborhood development depends on the success of strategies aimed both at specific economic sectors and at designated geographical areas. It also depends on a recognition of the complex interplay between these approaches, which is affected at any given moment by both economic and political forces. In many respects, the Navy Pier and South Works cases attest to that.

In the context of economic structural change and declining public resources, meeting the goal of job generation demands a sectoral strategy. Planners must identify economic sectors that have promise for providing high-quality, lasting employment locally or in the region (Mier, 1984a; Rhode Island Strategic Development Commission, 1983; Lewin, 1984; Luria & Russell, 1981). They must determine which opportunities within those sectors can be influenced by local government and direct available resources to them. Steel and apparel task forces specified in *Chicago Works Together* exemplify the sectoral approach.

On the other hand, the goal of neighborhood development requires an area development strategy. This is required as an end in itself, because Chicago, like many cities, contains vast tracts of predominantly minority, poverty-stricken neighborhoods that cannot be ignored. As in the sectoral strategy, however, scarce resources must be invested in those commercial strips or in neighborhood development projects that show a reasonable likelihood of success. A strategy might be the development of a supermarket/convenience store complex in an area where none exists, therefore guaranteeing a market.

There are also political reasons for pursuing both sectoral and area strategies. Each strategy is associated with a different constituency. For example, workers and local residents typically are the respective constituencies for the sectoral and area strategies. Sectoral and area strategies can, and should, be consciously designed to overlap and be mutually reinforcing. For those reasons Washington's task force on the apparel industry recommended the creation of a "needle trades" district, centered on a building designed and managed to nurture the growth of apparel and related firms.

Permeating much of economic development practice is the assumption that the pursuit of sectoral development will yield specific area development automatically because the benefits trickle down.[6] But many sectoral developments fail to affect local communities. For example, in Chicago there had been tremendous public emphasis on development of the financial services sector, supported by the belief that the benefits of that development would accrue to the neighborhoods of Chicago. While financial services and other subsectors of the services grew, however, employment held by Chicago residents in these sectors declined substantially. In reality, most new financial service jobs located in the central business district were (and are) held by suburbanites. Similarly, many area-specific actions, such as a neighborhood grocery store, have no sectoral rationale and can be questioned on efficiency grounds.

Chicago Works Together sought to coordinate sectoral and area strategies to reinforce each other. For example, the City's Department of Economic Development conditioned incentives for new businesses on locational choices. In addition, the administration made hiring agreements a condition for public investment in many developments, such as the O'Hare expansion project. The City targeted its own public purchasing to minority- and female-owned and Chicago-based businesses. The private sector joined the City with its own modest local purchasing program. Finally, the City funded a variety of local neighborhood-based development groups. Their activities ranged from launching businesses themselves to being financial counselors to businesses, providing technical assistance to businesses, and promoting local entrepreneurship. For example, four neighborhood waste-recycling businesses were created and three centers were established to foster expansion of small businesses.

4. Strategic planning processes in a reform administration must involve citizens. The most widespread citizen participation in the administration's strategic planning process occurred during the mayoral campaign. The actual writing and revising of *Chicago Works Together* did not involve citizen groups. A number of community organizations, while strongly supportive of the content of *CWT,* were critical of the lack of participation in the drafting stage. They argued that even though citizen participation was a stated goal of *Chicago Works Together,* they were not involved fully in the subcabinet's deliberations about the plan. They seemed to feel less ownership of *CWT* than of *The Washington Papers.* The administration subsequently updated *Chicago Works Together* in a manner designed to involve not only community-based organizations but civic groups, labor, business, interest groups, and other governments as well.

The Washington administration conducted neighborhood forums throughout the city that allowed citizens and community organizations to ask questions of the mayor and his cabinet. A variety of briefings were held on every budget well in advance of City Council votes. For example, City Council deliberations on the 1986 budget were preceded by more than 140 community budget briefings. Eleven task forces on key policy issues in 1985 involved more than 600 citizens in policy development and program design. Issues covered included homelessness, housing abandonment, waste management, linked development (linking the benefits of downtown development to Chicago's neighborhoods), the steel industry, the apparel industry, and energy.

Finally, community groups had a much closer working relationship with government as co-strategists on specific issues, such as plant closings and loft conversions.

5. Local government bureaucracy is, at present, ill equipped to conduct and implement strategic planning. Our efforts revealed a number of limitations in our capacity to engage in local strategic planning. At the institutional level, administration officials must address issues of staff capacity, communication, intercultural sensitivity, cooperative intragovernmental and intergovernmental working relationships, systems for monitoring and evaluating progress toward performance targets, and good relationships with key leaders and organizations outside government.

Mayor Washington took control of a bureaucracy that lacked those requisite qualities. Decades of civil service hiring, dominated by a powerful patronage system, had created a bureaucracy staffed by too many inadequately trained employees, including many planners in the development group. Even good professionals hired by the Washington development departments frequently were unable to be fully effective because of basic gaps in information and limited communication skills needed for development of sectoral and area development strategies (Mier, 1984b; Bolan 1985).

The second set of limitations we encountered was political. Individuals and groups with narrow political agendas often impede genuine attempts to do cooperative strategic planning. When local government planning and decision making are opened up, however, those with narrow agendas are challenged to broaden their perspectives. Under the Washington administration Chicago saw government, labor, and community interests converge on several occasions in plant closing situations (Giloth & Mier, 1986). We needed such coalitions to support a legislative agenda locally, in the state government, and ultimately at the national level.[7] These coalitions were also needed to offset local political parties' reluctance to take the lead in strategic planning.

The City administration also needed to overcome the continuing wariness of members of the business community toward Mayor Washington and cultivate their involvement with government.[8] The interests of government and business should not converge completely, but *Chicago Works Together* placed a high priority on cooperation between the public and private sectors around the goal of creating and retaining jobs.

6. National industrial policy should be developed in localities and should involve local actors. We argue that a political constituency for national industrial policy must be built on a constituency for local economic development planning. The origins of this belief are too complex to elaborate here, but it is our conviction that the tension between equity and efficiency—a driving force for economic planning—is too easily lost unless it is built on a local foundation. To say it another way, we believe that economic planning requires a constant rub of equity and efficiency (Giloth & Mier, 1986), but they can hide from each other too easily at the national level.

For example, local efforts to actively revitalize the steel and apparel industries sharpened the focus of local debate on free trade policy and antitrust legislation (Washington, 1985). It is not surprising, therefore, that local mayors and legislative bodies in the 1980s became involved in such national issues as nuclear freeze, banning leaded gasoline, and investment in South Africa.

Conclusion

Several points merit summarizing. We want to argue for the importance of using strategic planning to achieve specified social and economic goals that often are pursued under the aegis of reform or industrial policy. For example, we saw bureaucratic consensus and widening community support for placing emphasis on job development, neighborhood development, and affirmative action. In addition, there was sharp public debate about linked development and targeting job opportunities to Chicagoans who needed work.

Goals such as these often bring out the inherent rub between equity and efficiency, between open government and administrative efficiency. Budget priorities were being discussed and debated in public with literally scores of community hearings, and important budget decisions were made in response to those debates. For example, development departments gained public support for earmarking for development purposes the proceeds from land sales-resources that previously went to general City operations.

It is our experience that strategic planning is a promising vehicle for conflict resolution. For example, it provided a framework for development subcabinet departments to prepare joint budgets and for dramatic revisions to the public infrastructure program, which redistributed tens of millions of dollars from the central area to neighborhood infrastructure. These types of choices were concentrated on decisions within development and did not affect trade-offs between development and, say, human services. Nevertheless, our experience with the bureaucracy of Chicago's government suggests that it needs substantial overhauling if it is to deliver the programs essential to the accomplishment of strategic goals, and we suspect this is true of many government bureaucracies. Any attempt to implement municipal reform or industrial policy must address forthrightly the quality of the delivery system if it is to be successful.

Finally, because of the depth of the public debate in Chicago about goals and means, we think a consensus for alternative national policies can be built out of organizing at the state and local levels (Giloth & Mier, 1986). This organizing should be focused on political and policy objectives that are derived from concrete experiences of people involved in strategic planning and economic development activities. It is unlikely that national policy change will be implemented, let alone be successful, if it is not linked to local activities.

Notes

1. Of course, this defines an ideal type. The words *process, key, agree, careful, environment,* and even *strategies* describe a wide range of action or attributes that loosely fit the definitions. For discussions of strategic planning, see So (1984), *Business Week* (1984), and Public Technology (1984).

2. The development subcabinet included the mayor's office and the commissioners of cultural affairs, economic development, employment and training, housing, planning, and public works. Representatives of the offices of information and inquiry, budget, and law also attended for informational purposes.

3. The transition team had an oversight committee of 57 of Chicago's business, religious, academic, and community leaders. The oversight committee was supported by a network of task forces and work groups that involved more than 300 people.

4. The Rouse Company is the well-known developer of Harborplace, Baltimore; Faneuil Hall Marketplace, Boston; and the South Street Seaport, New York.

5. We reviewed several recent plans for this paper. *A Philadelphia Prospectus* (Hershberg & Rubin, 1982) assessed 12 sectors and identified four developmental roles for Philadelphia, 15 objectives, and 56 recommendations. *Cleveland Tomorrow*

(Cleveland Tomorrow Committee, 1981) identified six programs to assist anchor industries and foster growth industries in Cleveland. *Goals for Dallas* (City of Dallas, 1977) identified 205 goals in 17 subject areas. *Jobs for Metropolitan Chicago* (Commercial Club of Chicago, 1984) identified five primary objectives and 14 strategies to target economic development in Chicago. San Francisco's *Strategic Plan* (San Francisco Chamber of Commerce & Arthur Andersen, 1983) identified 19 strategies relating to housing, transportation, city finance, and job and business opportunities. In *The Greenhouse Compact,* the Rhode Island Strategic Development Commission (1983) established specific goals for job creation, unemployment rates, and wage rates in Rhode Island. It also completed a sectoral analysis of 15 industries and recommended strategies for expanding the existing industrial base, creating new businesses and industries, and improving the Rhode Island business climate. (See Silver & Burton, 1986.)

6. Compare the views of Lasater (1984) and Krumholz (1984) on the neighborhood effects of the development of the Washington University Medical Center in St. Louis, Missouri.

7. In the spring of 1985 Governor James Thompson proposed a $2.3-billion economic development program. The governor's program included $26 million for Chicago and only $130 million for Cook County. The City of Chicago proposed that a "municipal agenda" targeted to the needs of cities be added to the program. The resulting document (City of Chicago Office of Intergovernmental Affairs, 1985c) illustrated how one city can use resources for economic development. It served as a blueprint for other cities throughout Illinois during the 1985 legislative session. As a result of the municipal agenda, the legislature appropriated $55.5 million for Chicago programs. The Community Workshop on Economic Development (1982b) also submitted a statewide economic development proposal to Thompson.

8. Under the Washington administration there were several major efforts to involve the business community in government, including a task force examining municipal management practice and a financial oversight committee.

6 | Managing Planned Change

with

KARI J. MOE

This chapter presents the challenge the Washington administration faced in implementing Chicago Works Together on striking a balance between neighborhood development and mega-projects. An equally important focus is on building organizational capacity, and the organizational culture to sustain it, within the Department of Economic Development. The discussion details how the bureaucracy prevented problems from being tackled head-on. It shares the steps taken to create a climate that encouraged individuals to work cooperatively across departments to develop innovative solutions to problems and create a sense of ownership of new policy initiatives.

Introduction

This is the story of our effort to implement the Washington development policies. That this chapter covers so much territory, including history, ideas, and implementation details, is an accurate depiction of how we experienced this period. For 6

AUTHORS' NOTE: Adapted from Mier and Moe (1991) and reproduced with permission of the Center for Urban Policy Research, Rutgers University.

years, from 1983 through 1989, when we both left as Richard M. Daley became mayor, we were engaged daily in broad and diverse discussions and activities. We were constantly changing gears, from debates about the most effective approaches to citizen participation, to who on our staff was leaking information to the mayor's political opposition. We shifted between debates and decisions about why we were not paying community organization subcontractors on time, to how to get a better public return on public investment, to whether we should be handing out pens and watches in the employee morale program. There was no aspect of governing that we did not take on as a challenge to "do it better," because that was the nature of our mission as we saw it.

Our course was inextricably rooted in the history of minority and community political struggles in Chicago. Its direction was enabled and informed by the clear vision and legislative record of Harold Washington. He believed that politics and government could be a force for fairness, effective service delivery, and social programs directed toward the needs of neighborhoods. As community organizers and as urban planners, we believed that our role was to apply our best efforts to implement this vision, with strategies that had to include both democratic process and good results. In terms of our personal history, what we set out to achieve was, somewhat ironically, rooted in influential experiences in the military. Moe grew up in a U.S. Air Force career family in which "public service" was a watchword. I went to Vietnam as a U.S. Navy officer and adviser and my experiences became a foundation for my commitment to urban development.

On a decision-by-decision basis, guided by Washington's vision and commitment, we tried to address the desires of all neighborhoods for open, effective, and fair government. We worked to make their agenda a reality in both big and small ways. We changed budget priorities and implemented reform legislation that was dramatic for Chicago. But no detail was insignificant. For example, we personally took care to rewrite letters that senior staff had prepared for the mayor's signature, to make them sound less bureaucratic and more human. We also talked to secretaries about being "Harold's voice" to the citizen who had perhaps never called City Hall before.

Even with our best efforts, there is no denying the huge constraints we faced at every turn in the implementation process. One of our favorite metaphors was that we won the opportunity to drive a 1940s jalopy in a 1980s road race. Worse yet, the pit crew was either inexperienced, working for the mayor's opponents, or, often, both. Moe was fond of saying that trying to get things done was like fighting a war with someone else's army. The idea that winning an election is a cakewalk compared to governing was one that we grasped immediately.

We learned that positive, concrete changes can and did occur as the result of a visionary mayor who developed a progressive policy agenda and directed his administrators to implement these policies through programs, plans, procedures, and legislation. We were, however, humbled by the extreme difficulty we encountered every single minute of every day in office.

The Department of Economic Development (DED)

Assessment

Virtually all the departments in the government inherited by Harold Washington operated as if they were a 1950s organization. For example, there were no computers in the DED when we walked in. None of the financial staff was using electronic spreadsheets; everything was being done by hand. Department staff were calling on 3,000 businesses a year with paper records that were virtually inaccessible. This backwardness held for all City government systems, as diverse as the personnel system and the check-writing system.

DED was a young organization, having been created in 1982. It succeeded the Economic Development Commission, which then had been vested with some line authority. The new department was created by adding some units from the Departments of Planning and Neighborhoods to those in the Economic Development Commission.[1] When I started in the department, a large amount of DED's $35-million budget was for infrastructure development. The City had received counter-recession federal Economic Development Administration (EDA) funds, so it was building industrial streets and undertaking some commercial area improvements. DED also had a $1-million EDA revolving loan fund, and was packaging federal Urban Development Action Grants (UDAGs). There was a business contact program with 10 or 12 people in the field knocking on doors. The department supported chambers of commerce to implement marketing programs for their neighborhood commercial strips. There were about 45 community business organizations annually receiving about $1 million in grants.[2] A staff of 10 or 12 people managed the commercial strip program.

DED lacked a clear mission and identity, partly due to its newness. There was no marketing program. There was no program designed to provide comprehensive services to small businesses. There was only a limited industrial policy focus (Giloth, 1989).[3]

Although DED lacked a clear mission, it had an organizational culture. This departmental culture accepted that significant projects went through an essentially political decision process. Favored nongovernmental deal brokers handled the major projects or programs. Therefore, the department staff was relegated to less-significant work.

Staff accepted that they didn't have the resources or authority to commit the bureaucracy. This paradox fostered an individual behavior, on the one hand, of trying to sound responsive, while, on the other hand, not being able to deliver. Bureaucratic procedures existed to shove away problems while pretending to take them seriously. If anything, this problem was exacerbated with the coming of Harold Washington. His campaign promise to make government accessible to everyone had raised expectations. The scarcity of resources and the overwhelming nature of many problems lead to enormous "queuing" problems.

Another problematic aspect of organization culture was a serious lack of information and knowledge across departmental divisions. For example, there were about 10 people who contacted businesses through field calls. These 10 people had received no training regarding the loan programs of the department. If a business person wanted financial assistance, he or she couldn't find out about it from the department agents who were the first point of information. The business person had to go through the deal brokers. We identified several similar problems in this early analysis.

Organizing the Department

I took office in August 1983. By mid-October, several division heads who were sensitive to and capable of managing the Harold Washington agenda were in place.[4] But the mayor was still troubled by the presence of many staff people who were set in their ways. These staff ranged from apolitical bureaucrats, who had been stuck in a job for years, to political appointees, who were allied with the mayor's opposition. The consequences of this included low productivity, bad morale, and in the worse cases, sabotage.

My new senior staff and I knew that changing organizational culture and staff behavior throughout DED would take 2 to 3 years. This was too long a time frame to achieve organizational effectiveness. We wanted the ability, at a moment's notice, to seize opportunities to implement concrete projects that embodied the Washington agenda.

To provide a stimulus for innovation and keep a focus on larger strategy questions, Moe, still in the mayor's office, and I formulated the idea of a new research and development division within DED. In November 1983, we drafted the functions of the division. It would provide staff resources to line divisions when they engaged in entrepreneurial activities; work with community-based organizations engaged in policy research and development; improve information systems within the department; and manage special projects. The R&D division was launched in January 1984, when Moe transferred to DED (Giloth, 1991).

Redefining the Culture

With key managers in place, we knew that we needed to foster a different organizational culture. The components of the desired culture were in some cases linked directly to the mayoral campaign. One theme was respect for the processes of community empowerment. This required creating a different attitude in the bureaucracy, one that respected and responded to external initiative instead of being exclusively internally driven, or driven by the political apparatus.[5]

Consistent with themes of openness and democracy, we wanted to minimize bureaucratic boundaries and to create a climate of problem solving based on point-to-point communication and teamwork. I recognized and rewarded this kind of initiative. This discomforted the division heads, even ones I had appointed. Like Washington, I would symbolically reinforce an emphasis on point-to-point communication by doing it myself.

A major obstacle, which cannot be overemphasized and which impeded the creation of a different culture, was the predominant administrative rules and norms of the bureaucracy. DED was subject to personnel regulations, hiring rules, and fiscal control systems that slowed everything down and lowered employee morale significantly. Because of this context, we also promoted cultural change through traditional, formal approaches. Moe and I implemented orientation and training sessions for the staff regarding the new directions of the department. We revised operational procedures, emphasizing the need for openness and accessibility. We symbolically reinforced these actions with, for example, new marketing paraphernalia. Over time, we underscored all this by introducing performance evaluations and tying them to achievement of our departmental objectives.

Within months Moe and I began to have quarterly all-department meetings, where people would be rewarded for actions that best exemplified the new goals. When someone undertook an initiative supportive of the new directions, the episode would be shared with the entire department, emphasizing how it fit into the big picture, and then the employee would be rewarded with office memorabilia, such as a calling card case or pen set. High performers were also promoted whenever possible.

Moe and I placed a strong emphasis on the goal of equal opportunity. We were probably one of the earliest departments that made substantial inroads into equal opportunity hiring. A key was my personal involvement as Commissioner. I simply would not let people hire unless I was satisfied that they had really done an EEO search. Moe developed the departmental procedures for such a search. I set goals for divisions, sections of divisions, and occupational hierarchies. For this, I was accused of "micromanagement," but I firmly believe this important goal must take absolute top priority for success. When the Latino Commission did an evaluation of departments' EEO hiring efforts, they acknowledged DED as an model for other departments in terms of pursuing an EEO hiring program (Mayor's Commission on Latino Affairs, 1984).

Part of what we were doing was along the classic lines of good government reform—creating an organization that was responsible to the mayor, yet operating along lines that were clear and accountable to the public.[6] Mayor Washington wanted the departments to be accessible to the public and to constituencies directly, as distinct from having citizens go through aldermen or consultants. For example, John Halpin, Washington's Commissioner of Streets and Sanitation, made himself available directly to community groups so they could get their streets cleaned by talking to him directly.

Managing DED Programs

Once the policy agenda was set, we were faced with the task of implementation. By spring 1984, DED had been reorganized into five operating divisions: business services, neighborhood development, real estate development, international business development, and R&D. These divisions together were responsible for managing a wide variety of programs and projects, outlined in the appendix.[7]

Within each of these divisions we faced a number of common problems. Staff capacity was limited, and the bureaucracy continued to move too slowly. We had too little money for everything, from computers and books to loan program dollars. We faced intransigent historical and institutional obstacles, such as trying to initiate development planning in neighborhoods where no new development had occurred for several years. We experienced covert and overt political opposition within our ranks. The media was uninformed, hostile, and unwilling to cover neighborhood development stories. Finally, we experienced disagreements about strategic directions. Any two or three of these factors operating at once would make management in any organization challenging. All six together made it extremely difficult.

Each division and its programs could be the object of considerable analysis and evaluation. Instead of focusing on all of them, we will highlight one program area: neighborhood development through community-based organizations, because this was central to the Washington development agenda. One division had major responsibility for this program area, but it touched the work of all the operating divisions. In addition, we will describe a number of large projects that we managed during the second half of the mayor's tenure.

Neighborhood Development Program

In 1983, the year Mayor Washington took office, DED supported 48 community-based "delegate agencies." They provided a variety of services in their local neighborhoods. This arrangement was politically controversial because in some respects it circumvented the political ward organizations. It was also a system that put Washington directly in touch with his grass-roots constituency, which was also why previous mayors supported the concept to some degree.

Up until 1983 there was little oversight of the delegate agency program. The 35 groups receiving money were subject to few requirements, although some were performing quite admirably. To the extent that there was an evaluation system, it was superficial. Funding was based on a 3-year cycle, at which point the department wished groups to be self-sufficient. In reality, the criteria were unclear and few groups were ever defunded.

Based on campaign commitments and our philosophy of neighborhood development, we wanted to expand and improve the delegate agency program. We wanted to demonstrate that development services could be effectively delivered through community-based organizations. Within 2 years, the number of neighborhood based organizations or citywide groups supporting the neighborhood effort receiving direct funding from DED had grown to more than 100.

The expansion involved four types of groups. First, there were new local businessmen's organizations being created, often encouraged by one of the major network organizations like CANDO or CWED. Second, there were groups in other functional areas, most often housing rehabilitation, who were broadening their work to include direct business assistance or development. Third, there were particular efforts to encourage business organization development in low-income areas, such as within public housing projects. Finally, there were service groups brought in to provide technical assistance to new or growing neighborhood-based organizations. For example, the League of Women Voters received a DED grant to conduct board training.

DED rewarded groups that developed business service capacity, both by giving them more money and by letting them carry on a greater load of the work. When they evolved to what DED considered the most complete stage of development, they were given twice the amount of money any group had been given in the past. DED staff were then pulled out of that community. The local organization would become the City's first line of contact with businesses outside the central area. This final stage of development was called the Local Industrial Retention Initiative (LIRI).[8]

The LIRI program originated in the field operations division of DED, run by Arturo Vazquez.[9] It evolved from an identification of the half dozen local industrial councils or community organizations, among those routinely working with DED, that had the highest organizational capacity to step up their industrial retention efforts. DED and these groups tried to formulate a systematic and strategic methodology for dealing with industrial retention—what businesses should be approached, what they should be asked, what could be done to give them more confidence in the City, and, most important, what concrete problems the City could realistically tackle.

In varying degrees, other departments of the City that worked with neighborhood-based organizations were trying the same thing. The Department of Housing was supporting groups to rehabilitate housing for low-to-moderate-income tenants. The Department of Human Services supported neighborhood-based social service providers (Walker, 1991). The Departments of Health and Aging and Disability, and the Mayor's Office of Employment and Training, were similarly developing networks of neighborhood-based service providers.

Evaluation of the Neighborhood Development Program

The program of support to more than 100 community development organizations made programmatic sense, policy sense, and political sense. But it was always a very tough program to manage because of the varying levels of capacity and performance from the groups.

Performance evaluation was very difficult and labor intensive. It exposed the uneven skills of our staff and their varying capacity to assist the groups and assess their performance. We needed an evaluation system that could minimize the risk associated with widely divergent groups and widely divergent staff skills. By supplementing our staff with outside evaluators drawn from local technical assistance providers, we developed a workable system. However, evaluations continued to generate discomfort among groups being reviewed. This process was essential for both our own internal purposes, and for the public and City Council.

Frequently when we went before the City Council, some delegate agency contract was the object of an aldermen saying, "That group in my neighborhood isn't doing anything." We had to defend that they were doing something worthwhile. We were constantly risking being attacked for just dumping money on groups for political purposes. They really wanted to attack us on that and make the case that this was a political operation, not a professional operation.

Our critics could not make their case. In 4 years, they could not find a case to demonstrate that a group we proposed to fund was not performing adequately. This standard required accountability from groups, and every year we defunded five or six groups for nonperformance. These actions were often protested, but we held our ground. Opposition aldermen could never find a nonperforming group that we hadn't already found and were planning to defund.

The U.S. Department of Housing and Urban Development (HUD), which provided most of DED's funds through the Community Development Block Grant, was auditing DED on a case-by-case basis. They investigated every group we were supporting, and asked whether it met the HUD national standards. During the 4 years, HUD evaluated 100% of the DED projects. This close scrutiny created an atmosphere both within our staff and among business and community groups working with us that HUD was not supportive of what we were trying to do.

Large-Scale Development Initiatives

Several development initiatives were of such scale and importance that they transcended the capacity of any one department to direct. Examples include projects such as the renovation or replacement of professional sports stadiums, the construction of the new central library, the development of new transit stations and adjacent land, and the development of surplus land at the City's airports. Each of these projects tended to involve multiple departments from the development subcabinet, the City's legal and financial staff, departments with specific technical responsibilities like Public Works, and departments holding such key assets as land owned by Aviation or Public Works.

Because DED chaired the development subcabinet, and because the mayor wanted economic development considerations to be preeminent, its top management was expected to play a part in these projects. In addition, the mayor had gained confidence in our individual abilities to respond quickly and thoroughly to projects with complex requirements. Over time, I assumed major responsibility for many of them, and their dictates were superimposed over the normal functions of the department.

To a degree, Mayor Washington undertook such projects reluctantly. They were not consistent with his development philosophy of small, widely dispersed projects with lots of opportunities for community involvement. The large projects risked activating the urban growth coalitions and having them again run roughshod over neighborhood interests (Mollenkopf, 1983). As Hollander subsequently argues, the Mayor found he had little choice.

His first problem was that he had not been able to effectively market a "small is beautiful" development metaphor. This image never really took hold in the major media. Second, the media held him to a standard that would not have been placed on a white mayor. Reluctance to deliver mega-projects, the mayor increasingly feared, would be interpreted by the media as fundamental evidence of his inability to govern, where it would be judged as strategic choice for a white mayor. Early in stadium deliberations, Washington told Mier that he believed if he lost a professional sports team, even to the suburbs, neither he nor another other African-American candidate for mayor could win.

None of this was consolation to his community constituency, and these projects generated controversy. Neighborhood groups' views about the correct development course were clearly defined by their own interests. They tended not to prioritize projects with a citywide impact or benefit. Harold Washington's track record on major projects was not their concern. We will illustrate these dilemmas by means of the stadium projects and the central library, projects for which one or the other of us had major responsibility.

The White Sox

There were three stadium projects that surfaced during Mayor Washington's tenure. Because the Bears and the White Sox wanted new stadiums, the initial efforts were focused on finding a site that could accommodate a new stadium complex. After some early consideration of a domed stadium, it became apparent that neither team wanted to play indoors or on artificial surfaces. Further, they had vastly different needs in terms of stadium size, with football seeking a 75,000-person stadium and baseball a 45,000-person facility.

Other issues eroded the idea of a stadium complex. One team owner was reluctant to enter into any cooperative management arrangement with the other, and was not confident that scheduling conflicts could be amicably handled. Also, the Bears wanted to own their own stadium, whereas the White Sox wanted a publicly built one.

By July of 1986, any prospects for a stadium complex with two teams as tenants evaporated. The White Sox then announced that they were going to leave Chicago to play in west suburban Addison, Illinois. Needless to say, a community outcry erupted.

The ensuing process to "Save Our Sox" was dominated by community activists who were more baseball fans than they were connected to the neighborhoods around Comiskey Park. Their organizing efforts were complemented by political activists seeking to build an organizational base in the communities adjoining the baseball park. They focused their attention narrowly on keeping the White Sox in Chicago and retaining historic Comiskey Park. They built grass-roots support among White Sox fans. They did not really entertain the possibility that keeping the White Sox in Chicago might mean building a new stadium for them.

It is important that we failed to expand the issue into a broad community context. This was the first of the big projects with a direct community impact. Further, it did not really "fit" in any department. As such, the team appointed to negotiate with the White Sox and the state was led by Al Johnson, one of the mayor's key private sector advisers, and me. We were always trying to borrow resources from other departments.[10] City departments responded by trying to minimize staff effort.

By mid-fall 1986, support for the White Sox in Addison had eroded, and in early November they lost by a close vote in a local referendum. The White Sox were being quietly courted by St. Petersburg, Florida, and Denver, Colorado. With the Illinois State legislature due to convene for a brief session in late November, a window of opportunity for the mayor to "Save Our Sox" opened. He seized the opportunity.

Things moved very quickly. In a matter of 48 hours after Thanksgiving, a deal was put together that kept the White Sox in Chicago but called for a new stadium to be built in the vicinity of the current Sox stadium.[11] That choice was totally driven by costs—reusing existing infrastructure would save $30-$50 million. Within 5 working days, it was passed by the Illinois General Assembly. The new stadium would be financed by rent paid by the team, supplemented with a new tax on hotel and motel rooms, a tax base that would not have been available for uses other than those seen as benefiting the "visitor industry."

In the short run, there was widespread euphoria. After Mayor Washington's death, much controversy erupted that warrants exposition elsewhere. In a nutshell, the White Sox walked away from the deal, raised the stakes, and forced another $150 million of public subsidy into the deal. Also, the Illinois Sports Facilities Authority, empowered with building the stadium, was accused of running roughshod over the community, and in so doing, exposed the lack of community roots in the original community organizing and City planning efforts.

The Bears

After the collapse of the stadium complex idea, the focus also shifted to the Bears. Two forces shaped the direction that deliberations with the Bears took. The Central Area Committee became strong advocates for a privately financed stadium, and stood poised to organize the business community to purchase the luxury seating that could make such a venture feasible. A west-side grass-roots organization, the Midwest Community Council, organized a campaign in 1986 to bring any new Bears stadium to their neighborhood.

Mayor Washington was initially reluctant to consider the west side. Although there was considerable vacant land in the area being advocated by the Midwest Community Council, there also remained a significant number of occupied housing units. In late 1986, he proposed a site immediately north of existing Soldier Field. To complement the privately financed stadium, he proposed demolition of Soldier Field, the moving of parking off the lakefront to open up the space, and the creation of a museum complex to segregate football fans from visitors to the Museum of Natural History, the Aquarium, and the Planetarium immediately north of Soldier Field.

His proposal was immediately scorned by lakefront protection interests, and taken up as a major mayoral campaign issue by his opponents. Together, they captured the support of the *Chicago Tribune,* and the mayor reluctantly backed down. He created a site location committee, with a goal of deflecting the issue until after the election.

He was reluctant to include the west-side site in the committee's deliberations, but a strong group of organizations in that area demanded its consideration. In mid-1987 the committee recommended the west-side site. In the course of the committee's deliberations, strong local opposition to the site also emerged. The City project management team, again lead by Johnson and me, initiated and managed a broader community planning process around the Bears stadium, one that should have occurred with the Sox. The mayor realized the magnitude of the relocation problem on the west side. He encouraged community debate, and, working with both proponents and opponents, Johnson and I facilitated a process of community dialogue. We made a continual effort to reconcile community differences.[12]

As the community dialogue ensued, the cost of the community demands, although quite reasonable, began to mount. The mayor pledged to address the community needs and decided to subsidize community improvements with tax revenues from the luxury seating that would exist in a new stadium. He saw this as an opportunity to implement development policies of balanced growth and linkages between large and small projects.

In the end, the mayor proposed guaranteeing any dislocating households the option of physically moving and improving their home or building a new one of greater value. Further, he proposed holding them harmless for any increased costs they might encounter, such as increased taxes. He proposed a number of community facilities, like a library and park. Most of this would be paid from tax revenues derived from luxury seating.[13]

The conservative head of the Republican assembly, Pate Phillips, gave the best testimony on the Bears deal. He looked at it and said "This deal is dangerous. If we pass this it's going to set up a precedent that we can't live with elsewhere." After Mayor Washington's death, the Illinois General Assembly rejected the deal. The Bears are still playing at Soldier Field.

The Cubs

A 1982 proposal by the Chicago Cubs had aroused a fire storm of controversy in the neighborhood surrounding Wrigley Field. The well-organized, highly educated and articulate upper-middle-income community had engineered local and state legislation prohibiting lights. In 1984 the Cubs joined the chorus of dissident teams and proposed moving to the suburbs.

Mayor Washington agreed to take up the lights issue. He was partially motivated by a reluctance to avoid a thorny sports team issue affecting an upper-income white neighborhood when he was facing up to similar issues in poorer, largely African-American neighborhoods. Also, he saw the issue as a classic land use conflict and felt it had strong similarities to ones he faced in attempting to retain industry in Chicago.

He directed that an open public process be undertaken to find a way to partially accommodate the Cubs enough to make it difficult to leave the city. The process consisted of creating a negotiating committee comprising neighborhood residents, business leaders, and the Cubs. Their meetings were professionally facilitated, supported by considerable information-gathering that included the use of survey sampling, and a number of community meetings. A compromise resulted, hammered out over an almost 2-year period, which placed severe limitations on the number of night games (18) and which also specified starting times, a curfew for alcohol sales, and severe neighborhood parking restrictions. By all accounts, including those of the main "No Lights" advocates, the solution has worked quite well.

Chicago Public Library

The possibility of a new central library was another such large public development. This was a project that had been on the agendas of at least two previous mayors. Byrne's approach had been to put the new facility in a renovated department store on State Street—Goldblatt's. The site was subject to intense controversy because of questions about the suitability of the structure to carry library floor loads, its aesthetic qualities, and also because of questions about the process by which the site had been selected: a closed-door decision with no apparent appraisal or consultation with the Library Board.

Early in the Washington administration this decision was not reversed even though Washington had criticized the site selection process in his campaign. Initial engineering and architectural studies were under way in the Department of Public Works and within the library bureaucracy. The issue of the library project moved on to the mayor's large project development agenda by late 1985, around the time Moe moved back to the mayor's office.

This change in emphasis was due in large part to a campaign initiated by the *Chicago Sun Times,* the Better Government Association, and the Union League Club to scuttle the Goldblatt's site. The rallying metaphor became "world class library" and provided fuel for the argument that the Goldblatt's site would be exorbitant in expense and would never get the city the library it deserved. This public debate was raging during the time when the Washington administration was assessing both its accomplishments and its uncompleted agenda at mid-term.

A series of "mid-course correction" meetings occurred during late 1985 and early 1986 to do a critical assessment of essential work to be done. One such meeting was a retreat of the entire cabinet for a weekend at the O'Hare Hilton. One specific discussion asked the five subcabinets to prioritize projects for the upcoming 2 years. In the report-back session, the central library emerged as a priority for three of the five subcabinets. This was largely due to the realization that the Washington administration had to demonstrate its capacity to effectively implement large-scale development projects. This was against the background of the administration's rejection of the World's Fair and its inability to move the Navy Pier project in the face of opposition by the City Council's opposition majority.

Subsequent to this retreat, the mayor established an internal committee, chaired by Moe, to address the questions of the site—Goldblatt's or not—and the question of financing. The committee's job was to formulate a total implementation program. The committee included Economic Development, Planning, Library, Budget, Comptroller, and Public Works. The initial recommendation favored the Goldblatt's site mainly because of cost considerations and a concern for preservation of the Goldblatt's edifice as adaptive reuse of a historically important structure. The committee, as Planning Commissioner Elizabeth Hollander has related (1991), felt this would be a significant statement of a development objective.

Opposition continued, however, including a *Sun Times* front-page editorial and the intervention of Roman Catholic Cardinal Joseph Bernadin. Facing this, and internal disagreement within the committee, the mayor rejected the recommendation and directed the committee and library board to work together to find a new site and construction program for a new library. After consideration of several North and South Loop sites, the library board chose a site at State and Congress streets in the South Loop.

Because of the time pressure to deliver this project, and in light of the controversy surrounding cost overruns at such other projects as the State of Illinois Center and at McCormick Place, the mayor was searching for an approach that would deliver this project on time and within the budget. It was also more subtle: We all understood the way large projects were done to enhance the functioning of traditional development networks, with featherbedding of consultant costs, inflated change orders, and the like. We wanted to change this process. There was also a desire to change the process in a different way, by including a greater degree of public involvement.

The mayor established a Central Library Advisory Committee to advise him on the specifics of the development approach, in particular, completing the library as a "design-build" project. Using this technique, which Hollander (1991) describes in more detail, bids would be solicited to design and build the library within a specific cost. The developer would be selected based on both design and cost criteria. And significantly, the developer would be selected by a committee, following extensive public debate on the designs themselves. In this case the designs of the competing teams were on display at the Cultural Center and were the subject of extensive public hearings.

This approach was a fundamentally important departure from traditional approaches to development of such projects, not only in Chicago but also in the nation. It was so significant that it was the subject of a *Nova* public television program titled "Design Wars." In choosing the design-build approach, the mayor clearly understood that he was authorizing a process that was completely insulated from political influence in the development process, even influence that might work to his advantage.

The process worked beyond our imagination. Thirty thousand people viewed the design entries at the Cultural Center. In effect, a constituency for the new central library was developed through the process. The library opened in 1991.

Assessment of Large Projects

Our involvement with large-scale projects convinces us that it is both necessary and possible for a progressive local government to undertake them. To a degree, community attitudes toward large projects have been conditioned by decades-old "downtown versus the neighborhoods" community organizing emphases. These emphases were given teeth by the paternalistic tendency of old-fashioned politics, exemplified by the handling of the World's Fair by the Byrne administration, to treat large projects as too important to involve common people.

By 1987 the large-scale projects were being undertaken as if community people mattered. The library, fittingly named for the mayor after his death, may best exemplify this change in attitude. People throughout the city seem to claim ownership, and through it, can see a public interest that transcends local community interests. Finally, this public interest had been given teeth during the tenures of Mayors Washington and Sawyer by tight fiscal management and vigorous pursuit through contracting and purchasing of equal opportunity goals.

Conclusion

Because large projects are visible and dramatic, they can relatively easily obfuscate the important nuts-and-bolts work of making government function for people. Organizing the Department of Economic Development to deliver on a neighborhood agenda is an example of that work. Despite the efforts at participatory processes of development and implementation of large projects, some community activists felt priorities were being distorted (Brehm, 1991). But in parallel to the large-scale projects, substantial efforts at decentralization of policy-making and implementation were under way. The next chapter addresses those efforts.

Notes

1. The unit in Neighborhoods that was transferred to DED had itself been created in 1979, when some units out of the Department of Human Services had been transferred to the Neighborhoods Department.

2. Any nonprofit organization receiving a grant or contract from the City was referred to as a "delegate agency."

3. DED extensively used industrial revenue bonds and considered this almost singular tool an industrial policy.

4. This was a major problem for the entire Washington administration. Most of his supporters did not have experience in government. We needed people who were committed to the agenda, loyal to Washington, and technically competent. This proved to be extremely difficult for all 5 years.

5. See Giloth (1991) for how this was approached on one division, R&D.

6. An important distinction from classic reform efforts was Washington's emphasis on accountability to *all* citizens, rather than some form of elite accountability (Hays, 1970).

7. By virtue of a history dating back to the mid-1970s and the inception of the North Loop Development Plan, the Department of Planning had responsibility for central area development projects.

8. We acknowledge that this is a form of *privatization,* although one with substantially more community control than is normally associated with the term. We also invite the readers attention to our emphasis on "industrial" over "commercial."

9. Recall that Vazquez was a founding member of CWED and subsequently would run the Mayor's Office of Employment and Training during the administration of Mayor Eugene Sawyer.

10. Johnson was one of the more prominent African-American businessmen in Chicago. A former hospital administrator, he acquired General Motor's first minority-owned automobile dealership in the late 1960s. He became an important financial supporter of Operation PUSH, and the chairman of the Political Action Conference of Illinois (PACI). PACI played a major role in advancing the Illinois congressional, legislative, and aldermanic redistricting suits. Johnson was a significant financial backer of Washington's 1983 and 1987 campaigns, and served Washington as an ad hoc special assistant on business affairs and a member of the Mayor's Policy Advisory Council.

11. The City negotiations and the subsequent legislative effort were led by Johnson and me.

12. The group leading the opposition was the Interfaith Organizing Project (IOP). IOP subsequently represented the community in negotiations with the owners of the Chicago Bulls and the Chicago Blackhawks to build an indoor arena at the same west-side site.

13. It was one of the few cases where the concept of "tax increment financing" actually promised to work to the advantage of the more needy.

Appendix

Outline of the DED Development Program

The DED development program had the twin purposes of expanding employment opportunities in Chicago and linking work-needy Chicagoans to those opportunities. It had five essential components:

1. Strategy A: Focus on Export Businesses

    a. Business Calling Program

        i. Local Industrial Retention Initiative

Business calling program resulted in direct City contact with almost 10,000 businesses per year.

        ii. Critical Services

"Red-tape cutting" and general business advocacy within the City bureaucracy; 2,000 to 3,000 businesses per year were served.

iii. Economic Development Commission Ombudsman Program

Businessman-to-businessman advocacy program, with problems linked to City's critical services unit.

b. Commercial and Industrial Land Use Planning

Planning effort responding to a broad-based business development constituency as well as the recommendations of the Neighborhood Land Use Task Force. This effort was primarily executed by the Department of Planning.

c. Planned Manufacturing Districts

A major initiative to encourage targeted manufacturing expansion.

d. Industrial Parks Development

    i. Six City-sponsored parks

    ii. Three Economic Development Commission-sponsored parks

e. Industrial Infrastructure Investment

Use of six federal, state, and local funding sources to enable physical revitalization of local industrial areas.

f. Small Business Investment

    i. City finance programs

More than 10 different programs enabled selected and targeted financial assistance to expanding or modernizing businesses.

    ii. Chicago Equity Fund

Partnership with Chicago companies, financial institutions, and foundations to create an equity capital pool for small Chicago manufacturers.

g. Small Business Assistance

    i. Technical Assistance Program

City support of a comprehensive group of delegate agencies to support business development in virtually every neighborhood of the city.

    ii. Skill Training

Targeted training services coordinated by the Mayor's Office of Employment and Training (MET) in direct support of businesses facing new employee needs as a result of expansion or modernization.

    iii. Chicagoland Enterprise Center

Partnership with the Commercial Club, linking technical assistance from major Chicago corporations to small, growing, or modernizing manufacturing businesses with technical problems.

iv. Inventors Council

City-sponsored agency that linked small Chicago manufacturing firms facing modernization problems with inventors capable of creating technical solutions.

v. Chicago Association of Neighborhood Development Organizations (CANDO)

Network of neighborhood-based organizations provided technical assistance and served as a clearinghouse.

vi. Chicago Workshop on Economic Development (CWED)

A network similar to CANDO, but concentrating on development organizations in low-to-moderate income, largely minority neighborhoods.

h. Early Warning Program

i. Company Turnaround

Public/private partnership effort to prevent plant closing or relocation.

ii. Dislocated Workers Program

Comprehensive human service response to plant closings, coordinated by MET.

i. Export Program

Assistance to small to medium-size Chicago manufacturers in expanding their markets internationally.

2. Strategy B: Achieve Balanced Growth

a. Central Area Development

Focus on North and South Loop development, as well as construction of a new central library, coordinated by the Department of Planning.

b. Neighborhood Commercial Revitalization

Development projects in more than 50 neighborhoods, involving more than 75 neighborhood-based development organizations.

c. O'Hare Collateral Development

Development of nonaviation-related land at O'Hare International Airport, coordinated by the Collateral Development Task Force.

    d. Cultural and Recreational Development (Tourism)
        i. Stadiums
        ii. Exposition Facilities
        iii. Central Library
        iv. Navy Pier
    e. Economic Development Commission Strategic Planning Partner-
        ship effort to continually fine-tune the City's strategic develop-
        ment directions.
3. Strategy C: Employ Chicago First
    a. First Source Hiring

    Hiring agreements giving preference to Chicagoans.

    b. On-the-Job Training
    c. M/FBE

    Expansion of the mayor's Executive Order encouraging the use of minor-
    ity and female businesses into a wider range of development activities.

    d. Local Purchasing

    A goal to increase by 50% the amount of City purchasing done from
    Chicago-based businesses.

4. Strategy D: Reduce Business Costs Affected by Local Government
    a. Critical Services Unit

    See item a of Strategy A, above.

    b. Planned Manufacturing Districts

    See item c of Strategy A, above.

    c. Building Codes

    Modification of the codes to allow, where possible, adoption of a
    national performance-based code.

    d. Tax Relief

    Adoption of a set of procedures to achieve a more consistent and
    effective application of the Cook County authorized tax abate-
    ments.

    e. Energy Costs
        i. Commonwealth Edison Negotiations

    Negotiation of both the Franchise Agreement and the proposed rate
    increase to achieve a more favorable investment and development
    climate.

ii. Energy Savers Fund

Partnership effort to reduce residential energy consumption, coordinated by the Department of Housing.

5. Strategy E: Joint Development
   a. Read Dunning Mental Health Complex
   b. Rapid Transit Station at Howard-Paulina
   c. Bears Stadium
   d. White Sox Stadium

7

Decentralization of Policy-Making

with

WIM WIEWEL

LAURI ALPERN

The examination of policy-making switches from the administration to community organizations. This chapter details how the Local Industrial Retention Initiative program (LIRI) emerged from community organizations in much the same process as Chicago Works Together *evolved from* The CWED Platform, *developed by the Community Workshop on Economic Development (CWED). The importance of community organizations in developing and sustaining a bottom-up approach to industrial policy becomes evident in this chapter. It also discusses a different aspect of organizational culture than that presented in Chapter 6. Here, a set of working principles is elaborated. It was to be these principles, rather than manuals, organizational charts, or specific work rules, against which individuals would evaluate the appropriateness of their activities.*

AUTHORS' NOTE: Adapted from Mier, Wiewel, and Alpern's (1992) chapter in *Politics of Policy Innovations in Chicago*, with permission of JAI Press.

Introduction

A major element of the platform of Harold Washington when campaigning for mayor of Chicago was opening the policy-making processes of government to ordinary citizens, especially as their wishes and ideas became articulated through community-based organizations (Committee to Elect Harold Washington, 1983). Washington considered his political agenda a "progressive" one. By this, he meant that his goal was structural changes in policy formulation and decision-making processes. Early policy directions of Washington's mayoral administration, particularly in the development arena, derived directly from a community agenda-setting process (Mier, Moe, & Sherr, 1986; Bennett, Squires, McCourt, & Nyden, 1987). This chapter will examine both that agenda and the policy-making process, asking whether the progressive ideals were being reached in this one arena.

We address decentralized policy-making on three levels. First, we examine it as a dynamic interplay between the substance of development policy and the processes articulating and demanding it. Second, we are concerned with implementation of the development policy. Finally, we will close the policy-making loop by examining the feedback of the implementation experience on the processes of strategic planning and policy formulation.

To examine the interplay between policy substance and process, we will build on our earlier examination (Mier et al., 1986) of the shaping of the Chicago development plan, *Chicago Works Together,* by exploring the processes of its updating. We are particularly interested in the consistency between the Washington administration's approach and ideas promulgated by community-based organizations prior to Washington's election.

To bridge from policy formulation to implementation, we will examine strategic plans formulated by community-based organizations working under contract with the City's Department of Economic Development (DED).[1] As was discussed in Mier and Moe (1991), the Local Industrial Retention Initiative (LIRI) was a program that originated in the field operations division of DED. It evolved with approximately 10 local industrial councils or community organizations that had relatively high organizational capacity to design strategic industrial retention programs. As a condition of funding, the LIRI groups were each required to prepare strategic plans, and these plans will be reviewed.

We will focus directly on the activities of the LIRI groups—
what businesses they were approaching, what services they
were providing to them, the degree of correspondence between
the strategic plans of the LIRI groups and their actual activities.
The annual performance reports of the LIRI groups are available
for evaluation.

Finally, by way of examining the feedback between actual
operations and policy formulation, two community-based policy-
planning efforts will be examined. They are those of the Chicago
Association of Neighborhood Development Organizations (CANDO)
and the Chicago Workshop of Economic Development (CWED). In
addition, we will take a look at the directions of the current
Chicago mayor, Richard M. Daley.

Before we begin our actual assessment, we must say something about our evaluation methodology. Questions have been
raised about reliance on quality-of-life indicators as either a
useful or a fair method for measuring the achievements of a
progressive political movement (Mier, Fitzgerald, & Randolph,
1993). This methodology has led to a quick dismissal of limited
accomplishments without understanding the movement itself or
the goals of its constituents. Piven and Cloward (1977) point out
the risk of this narrow, positivistic evaluation tendency:

> While it is easy to point out that the . . . wrong organizational
> and/or political strategies were chosen, without demonstrating
> that it could have been done differently, given a set of social and
> institutional conditions, the criticisms are not useful in effecting
> social change. (pp. x-xi)

So, although we do not ignore immediate results, we believe
that the real aims of a progressive political movement are not
just the achievement of specific, quantifiable goals, but structural changes in policy formulation and decision-making processes. Measuring progress along these lines requires in-depth,
qualitative analysis, such as only a participant observation case
study or content analysis can provide (Schatzman & Strauss,
1973; Marris, 1987).

We hope to reach some conclusions about the degree of
success at decentralizing policy-making under Mayor Harold
Washington, and its endurance beyond his tenure as mayor. We each
played active roles in formulating or implementing Washington's

strategies, so we begin with biases that the policies were effective and will endure. This notion runs against local popular belief.[2] Thus we believe it in our interest to present as critical an evaluation as possible. We also hope to identify barriers to successful decentralization as well as forces impeding its long-term stability.

The Framework for Community Planning

The most widespread citizen participation in the Washington administration's strategic development planning process occurred during the mayoral campaign. Stages in that process have been codified in the CWED Platform (Table 4.1), *The Washington Papers* (Table 4.2) and *Chicago Works Together (CWT)* (Table 5.1). A number of community organizations argued that even though citizen participation was a stated goal of *CWT,* they were not involved fully in the subcabinet's deliberations about the plan (Mier et al., 1986). They seemed to feel less ownership of *Chicago Works Together* than of *The Washington Papers.*

In November 1985 Mayor Washington convened a broad and large task force to evaluate *Chicago Works Together* and the development progress of his administration.[3] The task force constituted 59 heads of citywide or umbrella organizations, reflecting business, neighborhood, labor, education, government, civic, and cultural interests, supplemented by individuals chosen for complementary expertise they could bring to the table (Chicago Works Together Planning Task Force, 1987). The task force worked for 18 months and held a number of full and subcommittee meetings. In addition, it convened an all-day workshop, attended by several hundred citizens, public officials, and representatives of businesses, community and civic groups, development organizations, and other special interests. In total, the task force considered more than 1,500 goal and policy recommendations.

In a general sense, the task force reinforced the basic directions of the Washington administration articulated in *Chicago Works Together.* They ratified three goals: increased job opportunities, balanced growth, and neighborhood development. They recommended two new goals:

1. Promote cultural development, reflecting the importance of arts and culture in economic development.
2. Provide quality education, acknowledging the interdependence between educational programs, a capable labor force, and Chicago's future development.

This latter goal was an original emphasis of *The Washington Papers.*

The most striking contribution of the task force was an emphasis on what they called "development principles." These were recurrent development themes that seemed, in their minds, to overarch a higher quality of development that they envisioned for Chicago. The principles were leadership, innovation, equity/ fairness, resource targeting, efficiency, building on the basics, citizen participation, and partnerships. The task force suggested that the principles ought to be city government's "organizational culture," although it seems that they were also talking about a civic culture. In words that could have come from an analysis of modern business practice (e.g., Peters & Waterman, 1982; Morgan, 1987), the task force said:

> If these shared values are effectively communicated to every member of the organization, they take the place of policy manuals, organization charts, and detailed procedures and rules. Everyone in that organization knows what to do in most situations because the new guiding values are clear. (Chicago Works Together Planning Task Force, 1987, p. 8)

The *CWT* update emphasized a number of themes that run consistently through the efforts at development planning which we have reviewed. When viewed against more mainstream approaches to development, their uniqueness is obvious (Krumholz, 1984; Luke, Ventriss, Reed, & Reed, 1987). They emphasized *job development* over real estate development. They emphasized *neighborhood development* instead of central business district development. They emphasized *retention and expansion* over attraction of industry. They emphasized *small business* over large. They articulated a belief in *targeting resources* rather than widespread distribution of all resources.

Also, they promoted conscious strategies to *target the work-needy* instead of relying on the labor market to distribute jobs.

They emphasized local actors—businesses and residents—over outside ones, with a push for *local purchasing* and *local hiring*. They saw *collective innovation* as more important than individual entrepreneurship. They saw an *aggressive public sector* rather than one that makes its role subservient to business. Finally, they saw *broader partnerships* involving community and civic actors.

Washington felt very confident in this agenda. In campaigning for re-election, he pledged to continue his emphases on job development, education, neighborhood improvements and housing, partnerships, planning, and innovation (Committee to Re-Elect Mayor Washington, 1987).

We now turn directly to community organizations. We will explore the degree to which these same themes are reflected in their own views. We are interested in the degree to which the themes become articulated in the organizations' planning efforts, both at the local level and collectively within networks of community-based organizations.

Community-Based Planning

Community Strategic Planning
Within a Policy Framework

The Local Industrial Retention Initiative (LIRI) evolved from an identification of the half dozen local industrial councils or community organizations, among those routinely working with DED, that had the highest organizational capacity to step up their industrial retention efforts (Mier & Moe, 1991). DED and these groups tried to formulate a systematic and strategic methodology for dealing with industrial retention—what businesses should be approached, what should they be asked, what could be done to give them more confidence in the City, and, most important, what concrete problems the City could realistically tackle. We will further analyze the strategic planning efforts of three of these groups, selected because they represent a cross-section of organizational types and communities.

The Industrial Council of Northwest Chicago (ICNC)

In the mid-1960s a grass-roots-based community organization on Chicago's near northwest side, the Northwest Community

Organization (NCO), began soliciting involvement and financial support from local industrialists for community improvement efforts. By 1967 it became clear that the industrial area had issues of its own, and NCO incorporated ICNC as a subsidiary. Early joint efforts included operation of training and placement programs targeted to local Latino residents.

Over the ensuing decade ICNC undertook a number of ventures, mostly with a training focus, with financial support from several federal government agencies. In 1977 NCO and ICNC leadership parted ways, and ICNC hired its own staff. With this separation, ICNC began to focus more on area development. In the early 1980s it acquired and began operation of what would become one of the nation's showcase industrial incubator buildings.[4] In 1985 ICNC became one of the City's initial LIRI organizations. One of the City's first requirements for ICNC was to undertake a local strategic plan.

The strategic goals identified by ICNC (Table 7.1) reflect a twin focus on business development and area development. In subsequent revisions of the plan, this distinction would be made more sharply as ICNC placed even more emphasis on offering through its incubator a wide range of direct business assistance services, including technology assessment (Industrial Council of Northwest Chicago, 1986). A clear shift of focus for ICNC has been away from its early emphasis on job training. Also, even though ICNC saw itself as a partner with the City in the LIRI program, its conception of it was one of "privatization."

Taken together, the set of ICNC goals closely resembles the goals, policies, and principles of *Chicago Works Together*, with more emphasis on direct business assistance and on the philosophy of privatization of public assistance.

Greater North Pulaski Development Corporation (GNPDC)

The GNDPC represents an area to the west and slightly north of that served by the ICNC, stretching to the city limits. It is an area that was historically anchored by large manufacturing firms, of which Helene Curtis Industries is the major remaining one. In the past 15 years the area has lost Schwinn Bicycles, Playskool Co., W.F. Hall Printing Co., and Pettibone Industries, which together employed more than 10,000 workers.

Table 7.1 Industrial Council of Northwest Chicago Strategic Goals

1. To improve the physical functioning of the movement of goods in and out of the area.
2. To change the area's land use status from an unsatisfactory mixture of industrial, residential, and commercial uses to 100% industrial.
3. To improve the physical environment for the security of personnel and property.
4. To encourage entrepreneurship and enhance the management skills of area businessmen.
5. To maximize the utilization of existing older real estate (both land and buildings) in the area and upgrade such through increased investment and new strategies for use.

SOURCE: Industrial Council of Northwest Chicago, 1986.

The GNPDC was formed, at the urging of the City in 1977, by a consortium of local business leaders led by the CEO of a area bank. From its inception, it pursued an agenda that sought to better tie local industry to the neighborhood. A major undertaking for GNPDC occurred in the wake of the 1985 Playskool shutdown (Giloth & Mier, 1986). GNDPC became a joint venture partner with a private developer in owning the vacated 600,000-square-foot Playskool facility. GNPDC's participation was capitalized with a grant from the Health and Human Services Administration. Within 2 years of acquisition, the facility was fully leased to a variety of small users.

The GNPDC interprets its strategic role as:

> [S]trengthening its base of small to medium sized industries. [It] focuses on identifying and addressing the problems of this sector, and acts as a link between the business constituency and the broader community within which it functions. This brings about the creation of private sector, unsubsidized jobs for community residents. (Greater North Pulaski Development Corporation, 1986, p. 2)

This agenda (Table 7.2) very closely reflects the strategic direction of the Washington administration. It emphasizes both job and neighborhood development, targeting opportunities to work-needy area residents, and forging whatever alliances are necessary to have an area impact.[5]

Table 7.2 Greater North and Pulaski Development Corporation Strategic
Goals and Objectives

Goal 1: To foster the retention and expansion of neighborhood industries.
  Objectives: A. Assist in early identification of plants likely to close.
                 B. Development and support intervention measures to avert
                    plant shutdowns.
                 C. Provide an ongoing, high-profile presence that encour-
                    ages businesses to stay and expand within the community.
                 D. Foster a positive business climate
Goal 2: To catalyze industrial and commercial development that create neighbor-
         hood-based jobs.
  Objectives: A. Complete the construction of Playskool Industrial Park.
                 B. Identify opportunities for industrial and commercial reuse
                    or development within the GNPDC area.
                 C. Begin the execution of at least one development that
                    substantially involves GNPDC.
Goal 3: To strengthen the links between business and the other sectors of the
         community.
  Objectives: A. Package employment and training programs as induce-
                    ments for "first source" hiring from the community, and
                    utilize these inducements with Playskool and all other
                    GNDPC developments.
                 B. Design a marketing plan for the Playskool Industrial Park
                    that aggressively solicits prospective tenants most likely to
                    hire from targeted populations.
                 C. Link businesses more directly to their community
                    through specific demonstration programs such as "Walk
                    Home," "Adopt a School," sponsorship of food and cloth-
                    ing give- aways, and youth athletics.

SOURCE: Greater North Pulaski Development Corporation, 1986.

Local Economic and Employment (LEED) Council

The LEED Council was created as a subsidiary of the New City
YMCA in 1982. Since its inception, it has been a tripartite
coalition of large and small business and community groups in
an area flanking the southern reach of the North Branch of the
Chicago River. Its service area contains some of the most sharply
contrasting and conflicting land uses in the Chicago metropolitan area. Its southeast corner is anchored by Cabrini-Green, a
10,000-unit, largely African-American resident Chicago Housing
Authority project. At its heart lies the city's largest remaining

steel-production facility as well as considerable developable land. Its northeast side is the site of considerable upscale residential and commercial development as Chicago's largely white "gold coast" moves west.

The New City YMCA is very conscious of its role of straddling and promoting harmony among socioeconomically and racially diverse communities. It strives to "be recognized as a significant partner with residents, families, businesses and organizations in community activities aimed at retaining current populations through empowerment of people within communities to promote stability and racial and economic diversity" (New City YMCA, 1989). The LEED Council plays a strategic role in achieving that goal by focusing on vitalizing the local economy and integrating work needy area residents into that economy (Table 7.3).

The LEED Council's outlook represents both a close reflection and maturation of the original CWED principles and *Chicago Works Together*. On the one hand, the LEED Council has had a unique organizational circumstance promoting this coincidence of values. The Council's founding executive director also participated on candidate Harold Washington's campaign issues committee, and has been vice-president of the board of CWED and president of CANDO. On the other hand, the LEED Council has probably been the most dependent on corporate and philanthropic donations of all LIRI organizations. These funding bodies have been the object of intense pressure from proponents of development.

From Strategy to Action

The strategic plans we have reviewed were written in the latter period of Harold Washington's tenure as mayor, with the LEEDS Council's being recently updated. It is important to consider the post-Washington actions of the organizations to judge the stability of their directions. Current activities of the three groups indicate the strategic plans that were based on Washington's development goals are more than just paper. In each case, the groups continue to actively pursue these goals. In many ways, they have expanded upon programs and even added new ones that are consistent with Washington's development policy.

Table 7.3 New City YMCA LEED Council Strategic Goals and Objectives

Goals
1. Support industrial retention and development.
2. Foster enterprises that maximize jobs, earning power, and hiring of local residents.
3. Develop a long-term balance of industrial, commercial, and residential land uses.
4. Encourage the development of innovative solutions to the housing problems of lower-income residents.

Objectives
1. Utilize the LEED Council's resources and unique capabilities to support and accomplish the goals of the New City YMCA.
2. Resolve land use-related conflicts among the residential, industrial, and commercial bases.
3. Find the appropriate resources for industrial/business development.
4. Generate income opportunities for lower-income residents.

SOURCE: New City YMCA, 1989.

For example, ICNC, has expanded upon its strategic focus to ensure that local residents are placed in new jobs created by businesses in the community. Through a partnership with the Greater Westtown Project, a community-based job placement network, every company that receives services from ICNC is asked to fill new jobs it creates with local community residents. Approximately 200 local residents have been placed in jobs in their community last year. Looking toward the future, the partnership would like to place local residents in all new jobs created in the community, not just with companies receiving service from ICNC (Goldsmith, 1990).

Greater North Pulaski is also expanding on Washington's development goals (Smith, 1990). Its strategic goal of strengthening the relationship between the business and residential communities is being realized through two new programs: the "Walk Home Program" and the community relations liaison staff. Both programs match resources of local businesses and residents to meet GNPDC's community development goals. For example, the "Walk Home" program enables community residents employed in local companies to purchase homes in their community through revolving loan funds established by the companies.

Participating companies have taken their roles even further and are now offering pre-purchase counseling to the residents. The community relations liaison facilitates development goals by working with local groups, such as block clubs and schools, to create strategies to improve city services, beautify the neighborhood, and support local organizing efforts.

The most significant contribution of the LEED Council has been the conceptualization and promotion of a Planned Manufacturing District ordinance, passed by the City Council in 1988 (Ducharme, Giloth, & McCormick, 1986; Giloth & Mier, 1988). In 1988 it also provided direct services to 66 local companies. These services ranged from packaging of financial assistance to assisting in job screening and placement.

The three organizations continue to view the retention and expansion of existing businesses, a policy originally established in *The Washington Papers,* as the cornerstone of their own community development strategies.[6] Active company visitation programs, in which at least 10 companies are called upon per week; watchdog efforts to maintain and protect all industrial land; and monthly seminars for businesses all continue to be key elements of the groups' operations. Greater North Pulaski's calling program has become so successful that they added additional staff to service all the requests for business services generated by their visits.

Bottom-Up Agenda Setting

During the 1970s substantial cross-fertilization occurred among Chicago community organizations. Organizations coalesced across class, across race, across issue areas, and across philosophy. Many of the organizations and organizers had been influenced by experiences in the civil rights movement, the antiwar movement, and Alinsky-style organizing philosophy, which focused on community empowerment. A major lesson from those experiences was the value of building networks, and the late 1970s were a period of development network building.

The resulting coalitions formed the foundation of ideas and a constituency for Harold Washington's neighborhood agenda. By the beginning of Harold Washington's mayoral campaign in

1982, several large and diverse neighborhood-based coalitions engaging in community economic development had emerged.

As we related in the Introduction, CWED was formed in 1982, and played a major role in articulating what would be the Washington agenda. It actually had been preceded by the Chicago Association of Neighborhood Development Organizations (CANDO), which started in 1978. At that time, about a dozen organizations had formed in working-class neighborhoods around the issue of commercial revitalization, and these organizations formed CANDO to lobby city, state, and federal agencies.

Both coalitions have grown and thrived in the decade of the 1980s. In many respects, the boundary between them is fuzzy, and many individual groups are active in each network.[7] CWED is perceived as being oriented more to low-income and minority communities, with a strong interest in policy issues, whereas CANDO is perceived as having more of a working-class, white ethnic focus, with an interest in industrial and commercial development. However, each possesses all these attributes.

Given its history, it is not surprising that CWED is closely tied to those activities that characterized the Washington agenda. In a recent communication, the CWED Executive Director said:

> [The CWED Platform of 1982] substantially reflects our current outlook. . . . We're still concerned about full employment, community ownership, community planning, increased public resources, targeted resource allocation, TA to CBOs, and affirmative action.

He adds:

> If anything, our policy outlook has become both broader and more specific over time as our demands have been fueled by our experiences. For example, we don't just advocate for community ownership, but we advocate for support for (specific) community ventures. We don't just advocate for "meaningful input in planning," but we advocate for pro-active planning by communities themselves. (Snow, 1990)

CWED goals and objectives (Table 7.4) amply illustrate its broadening and deepening, with emphasis on community ventures, community-based planning and entrepreneurship, public housing,

Table 7.4 CWED Goals and Objectives

Goal A: Community ventures.

      Objectives: 1. Improving the management of existing Community Ventures to draw an additional $500,000 in funding.

                    2. Extending the Community Ventures concept to youth and school-based enterprises.

Goal B: Community-based planning.

      Objectives: 1. Facilitating community-based planning efforts in eight communities.

Goal C: Community-based entrepreneurship.

      Objectives: 1. Expanding entrepreneurship training to two new communities.

Goal D: Public housing community economic development.

      Objectives: 1. Organizing CWED member organizations involved in public housing communities.

Goal E: Coalition-wide advocacy.

      Objectives: 1. Organizing new community-based development initiatives targeting state and local government resources and individual resident participants and donors, and helping to set the agenda for community-based development in the next decade.

SOURCE: Community Workshop on Economic Development, 1990.

community economic development and coalition-wide advocacy (Chicago Workshop on Economic Development, 1990).

CANDO also feels that it operates in the 1990s in a manner that is quite consistent with the mission articulated in the late 1970s. Like CWED, it believes its approach to development is richer in detail and strategically appropriate to the times. CANDO's 1990 strategic objectives (Table 7.5) include proposals for resource commitments to neighborhoods, specific funding targets for operating agencies with neighborhood agendas and for neighborhood capital improvements, and more of a real estate development emphasis than its original agenda of 1979 (Chicago Association of Neighborhood Development Organizations, 1990).

Is There a Washington Legacy?

The Washington administration was cut short by the mayor's sudden death in November 1987. Many of his goals and plans remained unfulfilled or barely started. The immediate collapse

Table 7.5 CANDO Goals and Objectives

Goals

1. Foster and promote the revitalization of urban neighborhoods, especially in the areas of commercial and industrial revitalization.
2. Support individual and citywide neighborhood revitalization efforts.
3. Serve as liaison between neighborhood development groups and agencies, foundations, media, private professional societies, and other organizations.
4. Expand private and public sector economic development opportunities for residents and local business people.
5. Enable community-based development organizations to assist and undertake reinvestment in their neighborhoods.
6. Encourage a diversity of approaches to neighborhood revitalization and the dissemination of successful revitalization techniques.
7. Provide a focus for community- and citywide organizations in formulating or responding to public and private policies and programs.

1990 Objectives

1. Increase City funds for neighborhood economic development projects.
2. Increase the number and funding level of corporate donors.
3. Use existing federal funds more efficiently by recycling UDAG repayments and CD "float."
4. Restore City-owned land and property to productive uses.
5. Initiate a small business loan program backed by state and municipal pension funds.
6. Pass an Economic Development Financing Bond.
7. Include substantial funds for economic development in a future General Obligation (GO) Bond.
8. Develop a strategic policy for the use of Tax Increment Financing (TIF).

SOURCE: Chicago Association of Neighborhood Development Organizations, 1990.

of his political coalition into warring factions appeared to leave little hope for a continuation of his programs and policies. Nevertheless, 4½ years turned out to have been enough to establish a new set of priorities and confirm a different style of policy-making.

One measure of the extent to which Washington's development policies survived him and remained in force is the virulence of attacks against them. Most notable among these was a series in the *Chicago Tribune*. In a series of seven articles of two full pages each, titled "Chicago on Hold," the paper launched a full-scale attack against community organizations that supported balanced growth and opposed neighborhood gentrification (McCarron, 1988a). The series attacked me, as well as African-

American and progressive aldermen who had championed Washington's development policies, and community activists who opposed large-scale gentrifying developments. The articles painted these organizations and leaders as misguided and naive at best, and corrupt and self-serving in some cases. The series specifically attacked the idea that saving manufacturing jobs was possible and suggested that the market forces leading to displacement of manufacturing jobs and low-income residents were largely desirable and, in any event, inexorable.

The series was an opening salvo for the 1989 mayoral campaign, and in many ways reflected the policy approaches of Richard M. Daley, who would go on to win the election. During his campaign, Daley stated his opposition to attempts to maintain manufacturing in the city, particularly the Planned Manufacturing District being pushed by the LEED Council (Horning, 1989). His strong support among real estate developers left little doubt that few obstacles would be put in their way, and that efforts at linked development programs would not go very far. Although few observers expected a wholesale return to the days of machine politics, Daley clearly would put an end to Washington's neighborhood-oriented policies. Indeed, even in a pre-election meeting with several neighborhood leaders, Daley showed little knowledge of, or interest in, their concerns.[8]

Daley easily won both the primary and the general election. Seemingly the only restraint on a major reshuffling of policies was that his election only to serve out Harold Washington's unexpired term would have him running again in 1991. Since his election, and subsequent re-election to a full 4-year term, policy changes have been far less than expected, and Daley has reversed himself on several issues, most notably in supporting the Planned Manufacturing District. As it turns out, Washington's policies, as well as his administration's process of decentralized policy-making, have shown a remarkable tenacity.

The most notable example of this tenacity is the issue of Planned Manufacturing Districts. As Ducharme (1991) discusses in detail, support for the concept of protecting the city's manufacturing in specific locations was built gradually and painstakingly over many years. The ideas and policy proposals arose out of the day-to-day work of the LEED Council, and it took several

years of research, organizing, and lobbying to obtain the support
of the Washington administration. Precisely because the process
took so long, and required a base of support separate from the
City administration, the thrust for protected manufacturing was
able to survive Washington's death and Daley's initial hostility.
The combination of strong support by area industrialists, many
individual business organizations and their coalitions, and research showing the benefits to the city of manufacturing over
other forms of economic activity, contributed to the Daley
administration's change in position.

Another major policy that has survived is the establishment of
clear numerical goals for City purchasing from minority firms.
First established in Chicago by Harold Washington, this policy
lost its legal footing due to a 1988 Supreme Court ruling requir-
ing clear evidence of discrimination prior to the establishment
of remedial policies. This ruling could have provided an easy
excuse for shelving preferential purchasing policies. The pressure
to pursue it anyway arose both from Daley's own political calculations as well as from a variety of minority-owned businesses, their
coalitions and business organizations, and mainstream African-
American organizations such as the Urban League.

The most comprehensive neighborhood-based policy-planning
effort is the one carried on by a coalition of the main membership
organizations of neighborhood organizations. A joint effort of
CWED, CANDO, the Chicago Jobs Council, the Chicago Rehab
Network, the Community Land Use Network, and the Neighborhood Capital Budget Group, "The Neighborhood Agenda" is
aimed at promoting major capital investment in neighborhoods.
Both in process and substance it recalls the similar effort of a
decade ago, which led to the formation of the CWED platform.
"The Neighborhood Agenda" also reflects the experiences of the
recent past, and is designed to be much more detailed and
oriented toward concrete programs and policies than the principles of the original CWED platform. The fact that four of the
six coalitions spearheading this effort did not exist a decade ago
is further evidence of the increased strength and sophistication
of the neighborhood development movement. Finally, Mayor Daley
and the City Council have committed to a $160-million infrastruc-
ture bond issue, a start toward the Agenda's $400-million program.

Conclusion

The analysis we have presented suggests several conclusions about the viability of policy innovations under conditions of relative political instability. These relate to the process of origination of such innovations, their institutionalization, and some limitations and contradictions that arise out of the institutionalization process.

First, what is striking in this and other accounts of the Washington administration (e.g., Clavel & Wiewel, 1991) is the importance of communication networks among key actors. The dissemination of ideas and the adoption of similar policies by a large number of organizations was facilitated by the frequent interaction of key actors throughout the seventies and early eighties. Thus both the CWED platform and the *Chicago Works Together* development plan were seen by many, not so much as new documents but as simply codification of what organizations and people had already been doing and saying.

It was also the existence of a shared system of beliefs that led to congruence between City policy and the strategic plans of individual organizations. This is shown most vividly in generative metaphors like "jobs," "neighborhoods," and even the theme of Washington's development plan, "Chicago Works Together," which became part of the lexicon of public/private/community partnership. Indeed, the follow-up by the Department of Economic Development on the content of the required strategic plans, or comparison between plans and achievements, was generally lacking. Thus the mode of operation was very much based on a "corporate culture" mode of motivating compliance, rather than a bureaucratic/hierarchical one (Morgan, 1987; Marris, 1987).

These communication networks bore perhaps their biggest fruit in the Washington administration, but they preceded and outlasted it. The roots of decentralized policy-making regarding neighborhoods go back to Chicago's rich tradition of neighborhood organizing, through civil rights fights, to campaigns against expressways and other forms of neighborhood displacement (Squires, Bennett, McCourt, & Nyden, 1987). The Washington administration formalized many of the substantive ideas coming out of this movement as its neighborhood development policy. It also helped institutionalize the decentralized policy-making process by providing resources to neighborhood groups and inviting their participation on a multitude of task forces, commissions, and boards.

Even during the Washington administration, however, this decentralized process was not fully subsumed by his program. Probably the ideological closeness between neighborhood activists and administration officials, and the fear of appearing disloyal to the first African-American mayor, stifled the independent neighborhood movement to some extent (Gills, 1991; Brehm, 1991). Nevertheless, independent efforts, such as those that had preceded his administration and indeed helped bring it about, continued. The Planned Manufacturing District campaign required just about as much independent organizing effort as it would have under a different administration. A coalition of organizations in the mostly white northwest and southwest sides of the city forced an extensive debate about linked development policies. They also initiated, and got passed, a home equity insurance program that was denounced as racist by African-American aldermen and opposed by the administration. Finally, even the relations between the city administration and CANDO and CWED, as well as their member organizations, were hardly peaceful or without criticism.

Both the continued independence and the enhanced legitimacy appear to have contributed to the survival of decentralized policy-making after Washington's death and his coalition's defeat. Although political expediency may be playing some role in Richard Daley's receptive attitude at this point, a process that has now been institutionalized for almost 10 years will likely have formed strong enough roots that it can no longer be extirpated easily.

Finally, the process of institutionalization creates its own contradictions and tensions. One of these is caused by the words and phrases used to communicate the policy innovation. As part of the system of shared beliefs among a network, a certain shorthand language develops, with code words signifying larger analyses. Examples of these in the present case were given before: neighborhoods versus downtown; manufacturing over services; economic development as jobs, not real estate. These metaphors are important both as an expression of shared beliefs and as public relations tools to communicate quickly and easily complex sets of ideas (Giloth & Mier, 1988).

However, this symbolic language may also cause people to misperceive reality. For instance, over time it became clear to the LIRI groups that the shortage of adequate industrial space was a key cause of job loss. Thus real estate development had to be a central part of a job creation and retention strategy. However, the artificial contradiction that had been set up between "jobs" on the one hand, and "real estate" on the other limited the legitimacy of a real estate development strategy. Similarly, the emphasis on manufacturing jobs as good jobs, and the dismissal of jobs in the service sector as "McJobs" led to neglect of a huge segment of the local economy. Even to the present, LIRI industrial representatives concentrate their business outreach on manufacturing companies, and therefore do little for the 80% of the local work force employed in nonmanufacturing firms.

Clearly, decentralized policy-making in regard to neighborhood development has survived into the post-Washington area. As such, it can be considered to be a successful policy innovation. More important, it continues to generate an intensity and sophistication of debate about the future of the city that is matched in few other places.

Notes

1. These organizations are labeled by the bureaucracy as "delegate agencies."

2. The first several years of the Daley tenure saw the local media full of articles like one appearing in the *Chicago Tribune* titled "Old Daley Clout Has Returned" (Davidson, 1990).

3. Mayor Washington frequently convened task forces as a vehicle to facilitate debate and participation (Alexander et al., 1987).

4. Mier and the University of Illinois Center for Urban Economic Development would play a major role in launching the facility.

5. These emphases parallel those of another LIRI group serving an older industrial area, the Southeast Chicago Development Commission (SEDCOM) (Southeast Chicago Development Commission, 1987).

6. The City's executive or statutorial economic development advisory bodies have been The Mayor's Committee on Economic and Cultural Development, the Economic Development Commission, and the Commercial District Development Commission. They also have advocated for a policy of industrial retention and expansion since the first of them was formed in the mid-1960s.

7. ICNC and GNPDC are members of CANDO. The LEED Council belongs both to CWED and to CANDO.

8. Approximately 15 people, including Wim Wiewel, attended this meeting on January 27, 1989, just a few weeks before the primaries. What was notable and worrisome was not just the substance of Daley's positions, but his apparent lack of real interest and knowledge about many of the issues of concern to the group.

8

Democratic Populism in the United States: The Case of Playskool and Chicago

with

ROBERT P. GILOTH

This chapter presents a different type of development choice from the one between neighborhood development and mega-projects discussed in Chapter 6. The story of the campaign to prevent a toy company, Playskool, from closing presents a choice between holding business accountable to the community and creating a "good business climate." In fact, this chapter reveals that the choice is based on a false dichotomy. Local manufacturers, who felt Playskool violated the public trust by not abiding by the conditions of its public development assistance, mobilized along with neighborhood stakeholders (community and labor organizations) to prevent the closing. As in Chapter 7, the mutual support between the administration and community organizations is revealed. The strategy for responding to the Playskool closing emerged from the community, and was supported by the administration.

AUTHORS' NOTE: This article was first published in *Cities*, Vol. 3, No. 1, February, 1986, pp. 72-74, and is reproduced here with the permission of Butterworth-Heinemann, Oxford, U.K.

Reeling from four defeats in U.S. national elections by conservative Republicans since 1968, the Democratic Party in the late 1980s was groping for a new formula and new directions.[1] Central to the Democratic quandary was the loss to Ronald Reagan's "conservative majority" of one of the party's foundation stones—populist issues and forces. With the exception of Henry Wallace's 1948 campaign, for 75 years the Democratic Party had captured the imaginations of those who cherished smallness and autonomy—the family, the neighborhood, the church, and the farm. With the emergence, however, of huge, often inert, liberal Democratic institutions such as the federal bureaucracy and labor unions, the party's connections with common people's concerns became obfuscated and tenuous (Lerner, 1988).

Those debating the future of the Democratic Party recognize the need to reconnect institutions capable of preserving or advancing civil and human rights as well as economic prosperity with immediate concerns of people chafing under the often repressive tendencies of large institutions. Nevertheless, there are few clues as to how to make these connections. One possible approach emerges from analysis of a recent plant closure in Chicago that stimulated unusual community, labor, and City government action. The significance of the case is accentuated because it occurred early in the first term of Mayor Harold Washington, a person widely perceived as touching a unique and promising chord in U.S. electoral politics.

The battle to maintain Hasbro-Bradley's Playskool toy plant on Chicago's west side took place in the winter of 1984-1985. That was a time when state governments were scrambling for the first plant to produce General Motor's new Saturn automobile, President Reagan was promising even more massive urban cutbacks, and doomsayers were predicting more doom for older industrial cities in the United States. The message for municipalities seemed clear. Amidst this depressing flurry, a community/labor coalition pressured the administration of Mayor Washington to sue Hasbro-Bradley to prevent the Playskool closure.

The settlement reached on January 31, 1985, between the City of Chicago and Hasbro-Bradley was much less than organizers hoped for but more than Playskool would have left in Chicago. Hasbro-Bradley promised to keep the Playskool factory open and retain 100 workers until November 1985, to operate a job-placement program that offered employers $500 for every ex-Playskool worker they hired, establish a $50,000 emergency fund for Playskool workers, and, with the City, to find a successor firm or donee for the Playskool facility. Hasbro also agreed to negotiate hiring agreements with new plant users that would give preference to unemployed Playskool workers. These commitments were in addition to the $2.3-million severance package negotiated by union and nonunion employees.

What is new about the Playskool settlement goes beyond the promise to "soften" the social costs of a specific plant closure. Playskool has spurred widespread interest in local industrial policy and has encouraged grass-roots and municipal efforts in Chicago and across the country to develop more responsible approaches to public/private partnerships.

Playskool—an old Chicago toy manufacturer of Lincoln Logs—was bought by Milton-Bradley in 1968, which in turn was bought by Hasbro in September 1984. The facts about the Playskool closure include repeated public financial assistance, multiple plant closures and relocations, the rise and fall of electronic games, and corporate mergers.

Public assistance may have fueled Milton Bradley's plant closure strategy. Employing 700 workers throughout most of the 1970s, Chicago's Playskool plant jumped in employment to about 1,200 in 1980, a result, in part, of the closure of plants in South Bend, Indiana, and Skokie, Illinois. South Bend Toy expanded in the late 1970s, with the aid of a $7-million public low-interest loan. A subsequent City of Chicago loan for new equipment eased the closure of this plant and the transfer of production to Chicago. Finally, Milton Bradley received a $1-million loan from the Massachusetts Industrial Development Authority for their East Longmeadow plant, the facility to which Chicago Playskool productive assets have been moved.

Losses and overexpansion—particularly related to electronic games—led Milton Bradley to choose plant consolidation in the East and the closing of Playskool. Hasbro bought this decision, announcing the layoff of 750 mostly Latino and African-American workers on September 19, 1984, shortly before the Christmas buying season began.

Breach of Trust

Shutting down did not distinguish Playskool. What angered people in Chicago was that Playskool "drank at the public trough" and 4 years later reneged on its public/private partnership. In so doing, Playskool failed to create the 400 jobs it promised the City of Chicago in exchange for the substantial interest savings to be achieved during the life of the City's loan. In addition, Playskool hid its relocation plans even from fellow businessmen on a west-side industrial council, the Greater North and Pulaski Development Corporation.[2] Public uproar branded their acts a "breach of trust." Chicago's media were quick to connect Christmas, toys, and layoffs.

What was so unusual about the Playskool plant closure that it sparked community uproar and a court settlement? One interpretation—focusing on grass-roots coalition building—is that community/labor action pressured a reluctant although sympathetic City government into action. A second emphasizes the risktaking and negotiating power of the City of Chicago, once pushed into action by community outcry. A final Playskool theme, more environmental in nature, argues that the circumstances of the Playskool drama were unique—the seeming breach of the loan contract, the Christmas season, toys, and Chicago politics—and that these issue attributes, not the competence or risk-taking of coalitions or local governments, accounted for the take-off and success of the Playskool confrontation.

A blending of these perspectives better tells the story. The Westside Jobs Network (WJN), a group of Chicago community and labor organizations, began to organize one week after Hasbro-Bradley's September 19, 1984, announcement of the closure of Playskool. The City had funded them to establish an early warning plant closing system. The Network sent letters to Mayor Washington and Steven Hassenfeld (the president of Hasbro-Bradley), and held a press conference in early October that produced the first round of press coverage. Dismay at the closure provoked widespread community interest.

The WJN and its supporters were responsible for the public perception of "community uproar" about the Playskool closure. Images of picket lines, unemployed families, toys, and broken promises soon appeared in newspapers, radio broadcasts, and on television news coast to coast. Playskool became the symbol for all that was wrong with the Chicago economy. The WJN organized picket lines on State Street during Christmas shopping. And on December 8, at a large public meeting at a neighborhood church, they declared a national boycott of Hasbro-Bradley toys.

WJN action inspired other local and national responses to the Playskool closure. More than 100 Playskool workers supported a lawsuit by workers to intervene in the City's case. A local religious coalition filed a "friend of the courts" brief on behalf of Chicago citizens. And economic justice groups from around the country bombarded Hasbro-Bradley with telegrams and phone calls.

The WJN pressured the City to act. They made Playskool a public priority that had to be dealt with decisively. As a consequence, the risks of unusual City government action were momentarily lowered while community uproar heightened the risks of the City's not taking action.

Here was a jobs issue that tested the Washington administration. Harold Washington's 1983 mayoral campaign promised jobs and open government; and Washington had been fighting for new and more equitable approaches to economic development that would distinguish his record from past Chicago administrations and from many others U.S. cities.

Legal Alternatives

The City initially moved cautiously. Due to a complete absence of U.S. regulation of plant closures, it had limited tools to intervene in the Playskool case, and there were no obvious precedents to guide City intervention. City staff explored the City's legal alternatives, the possibility of sending a business task force to talk with Hasbro-Bradley, and other similar public incentive-related cases around the country.

By December, public outcry and City Council pressure demanded forceful action, and the month began with Mayor Washington, in an unprecedented action, directing City attorneys into court. Chicago's suit charged Hasbro-Bradley with a breach of contract and claimed damages. The Mayor announced the court action, surrounded by members of both sides of Chicago's often contentious and acrimonious City Council and by WJN representatives. Such unprecedented municipal action launched the Playskool drama into the national spotlight.

Playskool ignited multiple fronts of action for the City of Chicago besides a path-breaking lawsuit. The Playskool affair erupted at the outset of the City's volatile 1985 budgeting season, prompting critical questions about the City's business loan program. The City had to speak clearly about the job performance of all its loan recipients (approximately 250 in the previous 6 years), and particularly those publicly assisted businesses, like Playskool, that had closed their doors. A parenthetical lesson was more clearly seeing public assistance as a job-retention rather than a job-creation device.

The December court action set a context to negotiate a settlement. The City attempted to structure an accountable relationship with the WJN to work out an acceptable settlement with Hasbro-Bradley. Formulating a settlement tested the confidence of the community/labor coalition in the City and the unity of the WJN: Member groups were torn between wanting to keep jobs, achieving more equitable severance for the workers, protecting the local industrial community, and making sure business development could occur in the future. These were difficult demands to balance.

Despite direct negotiations between Mayor Washington and Hassenfeld, Christmas passed without a fast conclusion in sight. In response, the WJN turned up the community heat on Hasbro. Toy retailers were asked to lobby Hasbro-Bradley. Picket lines returned. And a national telegram campaign got under way, with telegrams from at least 25 states reaching Hassenfeld by the end of January.

Negotiations concluded on January 31, 1985. Hasbro threatened unilateral action if a settlement was not reached, including the start of a job-placement program to be headed by a Chicago football star, Gale Sayers. Both sides compromised. The City and the WJN lowered their severance demands while Hasbro capitulated on an emergency fund for workers and put their company-controlled job-placement program in the final settlement agreement.

The Battle

The Playskool battle, however, was not won in the courtroom or at the bargaining table alone. The final, environment-oriented perspective on the Playskool closure centers not on the WJN nor the City, but on the characteristics of the Playskool issue and the climate of opinion that supported its dynamic of controversy. Good issues, a responsive public, and media attention can make or break organizing.

Certainly, the basics of Playskool stand out. A toy manufacturer decides to close its plant at the beginning of the Christmas season, seemingly working its workers, like Scrooge, to the very end, only to reward them with unemployment and what many thought to be a substandard severance package. There is also the matter of the $1-million loan in 1980 and a perceived "false promise" of job creation: Playskool's substantial underachievement of job projections was difficult to explain by a mere downturn in business conditions. Playskool seemed profitable. It appeared to the public as a calculated "hit and run" on the public trust. Playskool's relocation deception insulted fellow businesses on Chicago's west side and throughout Chicago, thus providing key business participation in the Network and forestalling corporate opposition to Chicago's court action.

The nature of the toy industry made community organizing easier. The brand conscious toy industry is vulnerable to negative product association and boycotts. Its consumer base consists of parents. During this Christmas season, Hasbro also came under consumer and media attack for distribution of a "schizoid doll."

Political Environment

Another unusual feature of the Playskool drama was the volatile nature of Chicago's political environment. One can be sure that if a public issue gets more than passing media attention in Chicago, there will be a competitive struggle to capitalize on it for political advantage. Economic development, in particular, is at the center of controversy; it was the heart of Mayor Washington's platform for urban political change.

A final distinguishing feature of the Playskool closure was the public sentiment, tapped during organizing, that enabled the issue to unfold. The campaign touched a raw nerve. These public feelings valued local control, stability of community, integrity in business and government affairs, and hard work and family.

Many people not involved in the organizing stopped buying Playskool toys. The City probably would not have taken such aggressive action without pressure from a community/labor coalition. The risks would have seemed to high.

Would a court suit against Hasbro-Bradley have occurred if Chicago's mayor was insensitive to community concerns and unwilling to consider unconventional action? Not likely. A city-sponsored early warning plant closing network would not have existed. Much organizing would have been required just to get the City to listen to the Playskool story, thus sapping scarce citizen organizing resources. Negative business opinion might have been unleashed. And City mayoral action would probably not have resulted until Playskool had left Chicago.

Conclusion

Can any of these individual Playskool perspectives explain the success of the Playskool fight? Not any plant relocation or public loan "breach of trust" could have unleashed a Playskool dynamic. Bad faith in conjunction with toys, Christmas, and profits created an organizing and media opportunity not to be missed.

This chapter has emphasized the importance of an open and risk-taking city government, a community/labor coalition, and the right issue at the right time. The result has been concrete benefits for workers and the community, and perhaps a model for private sector responsibilities in public/private partnerships.

More important, the Playskool drama has a moral for urban populism and Democratic politics. Citizen organizing should not be discouraged when reformers are elected to office. In many cases, the articulation of change will still need to come from the grass roots. But open, sympathetic government may make such organizing less painful, and outcomes resulting in greater public good more probable. Real benefits for those most in need can be achieved without upsetting the prospects for economic development.

By no means did the court settlement end the Playskool closing. The settlement required enforcement, and the Playskool facility had to be redeveloped. A monitoring of the performance of the Playskool Jobs Center by community organizations showed that few blue-collar workers obtained job placements, particularly female Latino workers. Women who eventually found work had

average wages of $3.50 an hour, much less than the $5- to
$8-an-hour jobs at Playskool (Kleiman, 1988). On the develop-
ment side, the Playskool facility has been redeveloped as a
mini-industrial park. The GNPDC is a joint venture partner in the
redevelopment. Unfortunately, early hopes to link the redevelopment of the Playskool facility to the employment and retraining needs of dislocated workers have not been met because of
developer reluctance.

Beyond the Playskool settlement and aftermath, there were
other impacts. Most important, alternative development ideas
were reaffirmed, leading to further experimentation with early
warning intervention (LaBotz, 1986; Moberg, 1987). In 1985
many of the same community and labor groups initiated the Coalition to Keep Stewart Warner Open. In contrast to organizing after
a plant closing announcement, this multifaceted coalition was truly
early in its identification of disinvestment in this company that
employed 2,000. Local managers of another company, Precision
Scientific, contacted the City and a neighborhood industrial council because they saw their nonlocal owners disinvesting. By 1987
a local manager buy out was achieved for this company, and 375
jobs were retained. A government, union, and company agreement
was reached to retain ECKO Products in Chicago—a recent lever-
aged buy out of a local firm employing 500. Other, less-concrete
successes included two worker buy out feasibility studies by WJN
in 1984-1985 and union, community, and City cooperation to
respond in 1986-1987 to the closing of LTV, Chicago's last integrated steelworks and an employer of 1,000 workers.

The Playskool legal action also added to the groundswell of
concern about plant closings and the abuse of public incentives
around the United States. In particular, local challenges to closures in Boulder, Duluth, and Louisville have used the Playskool
experience. Nevertheless, while Playskool encouraged other
creative plant closing responses, federal and Illinois plant closing legislation remained elusive until recently.

Notes

1. At the time of this writing, in late 1992, it is unclear whether the Democratic
presidential victory embodies that new formula and direction.

2. GNPDC was extensively discussed in the previous chapter.

9

Spatial Change and Social Justice

with

ROBERT P. GILOTH

This chapter supplements the Playskool analysis of Chapter 8 with two additional case studies: an effort at industrial retention through land use control, and the establishment of industrial task forces in the steel and apparel industries. The significance of these stories is that they move beyond reacting to plant closing announcements to more proactive strategies to maintain important industrial sectors. Combined with the Playskool case detailed in Chapter 8, these stories present three distinct approaches to industrial policy: The Playskool campaign was firm specific; the planned manufacturing districts represent a geographic approach; and the industry task forces detail a sectoral approach. This three-pronged strategy demonstrates the importance the Washington administration placed on manufacturing employment, despite ongoing resignation in many quarters that its decline was inevitable.

AUTHORS' NOTE: Adapted from Giloth and Mier (1988). We thank Wim Wiewel, Diana Robinson, and Bob Beauregard for their thorough and thoughtful criticism of earlier drafts.

144

The 1992 presidential election has seen the candidates counseling the limitations of local action and promising a national strategy that confronts the global political economy. To put it another way, the contemporary viewpoint about urban social and spatial changes sees recent upheaval in inner-city industrial and working-class zones, as determined by national and international economic restructuring beyond the influence of local planners and communities (Brandy, 1987; Fainstein & Fainstein, 1987).

We believe the presidential debates, with their focus on the global economy, have overlooked recent local experiences that contain lessons for a new national strategy. We suggest that distinctive local responses to events of economic restructuring, such as plant closings, show that there are continuing opportunities at the local level to articulate new development ideas and practices, to cultivate new coalitions, and to explore new relations between government institutions and social movements.[1] Further, we suggest that these local experiments, although adding to the growing list of challenging development efforts around the United States, are also nurturing principles of social justice, fairness, openness, and participation as seeds for a national strategy (Bruyn & Meehan, 1987; Clavel, 1985). Yet we argue, in contrast to those who overemphasize the rhetoric of "equity planning," that such community experimentation faces enormous obstacles in the form of growth coalitions, community fragmentation, unresponsive bureaucracies, and intractable local problems (Squires et al., 1987; Krumholz & Forester, 1990).[2]

We continue the exploration of the potential of local efforts by further examining Chicago's experience between 1983 and 1987. Although we emphasize distinctive features of the Chicago situation, we are not arguing that Chicago is unique. First, we reexamine preconditions for experimentation as it emerged in Chicago. Second, we present two cases that illustrate the strategies in action: industrial displacement and the implementation of local industry task forces. In each example, we attempt to connect the Chicago response to similar efforts in other cities. Third, we reflect on this experience for lessons about strategy development, coalition building, community action, replication of responses, and the connection of local actions to national change.

A Climate for Experimentation

In Chicago during the 1980s, one would often find an unlikely set of groups and individuals coming together to promote a grass-roots vision of development: environmental activists helping small manufacturers with toxic wastes; industrial councils of small manufacturers collaborating on worker buy out studies; public housing tenant councils working with local businesspersons in starting small businesses; a social worker leading a task force to set up a capital fund for neighborhood manufacturers; and union leaders supporting legislation to prevent displacement of industries by downtown development (Greenhouse, 1986; "Help for a Day," 1987). This creative ferment had several distinctive elements: the diversity of innovations being explored simultaneously; the coalition approach to problem solving; the ongoing difficulty of stretching these coalitions across racial boundaries; and the turn to production-oriented issues, such as business investment by neighborhood activists.

This climate for local experimentation in progressive economic development had multiple roots (Gills, 1991; Mier & Moe, 1991). The first was the maturation of the extensive network of neighborhood organizations interested in economic development, including several specialized organizations within this network dedicated to innovation, technical assistance, and advocacy (Mier, Wiewel, & Alpern, 1992). The Westside Jobs Network is an example (Giloth & Mier, 1986). The second was the evolution of the development ideas in ways that enabled the framing of problems in new ways and the invention of distinctive solutions. The central ideas included an emphasis on the quality of life in Chicago's neighborhoods, especially the lower-income ones; a belief that small business and manufacturing were being neglected; a mistrust about the reliance on downtown and service sector development; and a anger that questions of who was paying and who benefiting from development were not part of the public policy debate.

The networks and ideas generated quite distinctive local responses to events commonly associated with economic restructuring—plant closings, industrial land-use conflict, and general industry distress. These types of events embodied both the negatives of restructuring as well as opportunities for new actors to define new solutions—opportunities for "social invention" (Whyte,

1982; Judd & Ready, 1986). The related economic processes help explain the impact of restructuring at the local level: industrial concentration/fragmentation; spatial concentration/dispersal; and a bifurcation of the labor market. Before turning to our case studies, examples of social invention, these three processes will be discussed.

Industry Concentration/Fragmentation

Some industries, like steel, showed strikingly different processes as they declined. The industry was concentrating in the Midwest as it declined nationally; but it was also fragmenting, with the emergence of specialty steel producers, fabricators, and distributors. As the fully integrated industry complex decomposed, new opportunities for collaboration around technology, infrastructure, and investment occurred. For example, one of our cases will describe how City government invested in industrial infrastructure in the vicinity of an old steel mill; and the mill's owners, its workers, and a neighboring grass-roots organization supported the City's controversial industrial retention policy.

Firms on the small end of size hierarchies, or firms in industries whose market and supplier linkages were being radically redefined, more often engaged in cooperative action to advance technology or establish new markets. Similar processes were happening in other Chicago industries—apparel and printing—as well as nationally in motion picture production and automobile manufacturing (Ranney & Wiewel, 1987).

The process of concentration/fragmentation mixed with ownership changes also accounts for many plant closings brought about by the consolidation of plants, disinvestment overseas, or a move to low-wage areas. The Playskool plant closing addresses just such a closing. Plant closings raise the question of whether the disinvestment calculus ignores local opportunities and skills and, as such, creates opportunities for local challenges to industrial restructuring.

Spatial Concentration/Dispersal

Geographic restructuring in cities has a number of dimensions, one being the expansion of downtown, its service firms, and related residential enclaves into surrounding industrial and warehouse districts and low-income neighborhoods.

In short, gentrification—the change of neighborhoods to higher-income uses—affects the productive base of cities as well as their residential space. The process pushes firms and industries out, raising the question of where firms go and whether spatial agglomerations for specific industries (e.g., printing) can be recreated (Ranney & Wiewel, 1987). One of our cases recounts the struggle to constrain this industrial displacement. On the other hand, in conjunction with industry fragmentation and specialty niches, the dispersal process also motivated the rehabil-itation and subdivision of former single-user factories in neighbor-hoods where major firms left, thus creating opportunities for neighborhood economic development (Ducharme et al., 1986).

Bifurcation of the Labor Market

The increasing bimodality of the urban labor market with concentrations of subemployment is another dimension of the industry and spatial processes described above. The emerging service sector is characterized by dual concentrations of high-skill, high-wage occupations, such as lawyers and accountants, and low-skill, low-wage occupations, such as busboys, chamber-maids, and kitchen workers. Plant closings and the contracting out that often accompany restructuring industries reinforce this labor market bifurcation. The resultant real estate pressures have led to extraordinary juxtapositions of land values with high-priced condominium developments abutting public hous-ing projects. Their respective tenants have become competing constituencies for further upscale residential and commercial development, on the one hand, and basic industry, on the other.

Cases

Two cases illustrate how diverse community networks and alternative development ideas may yield more equitable responses to industrial restructuring.[3] The cases, supplements to the case of the Playskool plant closing, are fighting industrial displacement on Goose Island and in the Clybourn Corridor, and task forces on the steel and apparel industries. Each case study presents the background of the event, including normal public and private responses; ideas and networks that framed the event in a new way, or that emerged during the course of the response; the story of what happened; and the outcomes, including replication of approaches and diffusion of development ideas. For each case, we draw attention to what seems most distinctive—whether framing the problem or opportunity, building networks, elaborating development ideas, or impacts. All of the cases continue to unfold, hence what is offered is a snapshot, one that is also colored by our involvement as participants.

Industrial Displacement

Questioning the costs, benefits, prerogatives, and impacts of downtown development is a risky undertaking. It confronts growth coalition boosterism, challenges the rational voice of the market, and questions the allocation of public subsidies and regulatory exceptions for downtown projects. Although most city governments unquestioningly promote downtown development, a number of examples exist in which downtown dominance has been challenged: linked development agreements and ordinances, stopping big projects, and altering the terms of public financing and ownership of downtown projects (Keating, 1986; Mier, 1984a; Shlay & Giloth, 1986).

This case study is about how Chicago is attempting to protect one of its industrial districts from displacement caused by an expanding downtown and upper-income neighborhoods (Schmidt, 1987). Industrial displacement became a public issue because of the research, education, and advocacy efforts of the neighborhood industrial council for the North Branch industrial district (Giloth & Betancur, 1988). The New City YMCA's Local Employment and Economic Development Council (LEEDS) is unusual among industrial councils because of its merging of industrial council activities, such as providing services to area manufacturers with neighborhood development, and advocacy. Moreover, the LEEDs Council is distinguished by its attempt to serve and link the Cabrini-Green public housing project and the adjacent North Branch industrial area.

Although business displacement was found to be as frequent as plant closings, its potential consequences were not well understood by the public. Except for community opposition to the upscale redevelopment of an old brewery complex in the late 1970s, normal City of Chicago planning practice was to do what developers wanted. Hence, research and public education about industrial displacement and the benefits of balanced urban growth is the theme of this case. In the process of education and advocacy, a loose citywide coalition of community organizations, networks, labor, small businesses, aldermen, and city agencies came together to advocate solutions to industrial displacement. This coalition was pitted against the developer community and its chief public interest advocate, the Chicago Tribune Company. As a result of this organizing, a number of redevelopment projects have been stopped or redefined, a Planned Manufacturing District (PMD) has passed the City Council, and Apparel and Printing Task Forces have made anti-displacement recommendations for downtown-based apparel and printing firms. Several of the negotiated settlements for the contested redevelopment projects have involved financial contributions for industrial land-use planning, commitments for nearby industrial development, and project redesign.

Chicago has not been alone in confronting industrial displacement. In fact, most older industrial cities in the Midwest and Northeast are experiencing similar displacement problems. New York has developed the most ambitious set of policy tools to protect industrial districts, primarily the apparel districts in Manhattan, and promote the industrial retention of relocating firms. Even Baltimore, mecca of downtown boosterism and waterfront development, is experimenting with zoning controls to protect industrial districts (Betancur & McCormick, 1985).

The North Branch manufacturing district is 2 miles northwest of Chicago's Loop and is part of the North River Industrial Corridor that houses 10% of Chicago's manufacturing jobs, and more than 50,000 total jobs. It includes Goose Island and the Clybourn Corridor, both of which are experiencing the piecemeal conversion of industrial property to residential and commercial uses. If speculative redevelopment continues, most firms in these areas are likely to relocate outside the district due to high rents and property taxes, evictions, lack of adequate space to expand, hard-to-refuse purchase offers, and conflicts with new land uses. Many firms will remain in Chicago, but others may choose to move out of the city altogether (Ducharme et al., 1986).

The City of Chicago and other units of government have pursued conflicting policies regarding the North Branch district. On one hand, they have supported local manufacturers with capital improvements, financial incentives, support for a local industrial organization, and city plans designating the area as industrial. On the other hand, the City encouraged redevelopment by granting zoning changes required for residential reuse and by allowing redevelopment proposals to reach near-fruition before public review. Other units of government, such as the Illinois Housing Development Authority, have made loans for upscale housing developments and have been insensitive to the needs of industry as they make riverfront plans and public works decisions.

River Lofts. Goose Island is the southern terminus of the North Branch district and is created by the split in the north branch of the Chicago River. Originally a feisty settlement of immigrants, Goose Island became a district of tanners, smelters, and manufacturers at the beginning of this century. In 1988 there were 25 firms and 2,000 jobs on Goose Island, along with vacant railroad land and empty factories. Once designated an industrial park under Mayor Jane Byrne in the late 1970s, this plan collapsed when the developer withdrew from the project. Even though many industries remain on Goose Island and others might move there if they were certain of its future, large projects for Goose Island surface with some regularity: the proposed 1992 World's Fair, high-income housing and boat slips, and a sports stadium.

Loft conversions have occurred on Goose Island. The fight over the River Lofts development illustrates the effort needed to convince officials and the public at large that there is industry on the island worth saving. River Lofts is an ambitious project proposed for the southern tip of Goose Island—a $20-million renovation of an old factory for 200 combined work and residence units and commercial uses, including restaurants. Conflict arose because Goose Island industries did not want residential uses on the island, although they did not oppose its commercial development. They reasoned that 24-hour users would eventually object to the noise, the smells, and the truck traffic from nearby industries. River Loft's developers were undaunted; they hired Chicago's premier zoning law firm, mobilized support from other loft developers, and played Chicago politics.

Industries and developers battered City government with letters, meetings, and telephone calls. A public hearing was held, and industries and developers met separately with City agencies. Developers offered a compromise that would reduce the number of work and residence units and include provisions intended to prevent the harassment of industries. Industries stood firm and told of their plans for $10 million in local investment. After multiple cancellations of the Chicago Plan Commission meetings and widespread press coverage, the alderman for the ward postponed consideration of River Lofts until after his reelection in April 1987.

A compromise agreement was reached in June 1987, only after political operatives communicated to the industries and their industrial council that permanent enemies would be made if their opposition continued. Complete victory for the industries seemed either impossible or too costly. Industries did not stop the development, but managed to gain future protection of their district.

The final settlement reduced the number of work and residence units and the scope of outdoor restaurants on the site. The developers further agreed to buffer their property from industrial neighbors, establish a mediation system to deal with environmental complaints, and forego other types of residential development on the island. The City agreed to investigate whether a cul-de-sac and traffic rerouting on the island could be accomplished to more completely separate River Lofts from its industrial neighbors. Finally, the alderman agreed to support passage of a Planned Manufacturing District ordinance for Goose Island. Before the agreement could be implemented, the real estate economy turned sour and the developer was unable to obtain financing for the project. The building still sits unused.

Planned Manufacturing Districts. A question posed early by neighborhood advocates and city planners was whether there were local public policies that could prevent industrial displacement and either avoid or set limits on case-by-case zoning fights. One approach, revealed in a survey of 13 cities, was New York's creation of protected manufacturing districts with zoning restrictions and relocation incentives (Betancur & McCormick, 1985). A legislative opportunity to advance such an approach occurred when the alderman of the ward including the Clybourn Corridor, immediately north of Goose Island, declared a moratorium on considering proposed changes from manufacturing zoning until the City developed a workable policy on industrial retention and zoning. He was under pressure from industrial representatives, developers, residents, and numerous City actors every time a proposed loft conversion surfaced.

The design of an industrial protection policy occurred concurrently with such zoning controversies as River Lofts. The Clybourn Corridor, in contrast to Goose Island, has many more loft conversions (including one residential condominium development) and is directly adjacent to the upper-income and ever-expanding Lincoln Park neighborhood. In the course of 2 years, there were between 7 and 10 proposed conversions of industrial property in this district for shopping centers, housing, and boutique complexes. Yet the area retained an industrial base of close to 2,000 jobs, including a major specialty steel producer. Also, it had received millions of dollars of public industrial infrastructure in the past decade, particularly roads and sewers. Public hearings on each of these cases, and the publication of a research study on the potential negative impacts of industrial displacement, provided the rationale for the moratorium.

The outcome of more than a year of ordinance drafting, boundary drawing, public hearings, legal strategy, the election of a new alderman, and a mayoral tour was a PMD enabling ordinance and a specific Clybourn PMD application. Chicago's City Council held a final set of public hearings in early 1988, and the PMD enabling ordinance passed in the spring of 1988.

The enabling ordinance allows the establishment of PMDs with core manufacturing areas where special and residential uses are limited, and buffer zones where a broader range of commercial uses are permissible. Properties in PMDs may be changed to nonmanufacturing only if they are marketed in a good faith manner for manufacturing, and new uses do not negatively affect industry.

The lengthy process of ordinance preparation revealed new complexities about industrial displacement. Surprisingly, several businesses opposed the ordinance because they were included within its boundaries; they wanted to get as much as possible for their properties—as their stockholders supposedly demanded. Other firms lobbied to be included in the district. Industries, in general, learned to argue their case in terms of their contribution to Chicago's economy, specifically jobs and taxes. Remnants of the blue-collar residential neighborhood endorsed the PMD concept, but other residential groups were ambivalent: They wanted more residential but reluctantly understood the economic development arguments for preserving industrial districts. A number of citywide groups and several union locals endorsed the PMD concept and became involved in the public hearings. At the penultimate community hearing in March 1987, a majority of the 200 residents and businesses gave their support to PMDs.

Industrial displacement and, more broadly, the goal of balanced urban growth are now a fixture on Chicago's public agenda.[4] Much discussion has ensued about the future of industry in Chicago, the nature and benefits of downtown growth, the development biases evident in regulatory processes such as zoning, and the distribution of public incentives and subsidies. In addition, a network of organizations, including unions, community organizations, and business groups, has emerged to promote alternative development ideas and respond to displacement cases in the neighborhoods. Indeed, cases in many neighborhoods, whether related to downtown expansion or shopping center developers, are being confronted with new confidence. At the same time, downtown growth advocates, developers, and machine politicians are fighting back.

Industrial advocates realize that the long-term industrial displacement challenge is to build industrial districts that are competitive. Industrial districts should have strategic plans to attract new firms, lower inner-city business costs, and help older firms expand and prosper. Compromises will have to be forged that accept light manufacturing and service-type firms, and, as in the case of gaining industrial protection, a partnership of business, the local industrial council, and municipal government will be required. This quickly occurred on Goose Island: Three months after the River Loft's settlement, a major developer announced a 1-million-square-foot industrial park for an empty 37-acre site.[5]

Industry Task Forces

This case examines the designing of local industrial policies through the creation of task forces, specifically for Chicago's steel and apparel industries. It differs from the previous case in several respects: Its focus is sectoral-specific, rather than firm-specific or geographic; it involves more formally deliberative problem solving; and the task forces are more narrowly municipal initiatives, although they include broad participation (Wiewel & Siegel, 1987). The task forces changed the perception that manufacturing was dead in Chicago; produced concrete initiatives in the areas of technology, dislocated workers, and business retention; and provided a framework for intervening in plant closings and undertaking legislative lobbying (Alexander, Giloth, & Lerner, 1987).

These industry task forces are indicative of an array of cooperative industrial policy-making that had taken place in Chicago between 1983 and 1987. In most cases, the City of Chicago provided some financial and staff resources. For example, a task force on the printing industry, sponsored by the Center for Urban Economic Development at the University of Illinois at Chicago, was completed in July 1987 (Ranney & Wiewel, 1987). The Capital Base Task Force designed the Chicago Capital Fund, an alternative equity capital fund for neighborhood manufacturers (Patterson & Sieros, 1985). The Center For Neighborhood Technology (CNT) has provided technical assistance to small electroplaters attempting to comply with environmental regulations, while advocating for more supportive public policies and cooperative waste disposal techniques (Basler & Kitwana, 1986).

Efforts to design local industrial policies in Chicago confronted opposition ranging from amused disbelief to hostility. There was a common belief that economic development was simply a matter of real estate development, particularly downtown development. Moreover, in 1984, the Commercial Club of Chicago, a gathering of major corporate leaders and the sponsor of Daniel Burnham's 1909 Plan for Chicago, published its strategic plan, *Make No Little Plans.* It made no mention of manufacturing. Even when manufacturing was acknowledged as important, a pervasive feeling existed that it was a national problem that localities could not affect. Changing the terms of the economic development debate in Chicago to focus on jobs and to include manufacturing was a theme of Mayor Washington's *1984 Development Plan* and a function of the industry task forces.

In 1984 Mayor Harold Washington appointed two industry task forces to evaluate the problems of Chicago's steel and apparel industries and to recommend solutions. He was a long-time advocate of manufacturing (his congressional district contained the steel communities). For both steel and apparel, the importance of the remaining jobs and signs of industry resurgence reinforced the need to address the economic and social dislocation resulting from industrial change. Since 1979 approximately 13,000 steelworker jobs had been lost in Southeast Chicago, and each plant shutdown led to further layoffs by suppliers and distributors. Whereas the steel crisis in Chicago was precipitous, the economic problems of Chicago's apparel industry resulted from long-term decline: In 1983, 365 apparel and textile mill firms employed 10,372 workers in Cook County, down from 29,000 workers in 689 firms in 1964 (City of Chicago, 1986a, 1987a).

Chicago task forces did bring new people and institutions to the table. The Task Force on Steel and Southeast Chicago had a policy committee of 12 members and working groups that contained an additional 30 persons. Its policy committee included lawyers, academicians, real estate experts, and union and management representatives. Task force staff initially felt that this membership mix was optimal, but in retrospect, representatives of steel-related companies—such as steel service centers and machine tool builders and unions—would have added another important dimension. A source of frustration was the unwillingness of a large, national steel company headquartered in Chicago to participate in the task force. As the task force progressed, however, the company expressed greater interest, eventually meeting with task force members and participating in a steel technology conference. The Apparel and Fashion Task Force, in contrast, included more numerous apparel manufacturers and designers in addition to union representatives and academics. Its policy committee had 20 members, and 23 additional persons were involved in working groups.

The interaction of research and task force deliberations enlivened both task forces. In the steel task force, in particular, the researcher's documentation of a regional Chicago steel industrial complex (i.e., an interdependent network of steel producers, users, and suppliers) and the emergence of steel service centers proved enormously influential in shaping the task force's conclusion that the local steel industry was not dead (Markusen et al., 1985). The apparel task force, in contrast, relied initially more upon the experiences and opinions of industry members, with formal economic and survey research being completed later in order to confirm and polish these insights.

Each task force reflected the problems and characteristics of its industry. The steel task force confronted an industry that was widely regarded as dying by local media and business leadership: Integrated steelworks were outmoded. The task force's first step was to overcome this negative perception. With extensive research, they argued that although Chicago's steel sector was undergoing fundamental changes in production methods, distribution patterns, and market position, it remained vital to the local economy. Chicago's steel industry represented a complex of steel users, producers, and distributors that accounted for 250,000 jobs regionally, and steel service sectors, in particular, showed growth. Moreover, as the steel industry rationalized nationally, the more modern, spatially protected, high value-added facilities of the Midwest exhibited relative strength.

The steel task force then identified concrete steps to assist local steel-related manufacturers and the Southeast Chicago community, and sought to involve as many groups as possible in implementation. The task force recommended area development and retraining strategies (City of Chicago, 1986a). Moreover, it realized that even if a mature industry such as steel became a world class competitor again, all the workers who were displaced from that industry would not be reemployed, and the positive economic impact of such a diminished industry on nearby communities would not be as extensive as the negative impacts from the earlier closings. Steel task force initiatives included a comprehensive program of technology application and research, an increased business retention effort in Southeast Chicago, actions to ease the impact of projected electricity rate increases, business development and major infrastructure investments, and a mobilization of resources to respond to the needs of dislocated workers. Finally, the task force identified multiple actors to implement both sets of recommendations: local industrial councils; public/private commissions; a regional steel network of unions, churches, and municipalities; and the mayor.

Many recommendations were acted upon during the life of the steel task force and in the ensuing 2 years. The task force helped to resolve a court suit (of which the City was party) against USX for closing its South Works plant. The result was the temporary saving of 800 jobs and the retention of the site as an industrial park, instead of a site for residential or commercial purposes.[6] The task force and the mayor effectively lobbied for the Keyworth Initiative—a federally funded program to advance research into revolutionary steel-making technology—and in February 1987, convened a steel technology conference with Argonne Laboratories and the University of Illinois at Chicago, which brought together steel management, labor, universities, and the public sector. A number of steel-related companies were aided, and the City received a major EDA grant in September 1987 to design specialized programs for steel service centers and for dislocated workers.

The Apparel and Fashion Industry Task Force confronted a smaller, less organized industry. Chicago's apparel industry consists of one major menswear producer, a few midsize women's wear firms, and a diversity of small firms. The industry's future strength appeared to be in high value-added, short batch, women's designer clothes. In fact, there were a number of new Chicago designers coming into prominence (Weiss, 1988). Yet, although the steel industry and labor representatives had a clear understanding and common outlook on these issues even before the task force began, bringing the key apparel industry actors together was itself a major step. Compounding the fragmentation within the industry was the highly competitive nature of apparel producers: Executives and designers needed to be persuaded that cooperation was important, and that their mutual interest lay in assuring one another's survival.

In response, the task force's recommendations called for the formation of a permanent Apparel Industry Board. Representing the same diverse constituencies as the task force, this body would continue the cooperative research and activities begun during the task force and work with the City and other actors to implement task force recommendations: a business incubator for designers and displaced firms, new technologies that could be shared cooperatively, increased training and retraining opportunities for apparel production workers, and a "Buy Chicago" program that would encourage the consumption of locally made garments (City of Chicago, 1987a).

The concrete accomplishments of the Apparel and Fashion Industry Task Force have ranged from convening Fashion Business Seminars for new designers to City lobbying for fair trade for the apparel industry. The City provided first-year funding for the Apparel Industry Board and, with partial funding from companies and unions, in 1988 concluded a preliminary feasibility study for an apparel incubator building that could also house firms displaced by downtown growth.

In spite of concrete initiatives, Chicago's industry task forces have failed initially to ignite a critical level of community, labor, and business commitment. The Economic Development Commission, a public advisory body made up of major Chicago business leaders, never set up a formal subcommittee to oversee the recommendations of the steel task force, in part motivated by the deep-seated belief that manufacturing is a dying sector. Many community groups and labor activists feel that the task forces did not go far enough—for example, the City failed to use eminent domain to landbank the closed Wisconsin Steel site or the closing LTV facility. Some unions and companies felt that the City did not lobby hard enough for trade protection and was unwilling to close down apparel sweatshops.

Conclusion

We have tried to examine how local development politics in Chicago became a context for a reaction and response to economic restructuring. Table 9.1 summarizes the two case studies, with particular attention focused on issue characteristics. As a point of comparison, it includes information on an important case of industrial retention we have discussed elsewhere, the Playskool plant closing (Giloth & Mier, 1986). Although it is largely self-explanatory, several points, taken together, highlight the political dimension of Chicago's efforts at economic development innovation. Specifically, we are concerned with the elements that emphasize network building: the role of leadership, communication within networks, and the potential for political mobilization (see Chapter 10).

The Playskool and industrial displacement cases originated in community advocacy. Beginning in a web of diverse organizations,

Table 9.1 Characteristics of Local Industrial Policy Issue

	Playskool	Industrial Displacement	Industry Task Forces
Origin	Community/labor network	Single-community organization	City initiative
Time frame	Immediate	Immediate/medium term	Long-term
Scope	Single firm, single neighborhood	2-3 neighborhoods/multiple projects	Industry/region
City stake	IRB agreement	Zoning regulation	Planning/incentives
Problem solving	Advocacy, court action, negotiation	Advocacy/research, legislation, negotiation	Planning, lobbying, marketing
Development ideas	Early warning, public trust, local ownership	Balanced-growth manufacturing	Manufacturing industrial complex
Allocation of costs/benefits	More workers and community benefits	Protected industries and jobs, developer contribution	Promotion of manufacturing
Challenges	Network building, public dialogue	Framing the problem, public dialogue	Framing the problem, public dialogue, implementation
Outcome	Settlement redevelopment	PMD ordinance, redesigned projects, manufacturing development	Many specific initiatives and responses
Problems	City/network friction, intracity friction	Developer/Tribune opposition, intracity consensus building	Lack of city/public mobilization
Mode of collaboration	Dynamic, multiple centers, mobilization	Dynamic, multiple centers, mobilization	Formalistic and institutional, city-centered, missing actors
Leadership	Strong, multiple, diffused	Weak, multiple, diffused	Weak, government, institutional

the process of network building was easier, and the potential for the emergence of multiple leaders greater. Because the closing of the Playskool plant was a real threat, while industrial displacement was more long-term (at least in Clybourn/Goose Island), the Playskool mobilization was not as difficult but not as lasting. Opposition to the closing was facilitated by the formulation of colorful metaphors and organizing language ("local ownership," "early warning," "breach of trust"). An industrial displacement strategy could build on the same language ("manufacturing," "blue-collar"), enrich it and link it with broader development metaphors ("balanced growth"), and broaden the network of participants (more "grass-roots," "labor," and "citywide participation"). Each case had multiple leaders, multiple centers of impetus, and broader support than the immediate neighborhood in which the major events were occurring.

A major impediment to this networking, however, is the challenge of social integration across racial boundaries. In their own ways, each case illustrates the difficulty of building multiracial alliances: It is easiest in the most concrete situation, that is, the one linking African-American and Latino workers, their neighborhoods, unions, and local groups—the Playskool plant closing. With the effort to develop Planned Manufacturing Districts in the Clybourn Corridor area, ties among African-American public housing tenants, Latino neighborhoods to the west, small businesses, and labor slowly emerged during the years of organizing. Yet these experiences did expand the language of development across racial boundaries such that metaphors like "balanced growth" and "linked development" had common meaning for different groups.

The industry task forces were, in important respects, the most abstract and politically elusive, and thus were the most difficult to evaluate. They were not the product of an immediate crisis, although each derived from decade-long sectoral disinvestment. As such, the task forces did not conduct their work in a mobilization atmosphere. To this extent, they more easily involved those formal organizations with planning and research orientations—units of government, universities, and business and civic organizations that routinely participated in civic study efforts. The greatest difficulty for these task forces was framing their problems in such a way as to build a constituency and articulate a distinctive and viable local government role. Nonetheless, they enriched public awareness that development opportunities remained, even in shrinking economic sectors.

Taken together, all three cases focused local political debate on industrial development. They testified for a development policy that was fair, redistributive, open, and participatory. Broad-based constituencies supported forceful political action, such as the suit against Playskool's parent corporation, Hasbro Industries. In the five-person aldermanic race in the area of the Clybourn Corridor, the two leading candidates made industrial preservation central to their campaign planks. Throughout his own re-election campaign, Mayor Washington maintained a focus on industrial retention and on a nuts-and-bolts approach to industrial development, even in the face of strong criticism from the *Chicago Tribune,* the city's largest newspaper. Finally, before his untimely death in November 1987, Mayor Washington planned to inject the basic philosophy and concrete approach of his development program into national politics, working first through the U.S. Conference of Mayors and then through the Democratic Party's platform-shaping process. He was confident that he could promise broad-based popular support for an agenda emphasizing people, jobs, and industry.

How does local experimentation connect and accumulate to become effective nationally? How do alternative ideas and networks expand beyond local boundaries, without becoming formalistic or diluted in meaning? More specifically, are Chicago's circumstances unique, especially given the extraordinary political vision and charisma of Harold Washington, the extenuated period of political conflict and mobilization (i.e., Council Wars) between 1983 and 1986, and Chicago's legacy of machine politics and racial segregation?

A number of recent works have begun to map the terrain of alternative economic development, although they have not directly focused on the diffusion issue (Bruyn & Meehan, 1987; Clavel, 1985; Fitzgerald, 1991; Fitzgerald & Simmons, 1991; Clavel & Wiewel, 1991). Distinctive responses to economic restructuring are occurring across the United States under very different political circumstances. Moreover, there is a growing infrastructure of technical assistance centers, organizational networks, and foundations that serves community economic development—one that may both expand networks and control local experimentation (Pierce & Steinbach, 1987).

Building local to national political connections is already occurring through professional associations and political structures, such as the Democratic Party and the U.S. Conference of Mayors. These routes are important but limited. Recent sociological thinking about community decision making underscores the importance of interorganizational linkages or social networks that connect resource-mobilizing individuals (Bellah, Madsen, Sullivan, Swidler, & Tipton, 1985; Brown & Detterman, 1987; Wiewel & Hunter, 1985). By exploring feminist consciousness-raising, working conditions, ethical values, and family life, social psychologists are increasingly examining the processes by which small support groups begin to network regionally and nationally (Gilligan, 1982; Rubin, 1985). These perspectives on expanding local connections complement and nourish more empirical work looking at a variety of modern populist social movements (Boyte & Riessman, 1986; Boyte, Booth, & Max, 1986).

Local experimentation that responds to economic restructuring in more equitable ways faces additional challenges. First, the downtown/neighborhood dialectic, although powerful, is limited. It tends to generate either/or trade-offs and muddled thinking about economic growth, development, and equity. Second, collaborative efforts among community, labor, and government often leave a residual of ill will that comes with compromise, thus giving incentive for urban actors to pursue more solitary advocacy. Third, no adequate body of organizing, public administration, or leadership theory exists to guide these collaborations through the thicket of community conflict. Fourth, experimental projects require long gestation and implementation periods that often exceed community political cycles and media attention spans. Fifth, experimentation that challenges economic restructuring eventually evokes opposition from the "powers that be," which in turn tests collaborative efforts even more, thereby aggravating all of the above. Finally, local governments have limits, yet experimental action raises expectations.

Notes

1. Our framework for understanding Chicago's experiments with economic development and the role of networks, ideas, and metaphors derives from Clavel (1985), Evans and Boyte (1985), Schon (1980), and Whyte (1983). Our thinking on how social inventions diffuse has been influenced by Goodwyn (1987) and Schon (1971).

2. Equity planning articulates the primacy of specific populations in need (e.g., the poor and disenfranchised) in planning goal statements, policy plans, or reformed government processes (e.g., zoning, capital budgeting).

3. Our case studies draw extensively from articles and reports written with associates with whom we collaborated during this period: Stephen Alexander, John J. Betancur, Donna Ducharme, Margie Gonwa, Joshua Lerner, Lynn McCormick, Kari Moe, Raffaella Nanetti, Irene Sherr, and Howard Stanback.

4. In his 1989 race for mayor, Richard M. Daley campaigned *against* PMDs. Within 6 months of his inauguration, he was supporting legislation creating the Clybourn Corridor PMD.

5. This development became a victim both of Mayor Washington's death and a depressed real estate economy. The site still awaits development.

6. South Works remained open until 1991. Some may look at that as failure, but we believe the 6-year prolongation of its life was an enormous social and economic victory for Southeast Chicago.

10 | Cooperative Leadership for Community Problem Solving

with

ROBERT P. GILOTH

This chapter, along with the next, summarizes the effort under Harold Washington to forge a social justice-based local development policy. It reexamines several of the cases presented in earlier chapters, as well as some new ones, through the lens of leadership. It argues that much of the process of developing an alternative agenda represented a new type of leadership in action, one more participatory in nature. It calls this bottom-up leadership "cooperative leadership," and it explores its characteristic attributes. Finally, it looks at ways cooperative leadership can be developed.

Introduction

In 1983 we probably would have denied the importance of leadership, perceiving it an elite construct. That belief was challenged in Harold Washington's campaign for mayor. Certainly, the campaign rode the back of a broad-based social movement. Yet, the movement itself probably would have faltered without his charismatic ability to inspire people, to draw out the ideas for change percolating through the community and to rivet people's attention on them, to find a language that helped diverse people see common circumstances and possibilities, and to build a collective faith in local action. Notwithstanding, there remained a tendency to view Washington as an aberration, one of those too rare individuals for whom the cloak of leadership might almost uniquely fit.

Almost a decade later, we now believe in leadership—although not the type written about in most biographies. Mayor Washington's death in 1987 was a watershed. No one has stepped in to fill the void, yet new ideas continue to well up from communities, alliances get forged, problems get tackled, and solutions invented. We believe this is a leadership of a new sort, evident in many of the stories in this book. We call it cooperative leadership and juxtapose it against public/private partnerships and other elite conceptions of leadership.

In the ensuing sections, we elaborate on our notion of cooperative leadership in five ways. First, we present some examples of what we consider good and bad civic leadership to help sharpen the distinctions we draw between "partnership" and "cooperation." We then step back and try to define cooperative leadership more precisely. Next, we focus on the personal competencies we see exhibited by people who excel as cooperating leaders. We then address the question of whether cooperative leadership can be developed. We conclude with a proposal for a new civic leadership agenda, built on our faith in the possibility of local development generated through participatory processes that pay attention to values of social justice.

Civic Leadership in Action

Rich and complex communities need leaders to build common agendas among diverse sectors, organizations, and populations of the community. These leaders must mirror community diversity, its neighborhoods, government, unions, businesses, and universities. Some will be professionals, while others will be emergent neighborhood leaders. Four examples illustrate the challenges for today's civic leadership. The first two illustrate cooperative leadership and the latter two, classic partnership approaches.

A Plant Closing

Our first example involves the Playskool plant closing (Giloth & Mier, 1986). The Playskool factory announced in 1984 the lay-off of 750 workers and its relocation to the East Coast. Community outcry over the impending closing was loud and demanding. Neighborhood businesses felt insulted. Workers and union officials scrambled to negotiate a severance package. Community, industry, and labor advocates organized to fight this "breach of trust," as it was termed. City government was supportive but cautious, having never challenged firms to make good on their promises of jobs in return for subsidies. The broader community was volatile.

Generally, nothing immobilizes local government more than a plant closing—to attempt to intervene raises the specter of government interference in the market. Yet, the Playskool case saw joint strategizing among business groups, labor, community representatives, and government officials aimed at crafting an unusual agenda. In an unprecedented action, the City of Chicago filed suit against the company to prevent the closing. Simultaneously, grass-roots organizations launched a national boycott. Ultimately, the City negotiated added benefits and kept 100 Playskool jobs in Chicago for another year. Throughout the struggle, the business community at large remained silent, and in their silence, supportive.

This agenda required trust and cooperation among often alien business, community, and government organizations as they played out new and untested roles. This cooperation created the context for innovative action. Together, a broad array of participants brought about a step forward in corporate accountability. Today, the old facility is owned by a joint venture, including the local industrial council, an active player in the coalition. It is almost fully occupied, with multiple tenants employing around 600 people, although it remains economically fragile.

A Sports Stadium

A second example of civic leadership concerns a new football stadium and where to locate it (City of Chicago, 1987b; Mier &

Moe, 1991; Mier, 1993). Like many cities, Chicago faced the poker game of stadium mania, in which cities ante up public dollars while sports teams threaten to move elsewhere (Mier, 1992). In 1986 downtown leaders and city officials announced a plan for a lake-front stadium on park land for the Chicago Bears football team. Immediately, civic and environmental groups objected, editorials lambasted private profit from public land, and candidates in the upcoming mayoral race took potshots at each other.

The mayor appointed a three-person stadium review commit-tee to undertake a public review of several possible stadium sites, including the lakefront. The ensuing process involved public hearings, neighborhood meetings, discussions with de-velopers, and intense debate. In particular, a west-side commu-nity was divided as to whether it wanted a stadium that would displace as many as 1,000 people, but might leverage new housing and economic development. On the one side was a long-time African-American community leader and her organiza-tion, which believed that by negotiating for a new stadium it could also obtain development resources that the long-neglected neighborhood desperately needed. On the other side was a coalition of local African-American ministers and their congre-gations, who fought stadium planning and proposed their own neighborhood redevelopment plan.

Here was an urban problem demanding cooperative leadership. One faction of a poor, African-American community wanted urban renewal. The other opposed it. Both sides took risks, and their conflicting efforts created a level of public interest that, in the end, gave credence to tough negotiating and community involvement in future renewal efforts. Ultimately, squabbling among owners of sports teams, not community conflict, undermined the football stadium scenario. Two years later, a unified community reached an agreement with two other team owners for a smaller, basketball/hockey stadium (Mier, 1991b). The team owners now are partners with the community in the construction of new housing.

A World's Fair

Unfortunately, community elites often prefer top-down, secre-tive solutions more than those that build from the ground up. This mirrors the skewed distribution of community power and resources, and the preference of many elites to deal only with people like themselves. Although this style may have met little resistance in the past, many communities are now resisting centralized, nonparticipatory solutions (Haider, 1986; Chicago Project, 1987; Wiewel, 1987). This fallacy of centralization, or we what have coined "The World's Fair Syndrome," is an affliction found in many cities, often disguised under the rubric of public/private partnerships (Porter & Sweet, 1984; Judd & Parkinson, 1990). Recounting the rise and fall of Chicago's proposed 1992 World's Fair illuminates a formidable obstacle to our conception of civic leadership.

Chicago business elites and public officials created a 1992 World's Fair plan in an act considered a model of public/private partnership (Shlay & Giloth, 1987). Winning fair designation by the Bureau of International Exposition was the easy part. Fair designation enraged many civic and neighborhood leaders, who feared residential and business displacement, tax increases, and environmental damage to the lakefront, and who opposed secretive development planning that used public parks. Instead of opening up planning when confronted by these concerns, however, business leaders closed ranks.

Upon his election, Mayor Washington, while nominally supporting the fair, called for increased citizen input and minimal public investment and risk. Corporate leaders failed to alter their course, and called for the mayor to remain the leader of the partnership structure. Instead, he backed away and encouraged wide-open public dialogue. After much acrimonious debate and many conflicting revenue, attendance, and investment projections, state legislative leaders turned down additional funding for the fair (Mier, 1993). Chicago's 1992 World's Fair plan was dead.

Was this outcome inevitable? Many fair critics admit that they were not altogether opposed to the fair but were dead set against closed and arrogant planning that put the public at risk. Big projects initiated by community elites are not necessarily suspect in themselves; often, this is the only way they can happen. But centralized, nonaccountable planning just will not work in many communities, and was the primary reason for opposition to the Chicago fair.

A Neighborhood Development Program

In another example of the World's Fair Syndrome, a philanthropic agency proposed to organize neighborhood development in Chicago by constructing a "development engine" that would facilitate the production of economic development deals.

The same group had co-sponsored a neighborhood development report the year before, which emphasized participatory planning across all segments of the community (Bradford, 1987; Capraro, Ditton, & Giloth, 1985). Courting the business community and local government in secret, the agency proposed a new centralized entity with three parts to drive the project: a seed capital fund; a small business development lender; and co-developer expertise and financing for neighborhood organizations.

This centralized solution—extremely attractive to downtown business leaders—quickly floundered because beneath its gloss were untested design assumptions, minimal neighborhood input, and competition with another business equity fund and community banks. Initial support wavered as public sector and neighborhood leaders left out of the process expressed their concerns. Fortunately, these leaders persevered and encouraged instead the creation of a neighborhood capacity development fund, the Fund for Community Development (Giloth, Orlebeke, Tichnell, & Wright, 1992).

What Is Cooperative Leadership?

For planning to be effective, communities require leadership to open up civic visions, to build new social relationships and institutions, and to solve social problems ("Chicago Project," 1987). Yet, leadership largely is an alien concept in planning discourse and education. By taking the conception of leadership for granted, planners too often fall back on limiting, elite-based structures of community problem solving, like those advancing the Chicago's World's Fair or the development engine. We believe there is another broad-based conception of leadership that is more compatible with an inclusionary and process-oriented tradition in planning, community development, and public administration (Forester, 1989).

With the dominance of the Weberian tradition on the understanding of the role of organization in society (Morgan, 1987), it is not surprising that planners and public officials most comfortably associate leadership with authority (Hunt, 1984). Thus, the literature on civic leadership concentrates on either individual leaders (e.g., Caro, 1971; Frisbie, 1991) or public/private partnerships (Judd & Parkinson, 1990). As a consequence, two images of community leadership are prevalent. The first are individuals who run roughshod over bureaucratic impediments, or who confront institutions to change community policies and values, some supporting urban redevelopment plans (Committee for Economic Development, 1982) and some opposing them (Alinsky, 1971; Krumholz & Forester, 1990). The second image, considered the model for the 1980s and beyond, is groups of elites who promote local growth, or charity, or respond to social crises, working hand in glove with a city's elected leaders. This latter image often is enmeshed in a leadership structure like a civic committee or an "arms length" nonprofit agency, applying tried-and-true "business-like" approaches. The unifying and generative metaphor is "partnership."

We believe that partnerships are inherently limiting in three respects. First, they generally represent a structural and generic response to what often is an particular problem (Perry, 1990). For example, what development official has seen a problem the past few years for which tax increment financing hasn't been offered as a solution? Second, the partnership approach often concentrates on a monumental project as the engine for development. In Chicago, in recent years, Mayor Richard Daley has offered up a $1-billion doubling of the convention center, a $2-billion casino complex, and a $7-billion new airport. Finally, partnerships narrowly focus on the production of wealth, ignoring redistributive and social justice dimensions of urban problems (Krumholz, 1984; Judd & Parkinson, 1990). Because of these limitations, a third type of leadership is emerging in many communities.

This new leadership is derived from collaborative efforts to create solutions to difficult and controversial problems, ones with seemingly intractable conflicts of group interests. The metaphor of "cooperation" replaces "partnership," and connotes bringing diverse interests to the table to engage in "social invention" (Whyte, 1982; Osborne, 1988; Mier & Fitzgerald, 1991). We believe many of the initiatives in Chicago during the tenure of Mayor Washington exemplify this. We call this new leadership "cooperative leadership." Such collaborations occur in task forces, ad hoc networks, innovative organizations, and partnerships born of struggle. Impressive examples, by no means unique to Chicago, are when workers and owners, bankers and neighborhoods, or local governments and community coalitions jointly create solutions to commonly perceived and experienced problems (Trist, 1981; Whyte, 1983; Fitzgerald & Simmons, 1991; Fitzgerald, 1991).

Cooperative problem solving is essential for tackling the planning problems of today's cities. Communities are complicated, diverse, and undergoing rapid change, all of which create unexpected problems and demand new approaches to action (Trist, 1981). Urban economies, for example, have dynamic sectors, relative manufacturing decline, fragmentation of megaindustries, spreading downtowns, and increasing absentee ownership, small business growth, and self-employment (e.g., Piore & Sabel, 1984). Parallel with these trends, communities are experiencing the dismantling of the welfare state—its resources, problem definitions, and bureaucracies—and the proliferation of "independent sector" organizations that do everything from self-help and day care to neighborhood economic development (Harrington, 1985).

Another parallel development is the unraveling of local political alignments and power bases, coupled with growing empowerment of African-Americans, Latinos, and neighborhoods (Clavel, 1986; Shlay & Holupka, 1993). Civic leadership requires new roles and skills to build bridges among diverse interests, in addition to relying upon the traditional leadership skills of vision, strategy, motivation, and communication (Bennis & Nanus, 1985; Gardner, 1987). It must succeed at team-building and, as Schon has phrased it, "reflection in action," or the constant reexamination of social values, group dynamics, problems, and goals (Schon, 1980).

In this context, the structures of cooperative problem solving are equally important. Recent sociological thinking about community decision making underscores the importance of interorganizational linkages or loosely coupled social networks that connect resource-mobilizing individuals. How widespread, representative, and interconnected community leadership is affects a community's capacity to engage in collaborative problem solving. Deep divisions in community life, such as race or class, may limit the potential for cooperative leadership in the short run

(Brown & Detterman, 1987). Such networks may become a long-term community goal.

Cooperative leadership is not appropriate for all problems. Many issues require community confrontation, elite initiative, or national-level leadership. Community problems that might benefit from this type of civic leadership involve a multiplicity of interests, are at a crisis stage, and are microcosms of bigger issues. Examples include land-use conflict, parent involvement in education reform, and the development of new industries.

Discussion of civic leadership raises fundamental questions about democracy and social change. Some critics argue that citizenship, not leadership, is today's real challenge (Bradford, 1985; Giloth, 1985), and that a "professionalized" leadership may undermine grass-roots action (Bookchin, 1987). Without resolving these debates, we acknowledge that our conception of cooperative leadership, if unreflective or misapplied, may become cooptive, gloss over inequities and institutional responsibilities, or paralyze grass-roots empowerment. We believe it also has potential for building progressive coalitions and solutions to seemingly intractable planning problems facing communities today. Yet, what does it take to make it work?

Competencies for Cooperative Leadership

Cooperative leadership, as we have defined it, can solve community problems. But such leadership will require new or underemployed competencies that leadership-training programs often overlook. By elaborating on appropriate leadership skills and educational models, we hope to aid communities wishing to increase their problem-solving capacities.

We outline 11 leadership competencies that fall into two categories: team-building leadership and tools for innovative communication. Although our examples are only from Chicago and are limited to the arena of community economic development, they illustrate the range of problems that a number of different communities face. The first 5 competencies emphasize collaboration; the second 6 involve communication tasks.

Collaboration Competencies

Organizing. Cooperating leaders should be action-oriented, not waiting in the wings to receive invitations or bless solutions proposed by others. The community organizer role is indicative because organizers are adept at making sense of open-ended and muddled situations: They study the environment, identify major issues, and take action. At heart, the organizer is a coalition-builder attempting to spur joint action around concrete objectives.[1]

Problem Identification. Problems are not simply givens ready for the solution mill (Schon, 1979, 1980). They often represent an ambiguous mix of values, facts, and causal relationships. In some cases, the challenges in problem identification may be the community's or organization's inability or unwillingness to focus, not the obscurity of the problem. Cooperating leaders should be advocates for problems and community attention (Whyte, 1992).

A recent example of problem identification involved an industrial district in Chicago's Clybourn Corridor whose factories and blue-collar jobs were being pushed out of the city by high-income commercial and residential development (Giloth & Betancur, 1988; Giloth & Mier, 1988; Fasenfest, 1989). Few community leaders believed industrial displacement was a real problem; it was just the outcome of a normal market process. The local industrial council spent 2 years documenting the problem, fighting individual displacement cases, and educating the public to recognize industrial displacement as a threat to the local economy (Ducharme, 1991).

Getting Unstuck. An all-too-familiar scenario is the promising project or organization that goes nowhere. What happens is that the group doing the project gets stuck: Issues are unresolved, energy dissipates, hard-and-fast lines of conflict are drawn, and participation fades. Reasons for these impasses are many: Sponsoring organizations are weak but unwilling to give up control; participants have dramatically different perspectives on what issues matter or how to proceed; the effort lacks resources; or the project is simply taking on an extraordinarily difficult problem. Disbanding in some circumstances may be the only way to rescue creative energies.

Getting projects unstuck requires leadership, because it is easy for participants to walk away and admonish everyone to get their acts together. It is also easy to attend meetings diligently, with smug resignation about the outcome. Getting unstuck requires understanding why things are at a standstill and how to motivate the people involved to turn them around.

Negotiation. Forging agreement among diverse interests is the bread and butter of our cooperative leaders. Whether running meetings, exploring problems, or negotiating solutions, they must turn conflict into creative energy, cynicism about backroom deals into commitment, and intransigence into a willingness to discuss mutual interests. The literature on negotiation and its application is flourishing.

The negotiations between the developer of a proposed high-income commercial project, called River Lofts, and local industrialists achieved a balance between new development and protection for industry. After being convinced by local politicians that continued opposition would be bad for business, industries came to the bargaining table in good faith, attempting to understand the developer's constraints while clearly communicating their fears about nearby residential uses (Giloth & Betancur, 1988). In the short run, they got the protection they wanted. In the longer run, the real estate market turned down, and the building sits empty.

Politics. A number of cities are opening up government and exploring new public roles for citizens who previously were shut out of local governance (Clavel, 1986; Beneviste, 1989). To function in these situations requires cooperating leaders to strategize with neighborhood constituencies, city councils, government agencies, and other civic leaders; operate in dynamic, rough-and-tumble political processes; understand the tension between political transformation and administrative reform; and have a political vision.

Planning for a new football stadium in Chicago illustrates this political dimension. Corporate interests wanted a top-down process, with the mayor at the top—pulling the strings and risking major political capital in the name of private development. City officials stressed that there were multiple neighborhood and citywide actors in addition to the mayor, and that these players, often in conflict or creative tension, needed to be included in stadium planning.

Communication Competencies

Comparative Knowledge. An unsettling lesson is that the best of leaders are often creative copycats. In most instances they do not have the time, resources, or knowledge to identify problems or design solutions from scratch. There is a large body of work that discusses the limitations of such comprehensive rationality (March, 1982; Forester, 1989; Mier & Bingham, 1993). The civic leader must have access to a collective memory of cases, situations, processes, and outcomes that can be adjusted for their fit or nonfit to new situations. Collective memory, however, is only as good as the ability to judge fit. Designers of a stadium site selection process, for example, emphasized an open public process because they knew how the World's Fair planning had floundered from secrecy.

Style of Communication. Communication establishes relationships as well as conveys information (Forester, 1989). Building new coalitions means operating on other people's turfs under diverse rules. Civic leaders must be prepared to help chip away at the communication barriers that may distort collaborative efforts. Cross-cultural communication among African-Americans, Latinos, Asians, and whites requires sensitivity to the building blocks of communication, history, and politics. Gender adds another communicative dimension (Evans, 1979; Tannen, 1990). Discovery of common concerns and objectives can help turn group differences into recognition that "the enemy is not us."

Metaphors. Metaphors help communicate the concreteness and richness of meaning (Miller, 1985; Morgan, 1987). In so doing, they help invent solutions. A metaphor often used to portray neighborhood economies is the "leaky bucket." It suggests how income leaks out of even the poorest community through absentee owners, disinvesting banks, or employees who live elsewhere. Accordingly, improving neighborhood economies requires "plugging the leaks" with neighborhood ownership and responsible banking practices. Metaphors also make strategies or events comprehensible (Mier & Bingham, 1993). In the Playskool plant closing example cited earlier, "breach of trust" captured the "breaking" of public morals that justified unusual public action.

Stories. Stories add a time and change dimension (Kaplan, 1986; Morgan, 1987; Delgado, 1989). Stories have convinced nonbelievers about industrial gentrification by conveying what happened when firms got upscale neighbors, or how a building attracted industrial users, even though developers argued there was no industrial market. Stories make business incubation understandable: A young designer knits designer dresses at home until the first show, then gets a few employees and moves into an apparel incubator; eventually, further growth leads to more employees and a manufacturing loft.

Data. Data offer a powerful method to communicate information and ideas about projects or problems. Several types of quantitative information are useful. One of the most common is the budget of a project or organization. Budgets present sources of revenue and expenditures and represent assumptions or priorities—for instance, market penetration or staff allocation. When these assumptions are altered, different bottom lines result, which in turn provoke new questions.

A good example of the public balance sheet was the negotiation between the City of Chicago and the World's Fair Authority to spell out commitments for public dollars.[2] As the balance sheet was explored, hidden assumptions about public responsibilities surfaced, which in actuality added approximately $150 million to the fair's financing and ultimately cast doubts about the project's feasibility (Mier, 1993).

Technology. There have been enormous strides in downscaling sophisticated technology capable of facilitating complex communication and networking. Even the most basic grass-roots organization office today frequently has capacity for facsimile transmission, desktop publishing, or computerized contact management, and electronic networks are becoming a more common tool.

Leadership Skills Summarized

A fundamental premise of cooperative leadership is the notion that all affected parties should have a place at the problem-solving table. Getting to the table is one goal—something addressed in Harold Washington's Chicago through politics. Being effective once at the table is another. We have reviewed 11 competencies that we believe cooperative leaders need to possess: organizing, problem identification, getting unstuck, negotiation, politics, comparative knowledge, style of communication, metaphors, stories, data, and technology. We have seen these traits in people comfortable in boardrooms, as well as those comfortable in church basements. But we just as often have seen them missing in both places. That raises the question of how people become competent cooperative leaders. Recognizing that many of these skills are developed in the trenches, we argue that they can be developed.

Developing Community Leadership

There is broad agreement that communities should vigorously develop civic leaders. Foundations and philanthropic organizations have had national conferences to define leadership, education models, and the roles foundations should play. While many communities have undertaken initiatives such as Leadership Atlanta or Leadership Greater Chicago, others have pursued grass-roots leadership training, such as the Highlander Folk Center in Tennessee (Schardt, 1986; Boyte, 1980). Few communities, however, have initiated explicit efforts to alter the community characteristics that influence collaborative problem solving (Brown & Detterman, 1987).

Current approaches to leadership education vary little, and there are basically four models of training: university courses in leadership, usually administered by business or public affairs programs; mid-career leadership programs sponsored by universities or training institutes; leadership training provided as part of community service programs; and leadership incubation programs, sponsored by foundations or coalitions, which enroll promising individuals and hone their leadership skills.

For all the attention given leadership, there are few evaluations of leadership training. Time frames are long; measuring successful leadership is difficult; and programs inevitably enroll the cream of the crop. Our sense is that current training overemphasizes university settings, great leaders, and the already successful members of the community, omitting diverse populations and the skill-building and networking development that are supportive of cooperative problem solving. Although neighborhood organizations often produce the type of civic leaders we advocate, often they receive little support for performing this important community function.

Without answering all the conceivable questions about cooperative leadership, we will attempt, in the remainder of this section, to discuss the suggested components of a broad leadership education: formal and informal learning, and career development. In the concluding section of this chapter, we present our ideas of how a community can design a leadership and training program. During our time as members of the Harold Washington administration, we each placed increasing value on the development of people working for and with us, and tried to play the role of mentor. That we take the time to dwell on the means of training cooperative leaders is probably the best indication of the importance we now place on leadership.

Learning to Lead

Leadership comprises skills and experiences required to interpret new situations, invent explanations and solutions, and motivate group action. Acquiring these abilities can be facilitated through formal courses, field experiences, and informal learning situations. Field or studio courses and continuing-education workshops are coming back in favor as a means to expose potential leaders to undefined problems and organizational contexts.

Informal learning through study groups, volunteer civic work, and political campaigns enables testing of leadership skills and exposure to group processes. The concept of "free spaces" within society, such as churches and neighborhoods, in which new values, cultures, and organizational forms are nourished, has been instrumental in nurturing leaders for the civil rights, neighborhood, and women's movements (Evans & Boyte, 1985). Again, free spaces are largely unrecognized, except by historians of social move-ments, for their role in leadership development (Morris, 1984).

Career Ladders

A common fallacy is the belief in one correct career path, frequently defined by status as a "profession." Indeed, coopera-tive leaders come from all directions, out of widely different careers, and have great variety in the breadth of their civic involvement. What distinguishes cooperative leaders is their legitimacy—achieved through hard work, risk-taking, and atten-tion to social values. A civic sense of career goes beyond place of work or profession. A cooperating leader's legitimacy is based on participation in networks, garnering trust and respect that over time extend beyond neighborhood, union, or business to the broader civic arena.

There is a trade-off between salary and status and the quality and accumulation of experience. Working for a neighborhood organization, for example, guarantees wide exposure to issues, constituencies, roles, and responsibilities that is unmatched. Yet burnout is an occupational liability in these organizations, and sometimes the biggest lesson they teach is survival. One disturb-ing outcome of increased public support of them is that neigh-borhood organizations are professionalizing and, in some cases, losing touch with their home bases.

A Leadership Program for Tomorrow

Most communities think about civic leadership in simple terms: strategic plans, funding, classes, and workshops. These are impor-tant, but not sufficient to create a leadership with a propensity for cooperative problem solving. We offer five ideas about how communities can nurture cooperative leadership. An important premise underlying our thoughts is that developing leadership is not amenable to one centralized solution.

1. Recognize the "free spaces," informal networks and organi-zations where leadership development is occurring. Provide support for these free spaces. Coalitions of groups should be given resources, just to promote networking among members.

2. Identify appropriate educational resources and changes in curriculum and field studies to address the civic leadership competencies that we have emphasized. New educational forums may be needed to nourish grass-roots leadership.

3. Create opportunities for young people to gain concrete community experiences, starting at a young age. Perhaps a community-sponsored VISTA program would make sense. Urge other institutions, whether churches corporations, unions, or political parties, to create similar opportunities.

4. Encourage leadership incubators, like an urban version of the Highlander Center, which truly bridges race, occupations, and organizational affiliations. Opportunities should also be created for established leaders to expand networks and to discover commonalities.

5. Reflect on the effectiveness of community decision making. Is the community succumbing to the Worlds Fair Syndrome? Does community divisiveness run deep? Are problems getting solved, and how? Is leadership training working?

Civic leaders for tomorrow will make a mark in their communities if they recognize that centralized solutions, beneficent paternalism, and old boy networks close rather than open opportunities to solve pressing urban problems. We have suggested that the community organizer serves as a role model, and that civic leaders will need to become adept at formulating and promoting collaborative community planning. We believe the attribute most clearly separating cooperative leadership from more elite partnership models of leadership is the willingness to reach for inclusivity, even in the face of the tremendous challenges of communication across race and class lines. In the final analysis, we have come to realize that social justice goals, like those pursued during the tenure of Mayor Harold Washington, can only be reached with the continued development of cooperative leaders.

Notes

1. For a humorous reflection on organizing, see Kennard (1982).

2. Intergovernmental Agreement, State of Illinois, City of Chicago, and the Chicago World's Fair 1992 Authority. May 31, 1984. Copies of this agreement are available in the Chicago Historical Society.

11 | Community Development and Diversity

This final chapter completes the effort at summarizing the experience of formulating and delivering the Harold Washington agenda. It sets the context for evaluation by telling a story of developing a neighborhood infrastructure program. It then focuses on the difficulty of evaluating a program with numerous small projects, but nonetheless attempts an impressionistic evaluation. It concludes that evaluation with an observation about the enormous impact of race on development. It illustrates that impact with four brief sketches of race-related development issues. Finally, it speculates about the meaning of the Washington experience beyond Chicago.

Introduction

I have tried using stories to convey the effort of forging a social justice-based development agenda in Chicago, an effort that culminated during the 1983-1987 mayoral tenure of Harold Washington. Many of the stories focused on changing the terms of public debate about development priorities. Beyond the 1983 campaign itself, the debate took many forms. Cases or stories talked about in this book include the reexamination and ultimate rejection of the World's Fair; the fight to retain steel production at the South Works and the enlistment of civic leaders to work with labor and community leaders on a steel strategy; the lawsuit to impede the Playskool closing; and the creation of the Apparel Task Force.

As public support for new priorities emerged, it was necessary to frame them in ways that aided ongoing decision making. The development of a strategic plan, *Chicago Works Together* (*CWT*), was crucial but did not stand alone. As has been told in earlier chapters, it had emerged from Chicago's neighborhood-based development community through *The CWED Platform*, and its goals were re-articulated at the community level in the local strategic plans of many of those same development actors.[1] It set a context for the shaping of stronger efforts to preserve manufacturing, like the creation of Planned Manufacturing Districts, and it molded a people-oriented approach to mega-projects like the new public library.

The preponderance of stories in this book has addressed these steps of creating a social space for new priorities and then articulating a new decision framework. To set the stage for concluding observations, I want to share one more story of taking action within that framework. The story is one of enormous development impact—Washington's first neighborhood capital improvement program. It also reveals the unrelenting role of race in local development policy.

The Neighborhood Infrastructure Program[2]

The debate over the World's Fair heightened community awareness about wide-ranging infrastructure needs around the city. In a series of monthly neighborhood meetings, the mayor listened to people passionately and eloquently articulating their concerns about collapsing vaulted sidewalks, streets full of potholes, clogged sewers, deteriorating alleys, undermaintained or nonexistent branch libraries, and overcrowded municipal facilities like health and social service centers. They were worried about jobs and income, and wanted the mayor to be their champion on these issues. But they understood the connection between the basic physical quality of their neighborhoods and their economic and social well-being. They expected the mayor to act—as a candidate, he had articulated a planning and development agenda with a neighborhood focus, and invited more attention on these goals with *CWT*.

His main obstacles in advancing this agenda would be resources and politics. Washington had inherited a $168-million operating budget deficit when he took office in 1983. By the end of his first year in office, he had arrested the deficit through a combination of personnel cuts and tax increases. With the operating budget under control, he began to look at the possibility of a capital improvements program.

This appealed to him for both fiscal and political reasons. Fiscally, his financial advisers proposed a combination of retirement and refinancing of older debt, especially debt incurred in the late 1970s when interest rates soared. If this was done, they predicted he could borrow for traditional public works uses, without a tax increase, an additional $100 to $150 million. Washington knew this move would draw political opposition, but suspected community support, based on what he heard at the neighborhood forums.

In late 1984, as he was cooling toward the World's Fair, Washington directed his capital improvement team (the planning, publics works, and infrastructure directors) to prepare a $120-million program, with primary emphasis on neighborhood infrastructure. Within about 2 months, a project package was developed that reflected the mayor's commitment to balanced growth with a relatively uniform distribution of projects across the city. The key to this was a proposal to resurface 5 miles of residential streets in each ward, at a total cost of $50 million.

Of particular significance was the addition of almost $20 million of infrastructure supporting commercial and industrial areas of the city. In Chicago, City-supported infrastructure programs had ignored these areas because they were perceived as lacking a political constituency.[3] Yet the mayor insisted on their inclusion of these business-oriented projects because he sensed from the community forums that Chicago citizens had developed a deeper understanding of economic interdependencies within and between their communities.

The mayor submitted this proposed package of projects as a bond issue to the City Council in early 1985. Despite the obvious benefit of the capital improvement program to the entire city, the proposal languished in City Council through the spring. Rivlin (1992, p. 267) reports the rationale of the Mayor's opposition in stalling the program through the cruel words of Alderman Richard Mell: "There are some who believe that to get rid of Harold Washington is good government because we simply can't take four more years of him. Maybe . . . two years of not having this (bond) issue is worth ten years of political stability in this city." Rivlin adds that "Mell and his allies opposed the proposal precisely because it would make Washington look good."

In the face of such staunch opposition, the mayor decided to take the issue to the streets (Reardon, 1990). Using a bus filled with reporters from print and electronic media, the mayor began to visit wards of key opposition aldermen. His goal was to shift four votes to support the infrastructure program. The mayor literally walked the streets, rang doorbells, and, with cameras rolling, asked residents for support to fix up their neighborhood.[4]

The opposition aldermen, especially in the wards visited by the mayor, came under intense popular pressure. Citizens clearly understood that a comprehensive neighborhood infrastructure program was within reach, and they would not permit it to get bogged down in partisan politics. The ultimate cost of the four "swing" votes was an enormous expansion of the program, ultimately to more than $160 million. Some of the growth was in citywide projects, like preliminary repairs to historic Navy Pier on Chicago's lakefront. Most of it was in commitments to rebuild antiquated residential streets on the southwest and northwest sides of the city. These streets originally had been Depression-era Works Progress Administration projects and did not meet City street code standards. Needless to say, these areas of the city constituted the heart of the mayor's opposition.

Passage of the neighborhood infrastructure program was only half the battle. Getting it built was the other half. The building challenge was compounded by the mayor's commitment, articulated in his *1984 Development Plan*, to open up the business of the City to contractors who had been excluded.

Among the reasons for undertaking an infrastructure program comprising diverse, small projects, instead of mega-projects, was that they afforded new opportunities for small local businesses. For example, it meant soliciting bids for 50 small street resurfacing jobs, instead of several large ones that only a couple of contractors had the capacity to undertake. This process increased exponentially the steps, from engineering through inspection, in the contracting and building process, placing an extraordinary burden on the public works and purchasing bureaucracies.

Such impediments notwithstanding, the administration of Mayor Washington had succeeded by 1987 in shifting more than 20% of Chicago's purchasing from non-Chicago to Chicago-based firms, by awarding bid discounts based on the concept of "net least cost purchasing." This approach recognized that Chicago-based firms were local taxpayers, and returned some amount of each contract to local revenue coffers. In total, the 20% shift meant a greater than $100-million per year impact on the local economy. There are few development opportunities that have the potential for such impact.

In many respects, the racial fear of Alderman Mell was warranted—over the balance of his tenure, Mayor Washington presided over hundreds of groundbreakings and ribbon cuttings in every neighborhood of the city. In 1986 court-directed special aldermanic elections were held in seven wards controlled by his Council opposition. Washington supporters won in four, giving the mayor control of City Council. In 1987 he won re-election. Following the election he introduced, and City Council passed with virtually no opposition, another neighborhood infrastructure bond issue, this one for approximately $120 million.

In earlier chapters, the stories were of efforts to shape and implement an alternative development agenda through larger, symbolic efforts. The infrastructure story represents numerous smaller scale efforts, like a micro-enterprise loan program, a program to link inventors with technological problems facing businesses, the creation with City support of the Women's Self Employment Project, and scores of similar efforts. Thus one important manifestation of the Washington legacy is hundreds of small projects involving hundreds more small local businesses and community organizations, many of whom had previously been excluded from opportunities for working with the City.

How Do You Judge the Washington Development Effort?

Grasping the meaning of the Washington effort is difficult, and it certainly will continue to be studied and dissected.[5] I am tempted to let others do the evaluation, and let the stories presented in this book speak for themselves. This partially is because I was a key actor in the stories and have no claim to objectivity. On the other hand, I do not believe in complete objectivity in evaluation and, furthermore, also feel it is an author's obligation in social discourse to speak from the heart.[6] Thus this effort at reaching some conclusions.

I want to begin with the economic context. Economic development evaluation frequently attempts to demonstrate achievement by codifying economic impacts. Yet, it is impossible to trace such impacts through thousands of projects into a precise aggregate impact picture. Nonetheless, I will take a stab at quantifying the economic impact, although I place less value on that evaluation than the impressionistic one that will follow it.

Measurable Success?

Bear in mind that Washington took office in the trough of the 1981-1983 recession, and that Richard M. Daley assumed the mayoralty in 1989, before the 1990 downturn.[7] A 1989 report by the State of Illinois confirms that Chicago gained jobs at a very strong pace during the tenures of Harold Washington and his interim successor, Eugene Sawyer. The Illinois Department of Employment Security (IDES) (1989) showed that the city gained more than 82,500 private sector jobs between 1983 and 1989. Chicago's reported total job base of almost 1.2 million stood at its highest level since the mid-1970s.

Another economic snapshot, taken periodically by the federal Bureau of Labor Statistics (BLS), reinforced this finding. According to BLS figures, 239,000 more Chicagoans were working in 1989 than in 1983. In a period of slightly declining population, this represents more than a 22% growth in employment.

As impressive as both these data series are, they probably are *underestimates* of Chicago's growth boom. The IDES estimate excludes most branches of government, many self-employed people, and some nonprofit institutions. Similarly, the BLS probably undercounts total employment because it captures only those willing to respond to a survey, often missing the elderly, recent immigrants, and poor people.

Putting all this together, I conclude that jobs in Chicago increased by more than 100,000, or 10%, between 1983 and 1989, and that employed Chicagoans increased by 250,000. These estimates are reinforced by reports of growth of commercial and industrial space utilization by firms such as Corporate Reality Advisors, Grubb and Ellis, and Coldwell Banker.[8]

Besides the difficulty of separating any local impact from that derived from regional and national forces, there are other reasons to be cautious about these numbers. It is not yet possible to judge the quality of jobs being created. I suspect that manufacturing held its own, probably declining in employment but gaining in productivity. In the shadow of a two-decade hemorrhage, that would be very significant. I also suspect many of the new jobs are in the low-wage areas of the service sector. Similarly, it is not known who is working. Again, I suspect the economic growth of the 1980s has not adequately reached into minority communities. I am not overly optimistic about accomplishments in this crucial area, although decades of abuse cannot be reversed overnight.

What Happened Beyond the Numbers?[9]

The Washington agenda for development had simple social justice objectives: Public development action ought to be biased toward the work-needy; the goal of the public action should be to attack subemployment by opening opportunities for meaningful work and helping people become prepared to seize those opportunities; and the actions should be pursued in the public spotlight, cooperatively, with all affected parties. Four of my co-authors of chapters in this book—Kari Moe, Bob Giloth, Irene Sherr, and Lauri Alpern—participated with me in the Washington administration in trying to pursue these objectives of fairness, employment, openness, cooperation, and participation. I believe I speak for them to say that we are comfortable we achieved a lot of what we set out to do. There was substantial work with and in neighborhoods, especially lower-income ones. Most of the work involved concrete projects: facilitating community-based development, helping smaller businesses, and encouraging housing construction and rehabilitation. We also made headway on the large projects, but believe we undertook them in ways to make them less onerous to neighborhood people.

We emerged from our experience with a powerful sense of the importance of basic service delivery. Despite our emphasis on process and planning, we spent the vast majority of our time trying to deliver projects and programs. Yet in thinking about accomplishments, it is important to reflect on the environment within which we were working. It is the way we and ordinary people like us now see and operate in that environment that may signal Harold Washington's ultimate importance.

Unlike previous Chicago mayors, Washington did not enjoy the confidence and support of the Democratic political establishment at either the national or local levels. In a pattern quite *unlike* other cities undertaking government management reform, he received only limited business community support until after the 1986 special elections. Finally, he inherited a bureaucracy dominated by political appointees of his opposition, who did not see it as in their interest for Washington to succeed.

We came to appreciate that the structure of local power was more complex than we realized in 1983. The entrenched machine the mayor sought to dissolve had substantial influence, if not outright control, over most of the major local public and private institutions. These included the sister local governments: the Housing Authority, the Transit Authority, the City Colleges, the Board of Education, and the Park District. Its influence reached deep into major financial and legal establishments, the unions, and even the Catholic Church. In fact, the metaphor of a machine is quite misleading. A machine operates in a consistent and predictable way. A weed, with its ever-spreading roots and tenacity, is a better metaphor.

The idea of a "power elite" had always been abstract to us, but our experience in government brought it to life. In Chicago, it is not a small, tight-knit club, but a large, multilayered, informal network bound together by corporatist ideology. It was an ideology that had a difficult time accommodating the notion of a strong, African-American mayor.

In addition to these obstacles, Mayor Washington faced enormous fiscal constraints. He inherited a $168-million current operating deficit, and in his first term saw federal revenue-sharing decrease by a total of almost $200 million. He found little slack in the local budget, with almost 70% of the resources committed to provision of police, fire, and sanitation services. These areas of increasing public demand for expansion virtually were immune to efficiency improvements.[10]

In light of these realities, Mayor Washington had to reach beyond usual constituencies for support and encouragement. He found it both in the base that elected him and in some new places. Within the base, the African-American churches and black talk radio continued to provide important forums to exchange ideas and solicit support (Miller, 1989b). Within the white community, civic groups like the League of Women Voters afforded him the respect they traditionally showed all Chicago mayors. Within the Latino community, local business groups became important connecting points. Across all parts of the city, community-based organizations played a crucial support role, including areas of the city, like the northwest and southwest sides, that had voted overwhelmingly against Washington in 1983. Given the historical connection between the community-development movement and Washington's election, community-based organizations became an essential constituency for the mayor's development agenda.

From the perspective of efforts within government at policy and program development and implementation, support of community-based organizations was a powerful countervailing force with which to face entrenched political or bureaucratic interests. In some cases, the quality of the support was so rich that the mayor could move boldly. Examples include the Playskool suit, the shutdown of Community Development-funded departments in 1985, and pursuit of Planned Manufacturing District designation.

We were constantly aware of the fragility of relations with community-based organizations: Many of our staff felt them to be alien and hostile, and the community organizations themselves were walking a fine line between being helpful and feeling coopted (Brehm, 1991; Ducharme, 1991). This led to a growing frustration on their part. The large-scale projects placed a particular strain on the relationship. Nonetheless, the continued capacity development of community-based organizations and their sophistication at agenda setting may be one important legacy of the Washington years (Giloth, Orlebeke, Tichnell, & Wright, 1992).

With the backing of community-based organizations, we were able to do many things differently. Most important among them was to attack discrimination and to vigorously pursue equal opportunity programs. For example, in the 10 years prior to Washington's taking office, the Department of Economic Development and its predecessor, the Economic Development Commission, had done 9 financial deals involving minority firms. Within three years of Harold Washington's inauguration, we did 60.

This achievement had multiple roots. Most important were the development of a small business lending program, which the City previously did not have, and the recruitment of African-American and Latino professionals to the staff, so applicants could talk to people more understanding of their situation. With these and comparable accomplishments, we believe we changed significantly the nature and distribution of the outcomes of government development efforts.

Our initial expectation that local government could play a substantial role in illuminating issues was borne out. It has capacity to focus attention, shape debate, endorse or invent language, and influence forums. In the context of promoting participatory decision making, this is a powerful conception of the roles of planning and public administration (Forester, 1989).

Throughout, we were aware that a progressive local government in Chicago would likely be temporary, and constantly tried to institutionalize our progress. Three means stand out. First, we recruited talented and politically progressive people into the bureaucracy. Thankfully, many of them are still there. Second, we tried to fix, with tradition and law, means of opening up government information to ordinary citizens. An example is the Freedom of Information executive order. Finally, by bringing all interested parties to the tables of discussion and debate, we hoped to build both capacity and expectation in citizens to participate in government decision making. Harold Washington was a great believer in democracy, and these means were vital to him. Ultimately, their stability and significance, we believe, will hinge on the state of race relations in Chicago.

We came away with a humbling sense of the enormity of the issues of poverty and race. Poverty seems an overwhelming issue, yet in Chicago, race is possibly even more intractable (Rivlin, 1992). Because poverty and race are so intertwined in this society, the inability to deal with race seems a major cause of the inability to deal with poverty (Betancur & Gills, 1993). Because of the severity of this issue and its impact on efforts to generate local economic development, I want to devote much of the balance of this chapter to race.

Race in Local Economic Development

I have argued elsewhere that achieving the type of understanding in economic develop that can inspire action requires exploring alternative ways of seeing and speaking about the development possibility (Mier & Bingham, 1993). This is something practitioners often do, and race is one dimension that surfaces as an aspect of the development problem, especially in urban areas. Usually, it is the *last* way the opportunity is seen or framed.[11] I believe the fundamental lesson I learned from the Washington years is that race should be the *first* way a local economic development or planning problem should be framed. I arrived at this conclusion through practical experience, some of which I want to share.

A Neighborhood Shopping Center

Vince Lane is probably the nation's best-known public housing director. He is a successful African-American businessman who chaired a signal effort by the prestigious Metropolitan Planning Council to develop a turnaround plan for the Chicago Housing Authority. Challenged to practice what he preached, Lane stepped in to implement the plan.

Lane grew up in public housing. After college, he worked for one of the nation's best-known community development corporations, The Woodlawn Organization (TWO). After almost a decade of working in the development arm of TWO, he went into the business of managing and developing housing. Much, but not all, of the housing under his control served low-to-moderate income households.

I met Lane in 1984 when he was trying to develop a small (approximately 150,000-square-foot) convenience retail center adjoining one of his housing developments. The development was similar to a half dozen others in which the City had participated during the early to mid-1980s, in neighborhoods of similar socioeconomic status, although this was the first in an African-American neighborhood. Although he had the development more than 70% pre-leased, he was having trouble obtaining financing. Ultimately, he was able to structure a deal that mixed private and public money. It took him almost 2 years, and the conditions for private participation were eye-opening.

Lane could not get a Chicago bank to participate, but finally found one in Wisconsin. The Wisconsin bank required a letter of credit to secure the loan. The issuer of the letter of credit required a Lloyd's of London insurance policy for a large portion of the letter of credit. Finally, Lloyd's required another letter of credit to secure a portion of their insurance policy. To this day, I am convinced that this layering of credit security would not have occurred if Lane were a white developer and the center was in a white neighborhood.

Minority-Owned Businesses

Since the civil disturbances in Chicago upon Martin Luther King's assassination in 1968, Chicago has had several high-profile civic leadership organizations dedicated to promoting better race relations. A noteworthy one involving business leadership is Chicago United. For two decades, the central goal of Chicago United has been minority business development. For example, in the mid-1970s, it created the Minority Purchasing Council to target some of the spending of majority businesses to minority firms.

In 1985, as my senior staff and I were taking stock of our efforts at minority business development, *Black Enterprise Magazine* published its annual list of the 100 largest African-American-owned businesses. By any measure, $10-million annual sales represents a small business. And yet, we discovered there were only five Chicago-based, African-American-owned businesses with sales larger than that threshold. Further, none of the five had reached this plateau with the help of Chicago's majority firms—three produced African-American-oriented consumer products, and two were auto dealerships. In other words, two decades of interracial business partnership had produced more smoke than fire.

Community Development Block Grant (CDBG)

This major federal revenue-sharing program had been one of the backbones of the federal poverty programs. Chicago's entitlement was running around $100 million per year, by virtue of its concentration of poor people and the age of its housing stock. Yet a significant amount of the spending was occurring in areas of the city that were neither old nor poor.

In 1984 we began to impose area- or individual-specific standards of need for projects supported by Community Development funds, instead of citywide standards.[12] This led to increased rancor with the City Council majority. It came to a head on July 1, 1985, when the mayor vetoed the Community Development budget because he believed Council was directing expenditures for ineligible activities. For a week, all CDBG-supported employees were laid off until the opposition backed down.

I am still incredulous at the interpretation of these events. Although all Washington's Council allies represented low-to-moderate income wards, including *all* the areas of deepest poverty, both popular and scholarly interpretation is that Washington's actions were simply the exercise of political power in order to reward friends and punish foes (Rivlin, 1992; Rich, 1992). That most African-Americans in Chicago are poor, thus an intended beneficiary of the federal poverty programs, and that most whites are not poor seems to have no bearing on the interpretation of Washington's actions.

First Source Hiring

A major disappointment to me was our ineffectiveness with regard to implementing a targeted hiring program. Early in the work of the development subcabinet, we identified a need to explore ways to link participation in business assistance programs with efforts to see that work-needy people benefited from the creation of new employment opportunities.

We explored efforts in other cities, and became excited at a program most fully developed in Portland, Oregon, called "First Source Hiring." Simply put, the program required business recipients of public assistance to enter into a contract with a mutually agreed upon provider of potential employees, to give that provider the first crack at any new jobs. In other words, a specified provider of potential workers would be the "first source" to which the company would turn. Essentially, this program attempted to supersede the informal social networks that are dominant determinants of placement success and failure (Mier & Giloth, 1985).

Our effort to implement this program in Chicago ran into a fire storm. It quickly got labeled "Harold's patronage program," an image we could never break through. We created a task force of business and labor leaders to work out the details of a Chicago program, but despite their support, the patronage image held the day. We eventually began to include "first source" hiring agreements in our loan deals, but these were never enforced after we left office.

Reflections on Race

Another reader of the four situations I describe might choose to emphasize aspects of each that would highlight circumstances, not the patterns I am implying. I know that Vince Lane's development was not risk-free (which is why there was public participation). I know that the most talented, business-oriented minorities are aggressively sought after and rewarded by major corporations, and thus are seldom willing to risk starting their own businesses outside the field of professional services. I know that the changing terrain of federal regulation of the CDBG program created some honest confusion. And I know implementation of a "first source" hiring program is extremely complicated, especially when businesses need workers quickly.

Yet, I do see patterns. Like Derrick Bell, (1992, pp. 109-126), I think of the situation of racial differences as a burden-of-proof problem. If you are not a white male, then there is an extra burden on you to disprove questions of risk. This is true if you are a female, a Latino, an Asian, and especially, if you are an African-American. However, lately, especially as I think back on Chicago during the Washington era and as I see similar patterns of discrimination in other cities, I am no longer so benign.

This interpretation closely corresponds to that of an increasing number of writers and researchers (e.g., Davis, 1989; Kozol, 1991; Bell, 1992; Goldsmith & Blakely, 1992; Hacker, 1992). For example, Hacker says:

> A huge racial chasm remains, and there are few signs that the coming century will see it closed. A century and a quarter after

slavery, white America continues to ask of its black citizens an
extra patience and perseverance that whites have never required
of themselves. So the question for white Americans is essentially
moral: is it right to impose on members of an entire race a lesser
start in life, and then to expect from them a degree of resolution
that has never been demanded of your own race? (p. 219)

This inexorable presence of racism is my strongest realization
from the Washington years. I now find it impossible to approach
an economic development challenge without immediately seeing the race and gender dimensions of it, especially those of
African-Americans. Thus it is impossible to see that situation as
anything less than a opportunity to pursue social justice. My
ex-City Hall colleague, former Planning Commissioner Elizabeth
Hollander, says it clearly: "I can never again walk into a room
without being instantly aware of who's there . . . and who's not
there. It makes *all* the difference in the world."

Conclusion[13]

In the final analysis, I want to address briefly the generalizabil-
ity of this Chicago story. Macro-economic and social forces
affecting Chicago also impact most large cities. Production has
become increasingly concentrated in a handful of firms able to
compete in national and international markets and able to seek
a least-cost location worldwide. Yet, simultaneously, vertical
disintegration within those same sectors—be it steel, automobile, or motion picture production—is yielding many small, independent firms performing specialized supportive or finishing
functions in locally or regionally competitive markets. The smaller
firms can serve, as they did in Chicago, as the foundation of a local
economic development strategy.

The impact of these trends on workers and their communities
is stressful. Production either contracts or it hops around the
country, the continent, and the world, leaving behind a dislocated work force with obsolete and devalued occupational skills.
And the emergent new production activity takes new skills. In
the pubic sector, fiscal stress and public policy that favors
unproductive investments have limited the degree to which
government has been willing, in the absence of strong local

pressure like that seen in Chicago, to attempt actions to mitigate these market changes.

Finally, on the social front, our cities are experiencing enormous diversification of their populations. Like Chicago, many of our major cities—New York, Los Angeles, Washington, D.C., Atlanta, and New Orleans among them—now have "majority minority" populations, and within the decade probably will be joined by several states, including New Mexico, California, and Texas (Hacker, 1992). Diversity is exploding as a work force, as well as an urban, issue (Williams, 1992; Yates, 1992; Fitzgerald, 1993).

What will be the consequence of this rather rapid transformation of our economic and social fabric? Robert N. Bellah and his colleagues (1985), in their highly acclaimed *Habits of the Heart,* argue that a breaking point will be reached when a movement for a new "social ecology" emerges that captures the spirit of the civil rights movement of the 1960s. I think this story of Chicago is an example of that.

I believe further evidence that this movement already exists lies in the demand for better-managed economic growth. To a degree, the 1992 presidential election was a mandate on demand. I think that the political movement of Harold Washington, Henry Cisneros, and the Rainbow Coalition—calling for rejection of a politics that places an unbearable economic burden on poor people, minorities, and women—will gain strength.

I predict the results of these twin forces—the demand for managed growth ("management") and the rejection of exploitative politics ("fairness")—will support future organizing for change. I am not suggesting, however, that the realization of this process is assured. The challenge is to find a coherent expression of the twin forces. I believe the key to achieving that coherence is to seek it in more microscopic situations where the inherent contradictions between "management" and "fairness" can be exposed and reconciled.

Indeed, my reading of history says the roots of social change flourish when they are nurtured in a symbiotic relationship with social and community movements. This symbiosis existed in Chicago in the 1980s, where there was serious pubic debate about and, in some cases, implementation of worker buy outs, early warning systems, linked development, industrial district preservation, negotiated development for equal opportunity, and participatory public decision making.

I base my optimism about change on the belief that, as occurred in Chicago, the stage is once again being set for a social justice agenda to become an important part of local development efforts. I currently see it happening in Hartford, Oakland, and Los Angeles, where there are evolving loosely knit, dynamic interplays of development professionals, planners in formal and informal roles, and community- or issue-based advocacy and interest groups. The interplay is seldom confined to formal, bureaucratic settings and procedures. And their vocabulary includes fairness, subemployment, openness, cooperation, and participation.

Ultimately, the success of these movements for social justice will hinge on their abilities to confront racism and sexism, instead of trying to minimize their importance in concrete problem-solving situations. Fortunately, as Giloth and I discussed in the preceding chapter, it is occurring in grass-roots organizations.

In the end, it is the grass-roots action that gives me the most optimism, a force for change from below. Like Bellah et al., I believe people will not let our social fabric disintegrate. Their response to disintegration will set the conditions for a vigorous, and reinvigorated, demand for social change. The development profession brings people, practices, and a tradition that will be useful and valued, but its ultimate value will be determined by the willingness of its practitioners to engage in an open, critical self-examination. I continue to have faith in social justice movements.

Notes

1. Among the devices for communicating the meaning of *Chicago Works Together* was a logo on the document, all City construction signs, City stationary and calling cards, and even lapel pins. (I personally handed out around 10,000 lapel pins.) Two subsequent mayors considered replacing the logo as a means of establishing their own identity, but found it too powerfully embedded in public consciousness—it not only represented the traditional "city that works" but added a willingness to face diversity by "working together." Thus 5 years after Washington's death, one of his important legacies visibly lives on.

2. This story is told in considerably more detail in Mier (1993).

3. To state it simply, small business owners represent a negligible vote, are modest political financial contributors, and generally opt out of the process of trying to influence politics.

4. I accompanied the mayor on these walks. Generally, city staff preceded us, distributing an informational brochure describing costs and projects. Along one street, I was stopped by an older man who asked if rebuilding his street would really

cost only $2.50 per year on his tax bill. This was our publicly estimated cost for a prototypical Chicago bungalow. I reassured the individual, grabbed his brochure, and did testimony by signing my guarantee. At the moment, the mayor walked up, saw what I was doing, and added his name to mine. A sheepish opposition alderman walking with the mayor added his signature.

About 2 years later, I received a note from the old man accompanied by photocopies of our signatures and his tax bill. His taxes for the infrastructure program had gone up $4 per year. His note said: "I knew it would cost more than you said, but I'm glad you did it anyway."

5. Grasping the meaning of Washington's mayoralty is becoming the object of books, like Clavel and Wiewel (1991) and Rivlin (1992), and dissertations, like Reardon (1990) and Brown-Chappel (1992).

6. White (1987, pp. 58-82, 185-213) speaks to objectivity in the telling of stories. With regard to historical narrative, he reveals enormous disciplinary pressures to speak and write in a more scientific fashion. Such narration, he argues, is sanitized of emotion and imagination, the stuff of social action. With regard to speaking from the heart as well as the mind, I have been inspired by Berger (1979, pp. 195-213) and Gordimer (1989).

7. I include the tenure of Acting Mayor Eugene Sawyer in this analysis because he served as the caretaker of the Washington agenda.

8. In fact, about the only people not reporting results like this were the Chicago media. For example, in a late 1988 series of articles critical of Chicago development during Harold Washington's tenure as mayor, the *Chicago Tribune* claimed that Chicago had *lost* 75,000 jobs (McCarron, 1988a). This estimate was low by more than 150,000. Most often such large errors result from over reliance on perceptions over facts, something to which the Chicago media was quite susceptible during the Washington years (Rivlin, 1992).

9. This section is adapted from Mier and Moe (1991) and reproduced with permission of Rutgers University Press.

10. To be blunt, the white neighborhoods felt unsafe with an African-American mayor, and Washington's opposition exploited those fears. For example, in 1984, Washington attempted to reduce the police force by 500 uniformed personnel, from 12,000 to 11,500. He argued that Chicago's force was one of the largest, on a per capita basis, in the country. By the time the mayor's Council opposition had fanned the flames, the police force was *expanded* to 12,500.

11. It is my suspicion that in most economic development and planning education, race is seldom addressed. This is based on talking to a number of educators, as well as recent graduates I was considering as prospective employees. When it is, race is usually presented as a lecture or partial lecture toward the end of the course, among a number of subsidiary issues.

12. In this effort we got an unexpected boost from the Department of Housing and Urban Development. They began to issue administrative orders more narrowly defining the intent of the enabling federal law with regard to needy populations and communities. It is my opinion that this federal action was not altruistically motivated. Rather, I believe it was one of a number of attempts emanating from President Reagan's administration to impede the expenditure of funds for programs that Congress was maintaining against the White House's will.

13. This section is excerpted from Mier (1987) and reproduced with permission of *Colloqui: Journal of Planning and Urban Issues.*

References

Alexander, S., Giloth, R., & Lerner, J. (1987). Chicago's industry task forces: Joint problem-solving for economic development. *Economic Development Quarterly, 1*(4), 352-357.

Alinsky, S. (1971). *Rules for radicals.* New York: Vintage.

Alkalimat, A., & Gills, D. (1989). *Harold Washington and the crisis of black power in Chicago.* Chicago: Twentieth Century.

Arrow, K. (1973, May). Some ordinalist-utilitarian notes on Rawls' theory of justice. *Journal of Philosophy, 70,* 245-262.

Barret, P. (1983). *The Automobile and the city.* Philadelphia: Temple University Press.

Basler, S., & Kitwana, M. (1986). *The impact of environmental regulations on small manufacturers in Chicago.* Chicago: City of Chicago Department of Economic Development.

Baumol, W. J. (1965). *Economic theory and operations research.* Englewood Cliffs, NJ: Prentice-Hall.

Beauregard, R. (1993). Constituting economic development: A theoretical perspective. In R. D. Bingham & R. Mier (Eds.), *Economic development in the United States: Toward a theoretical perspective.* Newbury Park, CA: Sage.

Bell, D. (1992). *Faces at the bottom of the wall: The permanence of racism.* New York: Basic Books.

Bellah, R. N., Madsen, R., Sullivan, W. M., Swidler, A., & Tipton, S. M. (1985). *Habits of the heart: Individualism and commitment in American life.* Berkeley: University of California Press.

Beneviste, G. (1989). *Mastering the politics of planning.* San Francisco: Jossey-Bass.

Bennett, L., Squires, G. D., McCourt, K., & Nyden, P. (1987, Fall). Challenging Chicago's growth machine: A preliminary report on the Washington administration. *International Journal of Urban and Regional Research,* 351-362.

Bennis, W., & Nanus, B. (1985). *Leaders: The strategies of taking.* New York: Harper & Row.

Berg, I. (1970). *Education and jobs: The great training robbery.* New York: Praeger.

Berger, J. (1979). *Pig earth.* New York: Pantheon.

Berger, P. L., & Neuhaus, R. J. (1977). *To empower people.* Washington, DC: American Enterprise Institute from Public Policy Research.

Betancur, J., & Gills, D. (1993). Race and class in local development. In R. D. Bingham & R. Mier (Eds.), *Economic development in the United States: Toward a theoretical perspective.* Newbury Park, CA: Sage.

Betancur, J., & McCormick, L. (1985). *Industrial displacement in major cities and related policy options.* Chicago: University of Illinois at Chicago Center for Urban Economic Development.

Bolan, R. S. (1985, November). *Planning theory and experiential learning.* Paper presented at the annual meeting of the Association of Collegiate Schools of Planning, Atlanta, GA.

Bookchin, M. (1987). *The rise of urbanization and the decline of citizenship.* San Francisco: Sierra Club Books.

Bowsher, P. (1980). *Making housing work for the poor.* Washington, DC: Prentice Bowsher Associates.

Boyte, H. C. (1980). *The backyard revolution: Understanding the new citizen movement.* Philadelphia: Temple University Press.

Boyte, H. C. (1982, Spring). Reagan vs. the neighborhoods. *Social Policy, 12,* 4.

Boyte, H. C., Booth, H., & Max, S. (1986). *Citizen action and the new American populism.* Philadelphia: Temple University Press.

Boyte, H. C., & Riessman, F. (1986). *The new populism: Politics of empowerment.* Philadelphia: Temple University Press.

Bradford, C. (1985, November 25). *Neighborhood reinvestment: The legacy and the challenge.* Paper presented at the National Neighborhood Coalition Conference.

Bradford, C. (1987, Jan./Feb.). Building a development engine. *Neighborhood Works, 10*(1), 1, 7-9.

Brandy, D. (1987, Spring). Local development policy in the 1980's. *Journal of Planning Literature, 2*(2), 136-152.

Braverman, H. (1974). *Labor and monopoly capital.* New York: Monthly Review Press.

Brehm, R. (1991). The City and the neighborhoods: Was it really a two-way street? In P. Clavel & W. Wiewel (Eds.), *Harold Washington and the neighborhoods: Progressive city government in Chicago, 1983-1987* (pp. 238-269). New Brunswick, NJ: Rutgers University Press.

Brown, L. D., & Detterman, L. B. (1987). Small interventions for large problems: Reshaping urban leadership networks. *Journal of Applied Behavioral Science, 23*(2), 151-168.

Brown-Chappel, B. (1992). *The black movement model of mayoral policy leadership.* Unpublished doctoral dissertation in Social Service Administration, University of Chicago.

Bruyn, S., & Meehan, J. (1987). *Beyond the market and the state: New directions in community development.* Philadelphia: Temple University Press.

Business Week. (1984, September 17). The new breed of strategic planner: Number crunching professionals are giving way to line managers. Pp. 62-68.

Business Week. (1975, December 1, 8, 15). Egalitarianism: Threat to a free market. Pp. 62-65; 86-90; pp. 86-88, respectively.

Capraro, J., Ditton, A, & Giloth, R. (1985). *Neighborhood economic development: Working together for Chicago's future.* Chicago: Department of Economic Development.

Caro, R. (1971). *The power broker.* New York: Vintage.

Chicago Association of Neighborhood Development Organizations. (1990). *A prospectus for neighborhood investment.* Chicago: Author.

Chicago Central Area Committee. (1973). *Chicago 21: A plan for Chicago's central area communities.* Chicago: Author.

Chicago project: A report on civic life in Chicago, executive summary. (1987, February 27). *Crain's Chicago Business.*

Chicago Works Together Planning Task Force. (1987). *Chicago works together II: Recommended changes to the 1984 Chicago development plan.* Chicago: Author.

Chicago Workshop on Economic Development. (1990). *The next step: Building on low-income capacity.* Chicago: Author.

Choate, P. (1982, Summer). American workers at the Rubicon. *Economic Development Commentary, 6*(2), 2-10.

Cities seek greater return on real estate investments. (1982, April 30). *Urban Economic Developments, 4*(4).

City of Chicago. (1986a). *Building on the basics: The final report of the mayor's task force on steel and southeast Chicago.* Chicago: Author.

City of Chicago. (1986b). *1986 strategic plan* [Draft]. Chicago: Author.

City of Chicago. (1987a). *Cooperation for survival and growth: New designs for apparel manufacturing in Chicago.* Chicago: Author.

City of Chicago. (1987b). *Final report of the mayor's stadium review committee.* Chicago: Author.

City of Chicago Department of Economic Development. (1984). *Chicago works together: 1984 development plan.* Chicago: Author.

City of Chicago Office of Intergovernmental Affairs. (1985a). *An urban agenda for tax reform.* Chicago: Author.

City of Chicago Office of Intergovernmental Affairs. (1985b). *Chicago federal agenda: Legislative and budgeting issues.* Chicago: Author.

City of Chicago Office of Intergovernmental Affairs. (1985c). *Municipal agenda for build Illinois.* Chicago: Author.

City of Dallas. (1977). *Goals for Dallas.* Dallas: Author.

Clavel, P. (1986). *The progressive city: Planning and participation, 1969-1984.* New Brunswick, NJ: Rutgers University Press.

Clavel, P., & Wiewel, W. (1991). *Neighborhood and economic development policy in Chicago: 1983-1987.* New Brunswick, NJ: Rutgers University Press.

Cleveland City Planning Commission. (1975). *Cleveland policy planning report* (Vol. 1). Cleveland: Author.

Cleveland Tomorrow Committee. (1981). *Cleveland tomorrow—A strategy for economic vitality.* Cleveland: Author.

Commercial Club of Chicago. (1984). *Jobs for metropolitan Chicago.* Chicago: Author.

Committee for Economic Development. (1982). *Public-private partnerships: An opportunity for urban communities.* Washington, DC: Author.

Committee on Economic Development. (1980). The negotiated investment strategy: Review of concepts and implications for revitalizing cities. *A report by the subcommittee on revitalizing American cities.* Dayton, OH: Kettering Foundation.

Committee to Elect Harold Washington. (1983). *The Washington papers.* Chicago: Author.

Committee to Re-Elect Mayor Washington. (1987). *Mayor Washington's action agenda for Chicago's future 1987-1991.* Chicago: Author.

Community Workshop on Economic Development. (1982a). *The CWED platform.* Chicago: Author.

Community Workshop on Economic Development. (1982b, April 15). Letter to Governor James R. Thompson. Chicago: Author.

Corson, W., & Nicholson, W. (1980). *Trade adjustment assistance for workers: The results of a survey of recipients under the trade act of 1974.* Princeton, NJ: Princeton University Mathematics Policy Research Center.

Davidson, J. (1990, July 15). Old Daley clout has returned. *Chicago Tribune,* Sec. 2, p. 1.

Davis, M. (1989). *City of quartz: Excavating the future in Los Angeles.* New York: Vintage.

Delgado, R. (1989, August). Storytelling for oppositionists and others: A plea for narrative. *Michigan Law Review, 87,* 2411-2441.

Drucker, P. F. (1981). Demographics and American economic policy. In M. L. Wachter & S. M. Wachter (Eds.), *Toward a new U.S. industrial policy* (pp. 237-256). Philadelphia: University of Pennsylvania Press.

Ducharme, D. (1991). How a community initiative became city policy. In P. Clavel & W. Wiewel (Eds.), *Neighborhood and economic development policy in Chicago: 1983-1987.* New Brunswick, NJ: Rutgers University Press.

Ducharme, D., Giloth, R., & McCormick, L. (1986). *Business loss or balanced growth: Industrial displacement in Chicago, 1977-1984.* Chicago: City of Chicago Department of Economic Development.

Eckstein, O., & Tannenwald, R. (1981). Productivity and capital formation. In M. L. Wachter & S. M. Wachter (Eds.), *Toward a new U.S. industrial policy* (pp. 127-142). Philadelphia: University of Pennsylvania Press.

Einsweiler, R. C. (1980, December). What the top people are saying about central city planning. *Planning, 46*(12), 15-18.

Ellwood, J. W. (1982). *Background material on fiscal year 1982 federal budget reductions.* Princeton, NJ: Princeton University Urban and Regional Research Center.

Evans, S. (1979). *Personal politics: The roots of women's liberation in the civil rights movement and the new left.* New York: Knopf.

Evans, S., & Boyte, H. (1985). *Free spaces.* New York: Basic Books.

Fainstein, N. I., & Fainstein, S. S. (1987, Spring). Economic restructuring and the politics of land use planning in New York City. *Journal of the American Planning Association, 53*(2), 237-248.

Fasenfest, D. (1989). Race, class and community development: A comparison of Detroit's Poletown and Chicago's Goose Island. In J. Lembcke & R. Hutchinson (Eds.), *Research in urban sociology: Race, class and urban change* (pp. 101-134). Greenwich, CT: JAI Press.

Fitzgerald, J. (1991). Class as community: The new dynamics of social change. *Environment and Planning D: Society and Space, 9,* 117-128.

Fitzgerald, J. (1993). Labor force, education and work. In R. D. Bingham & R. Mier (Eds.), *Economic development in the United States: Toward a theoretical perspective.* Newbury Park, CA: Sage.

Fitzgerald, J., & Simmons, L. (1991). From consumption to production: Labor participation in grassroots movements in Pittsburgh and Hartford. *Urban Affairs Quarterly, 26*(4), 512-531.

Forester, J. (1989). *Planning in the face of power.* Berkeley: University of California Press.

Frisbie, M. (1991). *An alley in Chicago: The ministry of a city priest.* Kansas City: Sheed and Ward.

Gardner, J. (1987). *Leadership development.* Washington, DC: Independent Sector.

Giblin, J.-E., Vietorisz, T., & Mier, R. (1974, May). *Economic roots of the urban crisis.* Paper presented at the Annual Meeting of the American Psychiatric Association.

Gilligan, C. (1982). *In a different voice.* Cambridge, MA: Harvard University Press.

Gills, D. (1991). Chicago politics and community development: A social movement perspective. In P. Clavel & W. Wiewel (Eds.), *Harold Washington and the neighborhoods: Progressive city government in Chicago, 1983-1987* (pp. 34-63). New Brunswick, NJ: Rutgers University Press.

Giloth, R. P. (1981). *Disinvestment in South Shore's large rental properties.* Chicago: University of Illinois at Chicago Center for Urban Economic Development.

Giloth, R. P. (1985, Winter). Organizing for neighborhood development. *Social Policy, 15*(3), 37-42.

Giloth, R. P. (1989). *Industrial development bonds in Chicago 1977-1987: Subsidies for what?.* Unpublished doctoral dissertation, Department of City and Regional Planning, Cornell University.

Giloth, R. P. (1991). Making policy with communities: Research and development in the department of economic development. In P. Clavel & W. Wiewel (Eds.), *Harold Washington and the neighborhoods: Progressive city government in Chicago, 1983-1987* (pp. 100-120). New Brunswick, NJ: Rutgers University Press.

Giloth, R. P., & Betancur, J. (1988). Where downtown meets neighborhood: Industrial displacement in Chicago, 1978-1987. *Journal of the American Planning Association, 54,* 279-290.

Giloth, R. P., & Mier, R. (1986). Democratic populism in the U.S.: The case of Playskool and Chicago. *Cities: The International Quarterly on Urban Policy, 3*(1), 72-74.

Giloth, R. P., & Mier, R. (1988). Spatial change and social justice. In R. A. Beauregard (Ed.), *Economic restructuring and political response.* Newbury Park, CA: Sage.

Giloth, R. P., Orlebeke, C. J., Tichnell, J., & Wright, P. (1992). *Choices ahead: Community development corporations and real estate production in Chicago.* Chicago: University of Illinois at Chicago Center for Urban Economic Development.

Ginzberg, E. (1982, September). The mechanization of work. *Scientific American*, pp. 67-75.

Gitlin, T., & Hollander, N. (1970). *Uptown: Poor whites in Chicago*. New York: Harper & Row.

Goering, J. M. (1979, October). The national neighborhood movement: A preliminary analysis and critique. *Journal of the American Planning Association, 45*(4), 506-514.

Goldsmith, A. (1990, July 25). Interview with Lauri Alpern.

Goldsmith, W., & Blakely, E. J. (1992). *Separate societies: Poverty and inequality in U.S. cities*. Philadelphia: Temple University Press.

Goodwyn, L. (1987). *The populist moment: A short history of the agrarian revolt in America*. New York: Oxford University Press.

Gordimer, N. (1989). A writer's freedom. In S. Clingman (Ed.), *The essential gesture: Writing, politics & places* (pp. 104-110). London: Penguin.

Greater North Pulaski Development Corporation. (1986). *Strategic plan and two year work program, 1987-1988*. Chicago: Author.

Greenhouse, S. (1986, November 30). Chicago does its job hunting at home. *The New York Times*.

Grimshaw, W. (1984). Is Chicago ready for reform? Or, a new agenda for Harold Washington. In M. G. Holli & P. M. Green (Eds.), *The making of the mayor: Chicago 1983* (pp. 141-166). Grand Rapids, MI: Eerdman.

Guthrie, J. W., Kleindorfer, G., Levin, H. M., & Stout, R. T. (1971). *Schools and inequality*. Cambridge, MA: The MIT Press.

Hacker, A. (1992). *Two nations: Black and white, separate, hostile, unequal*. New York: Scribner's.

Haider, D. (1986). Partnerships redefined: Chicago's new opportunities. In P. Davis (Ed.), *Public-private partnerships: Improving urban life* (pp. 137-149). New York: Academy of Political Science.

Hampden-Turner, C. (1975). *From poverty to human dignity*. Garden City, NJ: Doubleday/Anchor.

Harrington, M. (1985). *New American poverty*. New York: Holt, Rinehart & Winston.

Harrison, B. (1982). *Rationalization, restructuring, and industrial reorganization in older regions: The economic transformation of New England since World War II*. Boston: Joint Center for Urban Studies of MIT and Harvard.

Harrison, B., & Bluestone, B. (1983). *The deindustrialization of America*. New York: Basic Books.

Harrison, B., & Gorham, L. (1992). Growing inequality in black wages in the 1980's and the emergeance of an African-American middle class. *Journal of Policy Analysis and Management, 11*(2), 235-253.

Harvey, D. (1973). *Social justice and the city*. Baltimore: Johns Hopkins University Press.

Hays, S. P. (1970). Reform in municipal government In A. M. Wakstein (Ed.), *The urbanization of America: An historical anthology* (pp. 288-314). Boston: Houghton-Mifflin.

Help for a day or even an hour. (1987, May 24). *The New York Times*.

Hershberg, T., & Rubin, M. (1982). *A Philadelphia prospectus: Overview of the city and introduction to the Philadelphia investment portfolio.* Philadelphia: Center for Philadelphia Studies, University of Pennsylvania.

Hinton, D. C. (1981). *Rethinking urban governance: An assessment of the negotiated investment strategy.* Menlo Park, CA: S.R.I. International Center for Public Policy Analysis.

Hoch, C. (1984, Summer). Doing good and being right: The pragmatic connection in planning theory. *Journal of the American Planning Association, 50*(3), 335-345.

Hollander, E. (1991). The department of planning under Harold Washington. In P. Clavel & Wim Wiewel (Eds.), *Harold Washington and the neighborhoods: Progressive city government in Chicago, 1983-1987* (pp. 121-145). New Brunswick, NJ: Rutgers University Press.

Horning, M. (1989). Daley reaches out to business. *Crain's Chicago Business.*

Hunt, S. M. (1984). The role of leadership in the construction of reality. In B. Kellerman (Ed.), *Leadership: Multidisciplinary perspectives* (pp. 157-178). Englewood Cliffs, NJ: Prentice-Hall.

Industrial Council of Northwest Chicago. (1986). *Strategic plan/business plan for the development of the Kinzie industrial corridor and the industrial council of northwest Chicago.* Chicago: Author.

Judd, D., & Parkinson, M. (1990). Patterns of leadership. In D. Judd & M. Parkinson (Eds.), *Leadership and urban regeneration: Cities in North America and Europe* (pp. 295-307). Newbury Park, CA: Sage.

Judd, D., & Ready, R. L. (1986). Entrepreneurial cities and the new policies of economic development. In G. E. Peterson & C. W. Lewis (Eds.), *Reagan and the cities* (pp. 209-248). Washington, DC: Urban Institute Press.

Kaplan, T. J. (1986). The narrative structure of policy analysis. *Journal of Policy Analysis and Management, 5*(4), 761-778.

Keating, D. (1986, Spring). Downtown development to broader community goals. *Journal of American Planning Association, 52*(2), 133-141.

Kennard, B. (1982). *Nothing can be done everything is possible.* New York: Brick House.

Kilpatrick, R. (1973, August). Income elasticity of the poverty line. *Review of Economics and Statistics, 55*(3), 327-332.

Kleiman, C. (1988, February 29). Stereotypes plaguing blue-collar women, too. *Chicago Tribune.*

Kozol, J. (1991). *Savage inequalities: Children in America's schools.* New York: HarperPerennial.

Krumholz, N. (1980, December). The loyal opposition speaks up. *Planning, 46*(12), 17.

Krumholz, N. (1984). Recovery of cities: An alternative view. In P. R. Porter & D. Sweet (Eds.), *Rebuilding America's cities: Roads to recovery.* New Brunswick, NJ: Center for Urban Policy Research, Rutgers University.

Krumholz, N. (1991, November). Equity and local economic development. *Economic Development Quarterly, 5*(4), 291-300.

Krumholz, N., Cogger, J., & Linner, J. (1975, September). The Cleveland policy-planning report. *Journal of the American Insitute of Planners, 41,* 298-304.

Krumholz, N., Costigan, P., & Keating, D. (1985, Summer). A review of Chicago works together: 1984 development plan. *Journal of the American Planning Association, 51*(3), 395-396.

Krumholz, N., & Forester, J. (1990). *Making equity planning work.* Philadelphia: Temple University Press.

LaBotz, D. (1986, January/February). How can communities fight plant shutdowns. *Neighborhood Works, 9*(1), 9-11.

Lampman, R. (1971). *Ends and means of reducing income poverty.* Chicago: Markham.

Lasater, D. E. (1984). A banker's view of redevelopment. In P. R. Porter & D. Sweet (Eds.), *Rebuilding America's cities: Roads to recovery.* New Brunswick, NJ: Center for Urban Policy Research, Rutgers University.

Lerner, M. (1988, January/February). The legacy of the sixties for the politics of the nineties. *Tikkun: A Bimonthly Jewish Critique of Politics, Culture, and Society, 3*(1), p. 44.

Levitan, S. A. & Taggart, R. (1974). *Employment and earnings inadequacy.* Baltimore: Johns Hopkins University Press.

Levy, P. (1979, September-October). Unloading the neighborhood bandwagon. *Social Policy, 10*(2), 28-32.

Lewin, T. (1984, June 10). Putting industrial policy to a vote. *The New York Times,* sec. 3, p. 4.

Lieske, J. (1984). The salvation of American cities. In P. R. Porter & D. Sweet (Eds.), *Rebuilding America's cities: Roads to recovery* (pp. 71-93). New Brunswick, NJ: Center for Urban Policy Research, Rutger University.

Longworth, R. C. (1981, May 10-14). City on the brink. *Chicago Tribune.*

Longworth, R. C. (1984, December 23). City in trouble: Business out to reverse economic trade. *Chicago Tribune,* sec. 5, p. 1.

Longworth, R. C. (1985, January 1). A sign of Chicago's decline. *Chicago Tribune,* sec. 1, p. 15.

Luke, J. S., Ventriss, C., Reed, B. J., & Reed, C. M. (1987). *Managing economic development: A guide to state and local leadership strategies.* San Francisco: Jossey-Bass.

Luria, D., & Russell, J. (1981). *Rational re-industrialism: An economic development agenda for Detroit.* Detroit: Widgetripper Press.

Magaziner, I., & Reich, R. B. (1982). *Minding America's business.* New York: Harcourt Brace Jovanovich.

Malizia, E. (1982). Contingency planning for local economic development. *Environment and Planning B, 9,* 163-176.

March, J. G. (1982). Theories of choice and making decisions. *Society, 20*(1), 544-587.

Markusen, A. (1989, November 24). City on the skids. *The Reader,* p. 1 ff.

Markusen, A., Learner, J., Patton, W., Ross, J., & Schneider, J. (1985). *Steel and southeast Chicago: Reasons and opportunities for industrial renewal.* Evanston: Center for Urban Affairs and Policy Research, Northwestern University.

Marris, Peter. (1987). *Meaning and action: Community planning and conceptions of change.* London: Routledge & Kegan Paul.

Mayor's Commission on Latino Affairs. (1984). *Chicago hiring update.* Chicago: Author.

McCarron, J. (1988a, August 31). The politics of poverty. *Chicago Tribune,* sec. 1, p. 1.

McCarron, J. (1988b, October 16). It's past the time we saw some results in the neighborhoods. *Chicago Tribune,* sec. 4, p. 6.

McGary, H. (1992). Rawls' logic of political argument: Political justification without truth. In B. Smit & E.C.W. Crabbe (Eds.), *Logic in political culture.* Edita, Neatherlands: Royal Dutch Academy of Arts and Sciences.

McGary, H., & Lawson, B. E. (1993). *Between slavery and freedom.* Bloomington: Indiana University Press.

Mier, R. (1983, Summer). High technology-based development: A review of recent literature. *Journal of the American Planning Association.*

Mier, R. (1984a). Job generation as a road to recovery. In P. R. Porter & D. Sweet (Eds.), *Rebuilding America's cities: Roads to recovery* (pp. 160-172). New Brunswick, NJ: Center for Urban Policy Research, Rutgers University.

Mier, R. (1984b, October). *Academe and the community: Some impediments to professional practice.* Paper presented at the annual meeting of the Association of Collegiate Schools of Planning, New York.

Mier, R. (1986). Academe and the community: Some impediments to professional practice. *Journal of Planning Education and Research, 6*(1), 66-70.

Mier, R. (1987a, Winter). A comment on "development planning as the only game in town." *Journal of Planning Education and Research, 5*(2), 142.

Mier, R. (1987b, Spring). A note on planning's future. *Colloqui: Journal of Planning and Urban Issues,* 52-54.

Mier, R. (1988, October 16). City official rebuts *Tribune's* development series. *Chicago Tribune,* sec. 4, p. 1.

Mier, R. (1991a, Fall). Baseball brinksmanship: Any economic development impact? *Michigan Partnership for Economic Development News, 4*(3), 1.

Mier, R. (1991b, July 15). A stadium deal that won't leave residents in the cold. *Crain's Chicago Business,* p. 15.

Mier, R. (1992, November). Where is Chicago's industrial policy. *Urban Land, 51*(11), 25.

Mier, R. (1993). Economic development and infrastructure: Planning in the context of progressive politics. In D. Perry (Ed.), *Building the public city: The policy, politics and planning of public works.* Newbury Park, CA: Sage.

Mier, R., & Bingham, R. D. (1993). Metaphors of economic development. In R. D. Bingham & R. Mier (Eds.), *Economic development in the United States: Toward a theoretical perspective.* Newbury Park, CA: Sage.

Mier, R., & Fitzgerald, J. (1991, August). Managing economic development. *Economic Development Quarterly, 5*(3), 268-279.

Mier, R., Fitzgerald, J., & Randolph, L. A. (1993). African-American elected officials and the future of progressive political movements. In D. Fasenfast (Ed.), *Economic development policy formation: Experiences in the United States and the United Kingdom.* New York: St. Martin's Press; London: MacMillan.

Mier R., & Gelzer, S. E. (1982, September). State enterprise zones: The new frontier? *Urban Affairs Quarterly, 18*(1), 39-52.

Mier, R., & Giloth, R. (1985, June). Hispanic employment opportunities: A case of internal labor markets and weak tied social networks. *Social Science Quarterly, 66*(2), 296-309.

Mier, R., & McGary, H. (1977). Social justice and public policy: An essay review of *A theory of justice. Educational Studies, 8,* 383-393.

Mier, R.,& Moe, K. J. (1991). Decentralized development: From theory to practice. In P. Clavel & W. Wiewel (Eds.), *Harold Washington and the neighborhoods: Progressive city government in Chicago, 1983-1987* (pp. 64-99). New Brunswick, NJ: Rutgers University Press.

Mier, R., Moe, K. J., & Sherr, I. (1986). Strategic planning and the pursuit of reform, economic development, and equity. *Journal of the American Planning Association, 52*(3), 299-309.

Mier, R., & Sherr, I. (1984). A review of *The contested city. Journal of the American Planning Association, 50*(4), 542-543.

Mier, R., Vietorisz, T., & Giblin, J-E. (1975). Indicators of labor market functioning and urban social distress. In G. Gappert & H. M. Rose (Eds.), *Social economy of cities* (pp. 361-394). Newbury Park, CA: Sage.

Mier, R., Wiewel, W., & Alpern, L. (1992). Decentralization of policy making under Mayor Harold Washington. In K. Wong (Ed.), *Politics of policy innovation in Chicago* (pp. 79-102). Greenwich, CT: JAI Press.

Miller, A. (1989a). *Climbing a great mountain.* Chicago: Bonus Books.

Miller, A. (1989b). *Harold Washington: The mayor, the man.* Chicago: Bonus Books.

Miller, D. (1985, December). Social policy: An exercise in metaphor. *Knowledge: Creation, Diffusion, and Utilization, 7*(2), 191-215.

Miller, H. P. (1973, October). Measuring subemployment in poverty areas of large United States cities. *Monthly Labor Review,* 10-18.

Mincer, J. (1973, March). Determining the number of "hidden unemployed." *Monthly Labor Review,* 27-31.

Moberg, D. (1987, August). Back from the brink. *Chicago Magazine,* pp. 99-101, 123.

Mollenkopf, J. (1983). *The contested city.* Princeton: Princeton University Press.

Morgan, G. (1987). *Images of organization.* Newbury Park, CA: Sage.

Morris, A. D. (1984). *The origins of the civil rights movement: Black communities organizing for change.* New York: Free Press.

Nagel, T. (1973, Summer). Equal treatment and compensatory discrimination. *Philosophy and Public Affairs, 2,* 348-363.

National Manpower Policy Task Force. (1974). *Adapting labor market statistics to policy needs: A policy statement.* Washington, DC: Author.

Nealon, M. (1977). *Factors related to the intention of Chicago manufacturers to relocate from their sites.* Unpublished master's project, School of Urban Planning, University of Illinois at Chicago.

New City YMCA. (1989). *Strategic plan.* Chicago: Author.

New development chief stresses jobs: Mayor's choice marks change in Chicago's hunt for industry. (1983, August 7). *Chicago Tribune,* sec. 6, p. 8.

Nozick, R. (1974). *Anarchy, state and utopia.* New York: Basic Books.

O'Connor, J. (1973). *The fiscal crisis of the state.* New York: St. Martin's.

Older industrial cities seek new support for neighborhood self-help public, private, community partnerships. (1982, Summer). *Building Blocks,* 1.

Orshansky, M. (1965, January). Counting the poor: Another look at the povery profile. *Social Security Bulletin,* 7-9.

Osborne, D. (1988). *Laboratories of democracy.* Boston: Harvard Business School Press.

Patterson, J., & Sieros, C. (1985). *Plan of action: Community equity corporation of Chicago.* Chicago: City of Chicago Department of Economic Development.

Pelissero, J. P., Henschen, B. M., & Sidlow, E. I. (1992). The new politics of sports innovation in Chicago. In K. Wong (Ed.), *Politics of policy innovation in Chicago* (pp. 57-78). Greenwich, CT: JAI Press.

Perry, D. C. (1990). Recasting urban leadership in Buffalo. In D. Judd & M. Parkinson (Eds.), *Leadership and urban regeneration: Cities in North America and Europe* (pp. 258-276). Newbury Park, CA: Sage.

Peters, T. J., & Waterman, R. H., Jr. (1982). *In search of excellence.* New York: Warner Books.

Phelps, E. S. (1973, August). Taxation of wage income for economic justice. *Quarterly Journal of Economics, 87,* 331-354.

Philpot, T. (1978). *The slum and the ghetto.* New York: Oxford University Press.

Pierce, N., & Steinbach, C. (1987). *Corrective capitalism.* New York: Ford Foundation.

Piore, M. Sabel, C. (1984). *The second industrial divide.* New York: Basic Books.

Piven, F. F., & Cloward, R. (1977). *Poor peoples movements.* New York: Vintage.

Porter, P. R. (1983, May 27). Personal correspondence.

Porter, P. R., & Sweet, D. C. (Eds.). (1984). *Rebuilding America's cities: Roads to recovery.* New Brunswick, NJ: Center for Urban Policy Research, Rutgers University.

Public Technology, Inc. (1984). *Strategic planning guide for cities and counties.* Washington, DC: Author.

Rainwater, L. (1970). *Behind ghetto walls.* Chicago: Aldine.

Rainwater, L. (1973, Spring). Economic inequality and the credit income tax. *Working Papers for a New Society, 1*(1), 50-61.

Rainwater, L. (1974). *What money buys.* New York: Basic Books.

Ranney, D., & Wiewel, W. (1987). *The graphic communications industry in the Chicago metropolitan area.* Chicago: University of Illinois at Chicago Center for Urban Economic Development.

Rawls, J. (1958, April). Justice as fairness. *The Philosophical Review, 67,* 164-194.

Rawls, J. (1971). *A theory of justice.* Cambridge, MA: The Belknap Press of Harvard University Press.

Rawls, J. (1985). Justice as fairness: Political, not metaphysical. *Philosophy and Public Affairs, 14.*

Rawls, J. (1987). The idea of an overlapping consensus. *Oxford Journal of Legal Studies, 7.*

Rawls, J. (1988). The priority of right and ideas of the good. *Philosophy and Public Affairs, 17.*

Reardon, K. (1990). *Local economic development in Chicago, 1983-1987: The reform efforts of Mayor Harold Washington.* Unpublished doctoral dissertation in City and Regional Planning, Cornell University.

Reich, R. (1983). *America's next frontier.* New York: Times Books.

Rhode Island Strategic Development Commission. (1983). *The greenhouse compact: Cultivating Rhode Island's fourth economy.* Providence: Author.

Rich, M. (1992). *Targeting to needy neighborhoods in the city.* Unpublished manuscript, Department of Political Science, Brown University.

Rivlin, G. (1992). *Fire on the prairie: Chicago's Harold Washington and the politics of race.* New York: Henry Holt.

Rubin, L. (1985). *Just friends.* New York: Harper & Row.

Sartorius, R. (1975). *Individual conduct and social norms.* Encino, CA: Dickenson Press.

San Francisco Chamber of Commerce and Arthur Andersen and Company. (1983). *San Francisco's strategic plan: Making a great city greater.* San Francisco: San Francisco Chamber of Commerce.

Scanlon, T. M. (1973, May). Rawls' theory of justice. *University of Pennsylvania Law Review, 121*(5), 1020-1078.

Schardt, A. (1986, May/June). Looking for leadership. *Foundation News,* 38-43.

Schatzman, L., & Strauss, A. L. (1973). *Field research: Strategies for a natural sociology.* Englewood Cliffs, NJ: Prentice-Hall.

Schemmer, R. W. (1982). *Business location decisions.* Englewood Cliffs, NJ: Prentice-Hall.

Schon, D. (1971). *Beyond the stable state.* New York: Random House.

Schon, D. (1979). Generative metaphors: A perspective on problem setting. In A. Ortony (Ed.), *Metaphor and thought.* Cambridge, UK: Cambridge University Press.

Schon, D. (1980). *Reflective practitioner.* New York: Basic Books.

Schmidt, W. E. (1987, December 10). Chicago plan seeks to prevent loss of factories. *The New York Times.*

Shlay, A. B., & Giloth, R. P. (1987). Social organization of a land based elite: The case of the failed Chicago 1992 World's Fair. *Journal of Urban Affairs, 9*(4), 305-324.

Shlay, A. B., & Holupka, C. S. (1993). Political economy and urban development. In R. D. Bingham & R. Mier (Eds.), *Economic development in the United States: Toward a theoretical perspective.* Newbury Park, CA: Sage.

Silver, H., & Burton, D. (1986, Summer). The politics of state-level industrial policy: Lessons from Rhode Island's greenhouse compact. *Journal of the American Planning Association, 52*(3), 277-289.

Smith, D. (1990, July 25). Interview with Lauri Alpern.

Snow, L. (1990, July 18). Letter to Wim Wiewel.

So, F. S. (1984, February). Strategic planning: Reinventing the wheel. *Planning, 50*(2), 16-21.

Southeast Chicago Development Commission. (1987). *Strategic mission.* Chicago: Author.

Spring, W. (1971, Winter). Unemployment: The measure we refuse to take. *New Generation.*

Spring, W., Harrison, B., & Veitorisz, T. (1972, November). The crises of the underemployed. *The New York Times Magazine,* pp. 42-60.

Squires, G., Bennett, L., McCourt, K., & Nyden, P. (1987). *Chicago: Race, class, and the response to urban decline.* Philadelphia: Temple University Press.

Tannen, B. (1990). *You just don't understand: Women and men in conversation.* New York: Ballantine.

Task Force on Navy Pier. (1986). *Window on the future.* Chicago: City of Chicago Department of Economic Development.

Task Force on Steel and Southeast Chicago. (1986). *Draft report.* City of Chicago Department of Economic Development.

Throgmorton, J. A. (1992, Fall). Planning as persuasive storytelling about the future: Negotiating an electric power rate settlement in Illinois. *Journal of Planning Education and Research, 12*(1), 17-31.

Thurow, L. (1974, November 2). More are going to be poor. *New Republic,* 26-27.

Travis, D. (1989). *"Harold," the people's mayor: An authorized biography of Mayor Harold Washington.* Chicago: Urban Research Press.

Trist, E. (1981). New directions of hope: Recent innovations interconnecting organizational, industrial, community and personal development. *Regional Studies, 13,* 439-451.

Tussing, A. D. (1975). *Poverty in a dual economy.* New York: St. Martin's.

United Neighborhood Organization of Chicago. (1985). *New facilities and new directions for city colleges.* Chicago: Author.

University officials get advice on developing research parks. (1982, September 27). *Economic and Industrial Development News, 1*(8), 1-3.

U.S. Senate. (1945). *Full employment act of 1945: Hearings before a subcommittee on banking and currency, 79th Cong., 1st sess. on S380.* Washington, DC: Government Printing Office.

U.S. Department of Commerce, Bureau of Census. (1992, March). Workers with low earnings: 1964-1990. *Current population reports* (Series P60, #178). Washington, DC: Government Printing Office.

Vietorisz, T., Mier, R., & Giblin, J-E. (1974). The concept and measurement of subemployment. *Selected Papers from the 1974 North American Conference of Labor Statistics.* Washington, DC: U.S. Department of Labor.

Vietorisz, T., Mier, R., & Harrison, B. (1975, March). Full employment at living wages. *Annals of the American Academy of Political and Social Science, 418,* 94-107.

Walker, J. (1991). Reforming the role of human services in city government. In P. Clavel & W. Wiewel (Eds.), *Harold Washington and the neighborhoods: Progressive city government in Chicago, 1983-1987* (pp. 146-164). New Brunswick, NJ: Rutgers University Press.

Washington, H. (1985, October 10). Letter to Illinois congressional delegation regarding the textile and apparel trade enforcement act of 1985. *Congressional Record* [Daily ed.], H8632.

Washington Transition Committee. (1983). *Toward a prosperous, compassionate and efficient Chicago.* Chicago: Author.

Weiss D. (1988, March). The Chicago look. *Today's Chicago Woman,* p. 11.

White, H. (1987). *The content of the form: Narrative discourse in historical representation.* Baltimore: Johns Hopkins University Press.

Whyte, W. F. (1982, February). Social inventions for solving human problems. *American Sociological Review, 47,* 1-13.

Whyte, W. F. (1983). *Worker participation and ownership.* Ithaca, NY: ILR Press.

Whyte, W. F. (Ed.). (1991). *Participatory action research.* Newbury Park, CA: Sage.

Wiewel, W. (1987). The Chicago project's corporate vision ignores the city's cast of thousands. *Chicago Enterprise, 1*(11), 12-13.

Wiewel, W., & Hunter, A. (1985). The interorganizational network as a resource: A comparative case study on the organizational genesis. *Administrative Science Quarterly, 30,* 482-496.

Wiewel, W., & Siegel, W. (1987). *Industry task forces as pragmatic planning: the effect of ideology, sponsorship, and economic context on strategy selection.* Paper presented at the annual conference of the American Collegiate Schools of Planning, Los Angeles.

Williams, L. (1992, December 16). Scrambling to manage a diverse work force. *The New York Times,* p. A1.

Wolff, R. P. (1977). *Understanding Rawls.* Princeton: Princeton University Press.

Wong, K. (Ed.). (1992). *Policy innovation in Chicago.* Greenwich, CT: JAI.

Yates, R. (1992, December 13). Racial, ethnic divisions top concerns of leaders. *Chicago Tribune,* sec. 7, p. 1 ff.

Index

About the Contributors

Robert Mier is Professor of Urban Planning and Public Administration at the University of Illinois at Chicago. From 1983 to 1989, he worked for the City of Chicago during the tenure of Mayors Harold Washington and Eugene Sawyer. He was Commissioner of Economic Development and Assistant to the Mayor for Development. In the latter role, he was responsible for the activities of the departments of Cultural Affairs, Economic Development, Employment and Training, Housing, and Planning. He also was the architect and chief implementor of Chicago's highly regarded *1984 Development Plan,* a national model for equity oriented local municipal development planning.

He is widely recognized for his policy research and consulting in the areas of economic development strategies, and for his teaching and professional training in public systems management. He is the author of over eighty scholarly or professional publications, and is a regular commentator on urban development issues in *Crain's Chicago Business* and on Chicago public radio. He is the co-editor with Richard D. Bingham of *Economic Development in the United States: Toward a Theoretical Perspective.* He has degrees in civil engineering from the University of Notre Dame and urban planning from Cornell University, and is a registered professional engineer in Illinois, Missouri, and California. He also is a decorated veteran of the Vietnam War.

Robert P. Giloth is Executive Director of the South East Baltimore Community Organization and President of the Southeast Development Institute. He is a former Deputy Commissioner of

217

Economic Development for the City of Chicago during the administration of Mayor Harold Washington. He has a Ph.D. in planning from Cornell University and has extensively published on community and economic development in *Economic Development Quarterly, Journal of the American Planning Association,* and *Social Policy,* among others.

Kari J. Moe is Chief of Staff for Senator Paul Wellstone (D., Minnesota). From 1983 to 1989, she worked for the City of Chicago during the tenure of Mayors Harold Washington and Eugene Sawyer. She was Deputy Commissioner of Economic Development, Commissioner of General Services, and Assistant to the Mayor for Human Services. In the latter role, she was responsible for the activities of the departments of Aging and Disabilities, Human Services, and Library as well as the commissions on Human Resources and Latino Affairs. She has a master's degree in urban planning from the Massachusetts Institute of Technology.

Lauri Alpern is Director of the Illinois Partnership for Business Development, Center for Urban Economic Development, University of Illinois at Chicago. She is a former Assistant Commissioner of Economic Development for the City of Chicago. She has a master's degree in urban planning and policy from the University of Illinois at Chicago.

Bennett Harrison is Professor of Political Economy in the Heinz School of Public Policy and Management at Carnegie Mellon University. He is the author or editor of seven books and nearly 100 scholarly and popular articles, including *The Deindustrialization of America,* co-authored with Barry Bluestone, and *The Great U Turn.* He has a Ph.D. in economics from the University of Pennsylvania and, for 17 years, taught urban studies and planning at the Massachusetts Insititute of Technology.

Howard M. McGary, Jr., is Professor of Philosophy at Rutgers: The State University of New Jersey. His research is on social philosophy and African-American philosophy, especially black historical thought. His most recent book is *Between Slavery and Freedom,* co-authored with Bill E. Lawson. He is on the editorial boards of *Philosophical Forum* and *Encyclopedia of Ethics.* He has a Ph.D. in philosophy from the University of Minnesota.

Irene Sherr is a private consultant. She was Assistant to the Commissioner of Economic Development for the City of Chicago, Executive Director of the Howard-Paulina Development Corporation, and Executive Director of the Hyde Park Development Corporation. She has a master's degree in urban planning from the University of Pennsylvania.

Thomas Vietorisz is Professor of Economics at the Graduate Faculty of the New School for Social Research, and a Visiting Professor of Planning at Cornell University. He is the co-author, with Bennett Harrison, of the seminal work, *The Economic Development of Harlem.* He has a Ph.D. in economics from the Massachusetts Institute of Technology, and for three decades has conducted research and consulted on international development, most recently in Mexico.

Wim Wiewel is Associate Professor of Urban Planning and Policy, and Director of the Center for Urban Economic Development, University of Illinois at Chicago. He has written a number of scholarly articles on community development and economic development strategies. He is the co-editor, with Pierre Clavel, of *Harold Washington and the Neighborhoods: Progressive City Government in Chicago, 1983-1989,* and, with Philip W. Nyden, of *Challenging Uneven Development.* He has a Ph.D. in sociology from Northwestern University.